LEADING WITH THE CHI
MASCULINITIES IN *ESQUIRE*, 1960–1989

Leading with the Chin focuses on the *Esquire* writings of James Baldwin, Truman Capote, Raymond Carver, Don DeLillo, Norman Mailer, and Tim O'Brien to examine how these authors negotiated important shifts in American masculinity. Using the works of these six authors as case studies, *Leading with the Chin* argues that *Esquire* permitted writers to confront national fantasies of American masculinity as they were impacted by the rise of neoliberalism, civil rights and gay rights, and the cultural dominance of the professional-managerial class.

Applying the methodologies of periodical studies and the theoretical concerns of masculinity studies, this book recontextualizes the prose and fiction of these authors by analysing them in the material context of the magazine. Relating each author's articulation of masculinity to the advertisements, editorials, and articles published in each issue, *Leading with the Chin* shows that *Esquire* reflected and helped to shape the forces that structured American masculinity in the twentieth century.

BRAD CONGDON received his PhD from Dalhousie University, where he is an instructor in Gender and Women's Studies and English.

Leading with the Chin: Writing American Masculinities in *Esquire*, 1960–1989

BRAD CONGDON

UNIVERSITY OF TORONTO PRESS
Toronto   Buffalo   London

ISBN 978-1-4875-0275-1 (cloth)   ISBN 978-1-4875-2216-2 (paper)

Printed on acid-free, 100% post-consumer recycled paper with
vegetable-based inks.

Library and Archives Canada Cataloguing in Publication

Congdon, Brad, 1981–, author
Leading with the chin : writing American masculinities in
Esquire, 1960–1989 / Brad Congdon.

Includes bibliographical references and index.
ISBN 978-1-4875-0275-1 (cloth). – ISBN 978-1-4875-2216-2 (paper)

1. American literature – 20th century – History and criticism.
2. Masculinity in literature. 3. Esquire. I. Title.

PS228.M37C66 2018   810.9'353   C2018-902728-2

This book has been published with the help of a grant from the Federation
for the Humanities and Social Sciences, through the Awards to Scholarly
Publications Program, using funds provided by the Social Sciences and
Humanities Research Council of Canada.

University of Toronto Press acknowledges the financial assistance to its
publishing program of the Canada Council for the Arts and the Ontario Arts
Council, an agency of the Government of Ontario.

For Krista, for everything

Contents

Acknowledgments

Leading with the Chin is the result of years of research and a not insignificant portion of my life. I've been working on this book, in some form or another, for the last seven years, and in that time I've built up a great debt of gratitude. Hopefully, I can now begin to repay what I owe.

Jason Haslam has influenced my thinking and writing at every stage of my research, from talking through theory and methodology to providing detailed feedback on each chapter. More than once, he has pointed out that what appeared, at first, to be a dead end was actually a new avenue of inquiry. It is because of his rigour and his generosity that I was able to see this long project through to the end. He is a model of academic mentorship.

Thoughtful feedback and criticism from Lyn Bennet, Carrie Dawson, Leonard Diepeveen, David Earle, and Anthony Enns helped me to see the forest for the trees and shape my research into the monograph it is today.

I've been lucky enough to get feedback on all or part of this manuscript from a number of smart, diligent reviewers, including Maggie McKinley, Daniel Worden, James Plath, the anonymous readers at *Critique* and the University of Toronto Press, and panelists and audience members at the conferences of the American Studies Association, the Canadian Association of American Studies, and the Association of Canadian College and University Teachers of English.

More generally, I've been lucky enough to be a part of a stimulating and encouraging academic community. Though my graduate-school cohort has faced declining wages and career prospects, they have never been anything but empathetic and supportive. None of us may end up with careers in academia, but all of us are rock stars.

Working with the University of Toronto Press has been a terrific experience. In particular, I'd like to thank Mark Thompson, who shepherded this book through the publication process; Barbara Porter, who saw it through to completion; and Michel Pharand, whose impeccable copyediting whipped this book on masculinity into fighting shape.

If, after all of this excellent help, advice, and criticism, weaknesses yet remain in the book's argument, style, or execution, then those faults are mine alone.

Were it not for early funding from the Social Sciences and Humanities Research Council, this project never would have begun; were it not for a grant from the Awards to Scholarly Publications Program (Federation for the Humanities and Social Sciences), this project may never have appeared in its current form.

LEADING WITH THE CHIN

Introduction

The Crisis of Masculinity and the Problem of Identity

Esquire aims to be the common denominator of masculine interests – to be all things to all men. This is difficult to accomplish, all at a crack, and we would be foolish to expect to work out the formula down to the last little detail, in the first issue. One of the things that are needed, for the ultimate shaping of this magazine into what will be its final form, is a frank reaction from the readers. We won't know how to please you in future issues unless and until you tell us what you think of the way we started out. The one test that has been applied to every feature that is in this first issue has been simply and solely: "Is it interesting to men?" How often were we wrong? Come on, let's have it – we're leading with the chin.

– Arnold Gingrich[1]

With the above words outlining the magazine's goals, editor Arnold Gingrich launched *Esquire* magazine in the autumn of 1933. *Esquire* may have seemed out of step with the times: focused on men's fashion and costing the then-outlandish cover price of fifty cents, the first issue went public during the height of the Great Depression. Gingrich, along with publishers David Smart and William Weinraub, needed to quickly establish a readership if the magazine were to survive, let alone flourish. They did so by targeting men – specifically men of means – by providing them with a quality package of articles and fiction meant to edify them *as men*. If the content didn't grab them, then they were invited to respond to Gingrich's challenge. What "real" man could resist?

Esquire magazine is still published today, making it America's longest running – and at times most influential – men's interest magazine. In fact, *Esquire* represents "the first thoroughgoing, conscious attempt to organize a consuming male audience."[2] Central to its success was Gingrich's editorial policy, in which he treated the magazine as a three-ring circus, the rings being "fashion, off-beat masculine writing, and sex."[3] The editorial content of the first issue did much to establish the interests of the magazine and *Esquire*'s ideal readership. Though promising to be "all things to all men," Gingrich soon suggested a more restricted audience, stating that *Esquire* "never intends to become, by any possible stretch of the imagination, a primer for fops." On the contrary: *Esquire* would not burden its readers with "a lot of dress rules that nobody but a gigolo could possibly find either time or inclination to observe." The editor does claim, however, that there is nothing "effeminate or essentially unbusinesslike" about men attending to style.[4] In a few words, Gingrich moved from identifying a readership limited only by sex to one articulated in opposition to fops and gigolos, and further implied the class background of *Esquire*'s ideal readers: these thoroughly masculine men were also professionals. It was taken as a given (and reinforced in subsequent issues) that the readership would be primarily white. Though the magazine aimed to be "all things to all men," that final term was highly qualified.

The "men" that *Esquire* targeted were to be addressed *as men*. The opening editorial comments made it clear that *Esquire* would differ from the other available magazines, all of which supposedly appealed to a female readership. According to Gingrich, general interest magazines had "bent over backward in catering to the special interests and tastes of the feminine audience," and a male reader of such magazines was "made to feel like an intruder upon gynaecic mysteries."[5] Women's interests, so alien to men as to appear mysterious, were to be absent from the pages of *Esquire*, making it a "safe," homosocial space.

If these rhetorical flourishes were not enough, Gingrich dared male readers to respond, so that the magazine might get a better purchase on men's interests. Gingrich's pugilistic phrase ("Come on, let's have it – we're leading with the chin") challenged men to spar over the magazine's success in identifying and shaping American masculinity. By making this open challenge, *Esquire* enlisted its presumed readership in its ongoing project to appeal to men and to show them how to understand and master their own relationship to masculinity and the marketplace. While the specifics of this project have changed over the years, its goal remains the same, and exists as a phrase widely associated with the magazine: "How to Be a Man."[6]

According to the magazine, one task expected of "being a man" – and the one most important to this study – is reading the works of American authors. Since its inception, *Esquire* has cultivated an impressive reputation for the quality of its writing. As *Esquire* historian Hugh Merrill has noted, *Esquire*'s fiction has been its most enduring and influential feature.[7] The inaugural issue included writing by Erskine Caldwell, John Dos Passos, Dashiell Hammett, and Ernest Hemingway, the last of whom became one of the most frequent contributors to the magazine during the 1930s. The inclusion of these writers had an implicit ideological function. For the most part, these authors lent the fledgling publication prestige, but, as in the case of Hemingway, they also added much-needed masculine credentials. As the magazine's editor, Arnold Gingrich, later wrote, he specifically sought Hemingway's contributions to "deodorize the lavender whiff coming from the mere presence of fashion pages."[8] Hemingway's contributions – most of which were nonfiction essays, "letters" detailing his adventures travelling, fishing, and hunting – were meant to counteract any hint of effeminacy or presumed homosexuality that may have been inferred by male readers picking up a magazine devoted, in part, to lifestyle and fashion. In fulfilling this role, however, the prose and fiction of American authors may also articulate definitions of, and challenges to, masculinity that either compliment or complicate the image of masculinity being presented by the magazine.

Hemingway was not the only big-name author to frequent the magazine's pages. During its first decade, *Esquire* would also publish work by Ezra Pound, e.e. cummings, Langston Hughes, Aldous Huxley, and F. Scott Fitzgerald, among others. In the 1950s and '60s, readers were regularly treated to the works of Gore Vidal, Dorothy Parker, Diana Trilling, Tom Wolfe, Norman Mailer, James Baldwin, John Barth, Tennessee Williams, Thomas Pynchon, and John Cheever, to name only a few.[9] According to Gingrich, an independent survey in 1962, near the beginning of the period under discussion, identified fiction as the single most popular element of the magazine.[10] Though by the '70s and '80s the magazine had begun to dial back on its publication of fiction, often focusing on publishing excerpts of works in progress, it had by that point been firmly established as a high-end literary marketplace.

As Kenon Breazeale has argued, in the 1930s *Esquire*'s goal "to constitute consumption as a new arena for masculine privilege" was predicated on an almost absolute repudiation of femininity, resulting in what was a predominantly misogynist text.[11] *Esquire* used two strategies to make consumption safe and desirable for men: first, it included "cheesecake" pinups in each issue (first the "Petty Girl," later the "Varga Girl"); and second, it constantly offered men advice on food, clothing, decorating, and etiquette within a rhetorical context that claimed these areas of leisure needed to be rescued from the bumbling and inadequate hands of women.[12] The model created by *Esquire* – both in terms of the magazine itself and the construction of masculinity it proffered – was so successful that it was often emulated. The most obvious imitator of the original *Esquire* went on to be its most famous successor: Hugh Hefner's *Playboy*.[13]

When its original winning formula was coopted by its competitor, *Esquire* was forced to change tactics. Beginning in the late 1950s, *Esquire* became less urban and more suburban and, more importantly, became a home for experimental fiction and New Journalism. Though less reliant on blatant misogyny and less fixated on ostentatious wealth, this era of *Esquire* still aimed to tell its readership – who it presumed to be cisgender, white, heterosexual, middle-class, and male – exactly how to be a man in the changing social and economic climate of mid-century America. It is this period – that is, the end of the 1950s and into the 1960s – that this project takes as its starting point.[14]

As a venue for publication, *Esquire* enabled writers to think through national fantasies of American masculinity as those fantasies were challenged by historical change. From 1960 to 1989, Americans witnessed a number of transformative events. It was a period of great economic change: the end of the post-War boom; the "Nixon Shock" of 1971 that resulted in America's movement away from the Gold Standard; and the rise of what we now call neoliberalism. Socially, the era began with an intensification of the Civil Rights Movement, and subsequently experienced the Stonewall Riots, Second Wave Feminism, and the ensuing socially conservative Reaganism of the 1980s. Almost countless other significant cultural events could be added to this list: America's involvement in Vietnam; the assassinations of the Kennedys, Malcolm X, and Martin Luther King, Jr; and, relevant to a study of literature, the rise of postmodernism as a critical and aesthetic paradigm. Each of these factors challenged the dominance of white, heterosexual masculinity still found at the centre of American identity. Reading *Esquire* during this period is to see how hegemonic masculinity negotiated these challenges through promoting a certain type of masculine lifestyle.

Though the phrasing is, regrettably, rather clunky, I argue that *Esquire* has been engaged in a "hegemonic masculinity project." I will develop this concept throughout *Leading with the Chin*, but it deserves some preliminary explanation. "Hegemonic masculinity" is a term most commonly associated with the sociologist Raewyn Connell, who defines it as "the configuration of gender practice which embodies the currently accepted answer to the problem of the legitimacy of patriarchy, which guarantees (or is taken to guarantee) the dominant position of men and the subordination of women."[15] Connell's description of hegemonic masculinity as a "configuration of gender practice" points to the fact that the term does not refer to *actual men*, but to a type of *social practice* in which certain men might engage. This does not mean that it is entirely symbolic and unrelated to the "real" world: men in dominant positions – e.g., government, business, military – put hegemonic masculinity into practice. This is why Connell refers to masculinities as "projects, not fixed patterns."[16] *Esquire* engages in a hegemonic masculinity project by outlining the type of masculinity its readers should practice.

In other words, *Esquire*'s hegemonic masculinity project involves practicing a lifestyle of informed and distinguishing consumption. As Mike Featherstone explains, "lifestyle" is the primary way that individuality and selfhood are understood in contemporary consumer culture. Understood as lifestyle, "[o]ne's body, clothes, speech, leisure pastimes, eating and drinking preferences, home, car, choice of holidays, etc. are to be regarded as indicators of the individuality of taste and sense of style of the owner/consumer."[17] *Esquire* constructs and sells a lifestyle that promises to help men make sense of their place in the family, business, and leisure, and gain or maintain dominance in the face of social and economic change. However, as this study will demonstrate, for some men *Esquire*'s hegemonic masculinity project can also act as a form of "cruel optimism." As Lauren Berlant explains, cruel optimism occurs when a subject feels a deep intellectual and emotional connection to "a significantly problematic object."[18] In this case, an attachment to hegemonic masculinity in general, and *Esquire*'s project in particular, can lead men away from happiness and prosperity, and instead result in violence or despair (as demonstrated, for example, in my analyses of Norman Mailer and Tim O'Brien, below). Reading works of fiction in *Esquire* shows just how fraught and contradictory American masculinity can be.

Because major American authors played a central role in *Esquire*'s
masculinity project, at least for the first 50 years of the publication's
history, the goal of this study is to examine the role of masculinity
in works of prose and fiction by such authors as they were originally
published in the magazine. Specifically, in what follows I examine the
works of Norman Mailer, James Baldwin, Raymond Carver, Truman
Capote, Tim O'Brien, and Don DeLillo over a thirty-year period of
the magazine. As I demonstrate below, *Esquire* can fruitfully be used
as a tool for textual analysis, as a lens through which historically and
culturally specific arguments about masculinity can be made. In particular, situating these fictional texts in the pages of *Esquire*, among
its fashion advertisements and editorial content, is valuable for demonstrating how masculinities are constructed in relation to the marketplace. Readings of specific texts within the frame of *Esquire* show
that the works of contemporaneous authors were complicit with,
struggled against, or attempted to subvert the masculine codes and
behaviours promoted by the magazine. *Leading with the Chin* will demonstrate that gender is an always-present and always-contested factor in writing, sometimes obvious but sometimes subtle, and that the
gendered subtexts of written works can be brought to the surface
when read as part of a project dedicated to explicating "How to Be
a Man." Furthermore, this study demonstrates the value of conceiv-
ing of masculinity in relation to hegemony – that is, in viewing the
construction and maintenance of masculinities relationally and as
inseparable from other historic processes, such as the processes of
the marketplace. In so doing, *Leading with the Chin* reveals that the
market is a place where the discourse of masculinity is disputed, and
that the prose and fiction of male American authors contributes to,
and shapes, that very discourse.[19]

Theoretical and Methodological Background

In *Leading with the Chin*, I analyse masculinity by examining the relationship between *Esquire* magazine and the prose and fiction published
in its pages. To do so, I use a methodology adapted from periodical
studies (as well as Jerome McGann's concept of radial reading) and
the theories of gender current in the study of masculinities. Anyone
focusing specifically on the study of masculinities will very quickly
run into the work of Raewyn Connell, whose widely cited theory of
masculinities forms the framework for this study. Connell's theory is

well-suited to an analysis of masculinity in fiction: first, it complements the concept of cultural hegemony, most often associated with Stuart Hall and those affiliated with the Birmingham Centre for Contemporary Cultural Studies; second, its approach to masculinity is capable of accounting for the various levels at which gender operates (i.e., the symbolic, the ideological, the institutional, and the social). Moreover, Connell provides a series of terms – including hegemonic, subordinate, and complicit masculinities, gender regimes, and the gender order – that offer a framework for a formalistic analysis of masculinities. The section below outlines these terms, to orient readers for the analyses that follow.

In addition to hegemonic masculinity, Connell identifies two other types of masculinity pertinent to this study: subordinate and complicit. Because hegemonic masculinity is practiced by the dominant form of masculinity in a given set of gender relations, many other forms of masculinity are "subordinated" to or "complicit" with this dominant form. On the one hand, certain types of masculinity are "subordinated to straight men by an array of quite material practices," including "political and cultural exclusion," "cultural abuse," "legal violence," "street violence," and "economic discrimination." In America, gay men are paradigmatic examples of subordinated masculinities.[20] On the other hand, complicit forms of masculinity still benefit from the subordination of women and other men without practicing, or forcefully defending, hegemonic masculinity.[21] Straight, white, cisgender, middle-class men may not actively support a patriarchal system, for example, but they will still benefit from their privileged position by avoiding the types of discrimination felt by women and subordinated men. Indeed, the relationship of subordinated and complicit masculinities (and all women) to hegemonic masculinity can be understood as "symbolic violence." Pierre Bourdieu uses this concept to explain our "paradoxical submission" to an established order that perpetuates domination, privileges, and injustices.[22] For Bourdieu,

> the structures of domination ... are *the product of an incessant (and therefore historical) labour of reproduction,* to which singular agents (including men, with weapons such as physical violence and symbolic violence) and institutions – families, the church, the educational system, the state – contribute.[23]

The difference between hegemonic, subordinated, and complicit masculinities is a difference of their relationship to dominance, and one should understand masculinities as relating to one another hierarchically.[24]

Hegemonic, subordinate, and complicit forms of masculinity are highly visible within institutional settings. Connell uses the term "gender regime" to describe "the state of play in gender relations in a given institution,"[25] but which, I argue in chapter 4, might be associated with specific social spaces. Connell argues that a gender regime is "a pattern in gender relations," such as "who was recruited to do what work," "what social divisions were recognized," "how emotional relations were conducted," and "how these institutions were related to others."[26] Furthermore, different gender regimes generate different gender relations and different values.[27]

The movement from a gender regime to a "gender order" is the movement from the micro to the macro: the gender order refers to "wider [gender] patterns" which "endure over time."[28] Connell uses the gender order to discuss the pattern of gender relations in, for instance, the United States, rather than in a particular institution. It is in many ways harder to "think" the gender order without recourse to stereotypes and generalities; however, it is helpful to think of the gender order as reflective of the often "additive or complementary" relationship *between* regimes.[29] To use America as an example: if the institutions that have the most influence in a state – that is, what Louis Althusser calls the Repressive (e.g., the army, the police) and Ideological State Apparatuses (e.g., politics, the family)[30] – are themselves dominated by men (and each one dominated by a particular form of hegemonic masculinity), then we can posit that the larger gender order is one characterized by masculine domination.

Connell's theories provide a useful toolkit for an analysis of masculinities, especially one that takes into account the differences in cultural power and authority between and among men. To do the actual work of analysing masculinities further requires more radical gender critiques that have been widely influential in literary studies. *Leading with the Chin* therefore often turns to feminist and queer scholars to complicate and sometimes challenge the types of masculinity *Esquire* and the authors under discussion offer their readership.

Leading with the Chin argues that there is great value in bringing the methodology of periodical studies to the analysis of American masculinities. As a field, periodical studies insists that the most meaningful approach to analysing any serial text involves a wide and comprehensive selection of reading: rather than selecting individual items printed within the magazine, periodical studies argues for the significance of analysing complete issues and long-term print runs.[31] In this way, periodical studies recognizes each magazine's unique value of seriality, periodicity, and intermediality.[32] Published serially, magazines represent multiple authors and multiple interests, and respond to larger social forces. As Nancy Walker writes, a historical analysis of magazines reveals them to be "dynamic elements of American popular culture, responding to and interacting with events and ideologies that had wide cultural currency."[33] These characteristics make magazines privileged sites for analysing the historical forces that shape gender.

Published monthly, aimed at particular male audiences, and attuned to historic shifts and trends, men's magazines in particular provide an excellent venue for a study of gender keyed to the multilevel analysis of hegemonic masculinity. The research of several magazine scholars supports this assertion: the specific concerns of men's magazines crucially relate to wider cultural concepts of masculinity.[34] That is to say that though a certain magazine may have a limited circulation and a specific male audience in mind, it nonetheless responds to shifts in the larger gender order and can even represent certain aspects of local gender regimes.

Not only are men's magazines responsive to the larger cultural discourse of masculinity, but they also demonstrate how contemporaneous formulations of hegemonic masculinity are renegotiated. Peter Jackson, Nick Stevenson, and Kate Brooks assert that "magazines provide men with a kind of conceptual map for navigating safely through their contemporary gender anxieties, whether in relation to their health, their careers, their sexual relationships or their place in 'consumer culture' more generally."[35] Men's magazines offer men an understanding of their relationship to the world *as men* – that is to say, all relationships are understood primarily through the lens of gender. Accordingly, while magazines register supposed threats to masculinity, they also offer lifestyle choices, rather than significant change, as the means to neutralize these threats.[36] After all, magazines are in the business of making money, and they primarily do so by selling advertising, meaning that changes within gender regimes, or to the larger gender order, can also function as marketing strategies.

The serial, periodical, and intermedial nature of men's magazines makes them ideal for a historical analysis of masculinity. As Connell explains, "When conditions for the defence of patriarchy change, the bases for the dominance of a particular masculinity are eroded. New groups may challenge old solutions and construct a new hegemony ... Hegemony, then, is a historically mobile relation."[37] In particular, reading *Esquire* magazine over a period of months and years reveals the challenges to, and responses of, hegemonic masculinity.

As Stefan Horlacher notes, "literary discourses still remain a privileged site" for expressing the tensions inherent in hegemonic masculinity.[38] In addition, literary analysis can deal with ambiguity, ambivalence, and complexity. My method involves recontextualizing prose and fiction by male American authors in this dynamic, hegemonic cultural field. As Breazeale explains, "Magazines are both devised and experienced as a whole and can be most meaningfully studied as a system entire." Consequently, Breazeale argues that the pictorial content – the focus of her study – "can be understood as fulfilling a vital ideological function complementary to the text," but this approach to the magazine's cartoons can be extended to its prose, fiction, and advertisements.[39] This is not to say that magazines are "well-wrought urns," each part an equally significant and irreplaceable part of the whole; rather, the different parts of the magazine gain further significance in relation to one another. To examine this relationship, I use a form of what McGann calls radial reading, in which the immediate material context of each text influences its analysis.[40] My focus is not only on the "linguistic code" of each work, but on its relationship to its "bibliographic code." The bibliographic code of a work printed in a magazine includes the magazine's design features (including its cover, page layout, advertisements, and so on) and the accompanying contents (such as other works of prose and fiction, the letters to the editor, etc.). These bibliographic features help to situate the work in its original historical context.[41] The original work and its original context is therefore the starting point of analysis – each work gestures outwards, to the rest of the magazine, but also to the author's *corpus*, the products advertised, and, in the case of excerpted works, to the subsequently published (and sometimes revised) versions of the original text.

Significantly, *Esquire*'s bibliographic code is intimately related to masculinity. Following Stuart Hall's description of cultural hegemony, I understand *Esquire* as an "arena of consent and resistance. It is partly where hegemony arises, and where it is secured."[42] This means that *Esquire* is a place where hegemonic masculinity is established and fixed, but it is also possible to see it as a place where writers and other producers of culture can articulate counter-hegemonic discourses. As

Hammill, Hjartarson, and McGregor note, "The process of reading a magazine involves actively assembling the different components – articles, advertisements, illustrations, letters to the editor – into an unpredictable, idiosyncratic, and ultimately unstable whole."[43] The "ultimately unstable whole" of each issue of *Esquire* results in multiple messages about masculinity that are never wholly coherent. To adapt a point made by Walker in her analysis of women's magazines, it is precisely because *Esquire*'s constructions of masculinity are often clashing that a reader can see gender as "a contested and negotiated concept rather than a proscribed and stable one."[44] It is this contestation and negotiation of masculinity, inherent in each issue of *Esquire* and in the prose and fiction published in its pages, that *Leading with the Chin* seeks to decipher.

Leading with the Chin therefore focuses on the works of male authors published in the magazine, to demonstrate the workings and tensions *internal* to hegemonic masculinity. Though *Esquire*'s messaging changes from decade-to-decade, year-to-year, and sometimes issue-to-issue, its messages remain directed towards an ideal reader whose imagined identity remains surprisingly consistent. Despite an eighty-year period of publication, involving numerous changes in marketplaces and culture, the target audience has remained reasonably stable: *Esquire*'s ideal reader is a member of what John and Barbara Ehrenreich called the Professional-Managerial Class (PMC), that is, "a distinct class in monopoly capitalist society" comprised of, for instance, "technical workers, managerial workers, 'cultural' producers, etc." and "whose major function in the social division of labor may be described broadly as the reproduction of capitalist culture and capitalist class relations."[45] *Esquire* characterizes its own ideal readership in a number of ways: affluent, educated, and influential. Moreover, *Esquire*'s ideal reader has more-or-less remained the same straight, white man interested in leisure and sophistication whom Gingrich addressed in *Esquire*'s first editorial.[46] Given their choice of reading material, these ideal readers are also interested in "how to be a man": they are interested in practicing hegemonic masculinity in their given (white collar, professional-managerial) gender regimes.

Just as importantly, one of the primary ways they practice hegemonic masculinity is through *consumption*. If this were not obvious from the medium of the general interest magazine itself, it would become clear from a quick review of the scholarship: Breazeale sees *Esquire* as the "first magazine presenting an appeal to the desiring male subject (i.e., consumer) as a systematically developed editorial formula";[47] Tom Pendergast believes that early *Esquire* articles "rescued consumerism for a male audience";[48] Bill Osgerby discusses how *Esquire* furnished "upwardly-mobile male consumers with a repertoire of cultural codes and meanings ... which made intelligible their relationship with style, desire and commodity culture."[49] Indeed, *Esquire's* signature phrase "How to Be a Man" is always an invitation to consumption.

Stefan Cieply's analysis of *Esquire* from 1957 to 1963 makes a convincing case for the study of consumerism in relation to masculinity:

> how men define themselves as consuming subjects is directly implicated in the reproduction of the gender order. As men clothe their bodies, maintain their appearance through exercise, body products and/or cosmetic surgery and surround themselves with material goods, they look to mediated images of exemplary masculinity in their project of constructing the self. Thus, an analysis of how cultural intermediaries frame, produce and articulate masculinity is as vital to our understanding of the male consumer as the activities of actual male consumers.[50]

It follows that though *Esquire* invests in hegemonic masculinity, its masculinity project takes place squarely in the realm of consumption. *Esquire* advertised a particular hegemonic masculinity project as a lifestyle – that is, "an assemblage of disconnected consumer dispositions and proclivities that are brought together to express an individual style."[51] Nevertheless, men's relationship to consumerism is often problematic. Indeed, despite *Esquire's* longstanding investment in constructing a male consumer, this study will show that authors depict men – some men – struggling with their relationship to consumerism and domesticity. Moreover, in a capitalist society, men's relative comfort or discomfort with consumption is one aspect of the struggle for hegemonic masculinity.[52] No matter how fraught the relationship between consumerism and masculinity, it is through the marketplace that *Esquire's* hegemonic masculinity project would proffer its readers solutions to the "problem" of patriarchy.

Case Study: November 1958

To better demonstrate the theory and methodology behind this study, I turn to the November 1958 issue of *Esquire*. Published just prior to the tumultuous sixties, to which the first and second chapters of this study turn, the November 1958 issue demonstrates how the magazine made legible to its male readers the historical pressures on masculinity. This issue is not only notable for publishing Truman Capote's famous novella *Breakfast at Tiffany's*, but also for printing Arthur Schlesinger, Jr's "The Crisis of American Masculinity," one of the clearest appeals to a "crisis" narrative offered by the magazine. Far from offering a singular "*Esquire* Man," the magazine's articles cover many topics of masculine interest, including cognac, hunting, travel, Broadway musicals, religion, and literature, providing multiple avenues for masculine development.

Schlesinger's "The Crisis of American Masculinity" is one of several key texts published during the 1950s that sought to explain the causes and propose solutions to a supposed crisis of identity felt by the American male. As many critics have noted, the popular discussion of this crisis can be seen in a number of influential books of the period, most notably David Riesman's *The Lonely Crowd* (1950), C. Wright Mills's *White Collar* (1955), and William H. Whyte's *The Organization Man* (1956).[53] Each of these works, either implicitly or explicitly, deals with the supposed problem of being a man in an affluent, white-collar culture.[54] The white-collar worker, or what, following Whyte, I will call the "Organization Man," was a representative of "square" society. For Whyte, the Organization Man is a personality engendered by organizations; as Cieply explains, he "longs to be part of the group. In this sense, he willingly sublimates his own desires and needs to that of the group."[55] Timothy Melley finds at the root of *The Organization Man* a "story of declining individualism ... driven by a masculinist fantasy of resistance in which the only actors are 'the individual' and 'the organization'" and sees Whyte's prescription, in particular, as "nothing so much as a healthy dose of masculinity."[56] Of the three, Mills most clearly sees conformity as a specifically masculine problem, comparing white-collar workers to eunuchs.[57] These commentators identify 1950s American society as one in which men – largely divorced from production, manual labour, and land-ownership – have lost agency because of the movement towards an advanced capitalist society and white-collar work.

Schlesinger's essay seems a particularly well-timed contribution: *Esquire* had the previous month celebrated its 25th anniversary, and so the essay does some important work evaluating and re-articulating *Esquire*'s hegemonic masculinity project. Certainly the essay responds to the ongoing anxiety surrounding masculinity that the magazine had been developing throughout the 1950s. The American author and syndicated columnist Robert Ruark led the charge at the dawn of the decade, publishing chauvinist screeds such as "Mystery Unincorporated," an anti-cosmetic essay in which he calls the made-up woman "a decontaminated garbage heap,"[58] or the previous month's "What Hath God Wrought?" wherein he states that "The initial mistake was made in treating women like people."[59] Ruark's essays kept company with the likes of "Woman: The Overrated Sex," by J.B. Rice, in which the good doctor supposedly debunks the myth of female superiority.[60] When not attacking women, *Esquire*'s columnists sometimes complained about the treatment of men, as does the author of "Papa is a Patsy," who writes that television programs depict the American father as "ignorant, incompetent and immature" with "barely enough mechanical skill to tie his own shoes. All that's kept this oaf from going to hell in a basket are the tact and wisdom of his wife and kids, who treat him like a dear, retarded child."[61] Schlesinger's essay therefore not only takes stock of the current state of American masculinity, but also charts a course for *Esquire* and its male readership. Responding to the supposed, contemporaneous "crisis of masculinity" identified by Whyte, Mills, and Riesman, and played out in the magazine's pages throughout the decade, Schlesinger's essay directly addresses *Esquire*'s ideal male reader. As Cieply explains, Schlesinger "neatly, if unintentionally, defined *Esquire*'s imagined readership: a cadre of intelligent, sophisticated and well-rounded men eager to break the chains of conformity."[62]

The essay begins:

> What has happened to the American male? For a long time, he seemed utterly confident in his manhood, sure of his masculine role in society, easy and definite in his sense of sexual identity. The frontiersman of James Fenimore Cooper, for example, never had any concern about his masculinity; they were men, and it did not occur to them to think twice about it. Even well into the twentieth century, the heroes of Dreiser, of Fitzgerald, of Hemingway remain men. But one begins to detect a new theme emerging in some of these authors, especially in Hemingway: the theme of the male hero increasingly preoccupied with proving his virility to himself. And by mid-century, the male role had plainly lost its rugged clarity of outline. Today men are more and more conscious of maleness not as a fact but as a problem. The way by which American

men affirm their masculinity are [*sic*] uncertain and obscure. There are multiple signs, indeed, that something has gone badly wrong with the American male's conception of himself.[63]

It is important to note that, though Schlesinger is diagnosing American masculinity *in general,* he takes his evidence from literature (specifically from Dreiser, Fitzgerald, and Hemingway, all of whom published in *Esquire*), highlighting the role that fictional constructions of masculinity play in shaping "the American male's conception of himself." For example, he finds confused masculinity in the modern world when looking at contemporary literature, such as Tennessee Williams's play *Cat on a Hot Tin Roof.*

Several scholars have rightly objected to the reliance on crises discourses in studies of masculinity;[64] however, rather than propagating a myth of masculine crisis, gender historians need to understand the popular discourse of masculine crisis as an ideological tool for hegemonic masculinity.[65] This "crisis" discourse is mobilized so as to prompt a contemporaneous renegotiation of hegemonic masculinity. The "crisis of masculinity" asks men to renegotiate their masculinity in such a way that it is understood as a better "answer" to the "problem" of patriarchy. Men, responding to the "crisis" discourse, find new ways to establish dominance within their gender regimes and to feel comfortable in their relative positions in the gender hierarchy. This process is achieved in two ways: first, though "crisis" discourse recognizes underlying causal factors to the changes in contemporaneous masculinity, it asks men to understand that the problem is with masculinity, not with, for example, the economy. Despite identifying changing labour conditions as a cause, contemporaneous authors still label the crisis as a crisis of *masculinity,* not a crisis of capital. The second and related point is that this "crisis" discourse suggests that the solution to the crisis can be found in masculinity. Men are encouraged to change their behaviours and understanding of masculinity, rather than addressing underlying economic factors.

The reasons Schlesinger gives for this crisis are similar to those espoused by Whyte, Mills, and Riesman: men are increasingly performing "female duties" in the household, women are taking over higher-paying jobs, and homosexuality is "enjoying a cultural boom new in our history."[66] Modern heroes are "castrated," because "the conditions of modern life make the quest for identity more difficult than it has ever been before."[67] However, Schlesinger adamantly states that conservative sex roles will not solve this crisis, arguing that "Masculine supremacy, like white supremacy, was the neurosis of an immature society." Instead, Schlesinger prescribes three "techniques of liberation": satire, art, and politics. In other words, the solution Schlesinger offered the readers of *Esquire* was for them to read more *Esquire*, arguing that men could develop what he called their "lineaments of personality"[68] through engaging with the type of content that the magazine provided. Such a strategy offered *Esquire*'s readership the idea that societal change would not be a matter of class warfare, in which case *Esquire*'s ideal reader – who was, after all, a white-collar worker, with a problematic relationship to labour – would be on the wrong side of the divide; rather, it made the argument that social change, even radical social change, could be affected by the individual through the act of consumption.

Satire, art, and politics were three frequent features of the magazine. In this particular issue, satire is most easily identifiable in the numerous cartoons that adorn the pages, while Joe Kraft's article on "Washington's Most Powerful Reporter," Scotty Reston, certainly focuses on politics. Though the magazine attempted to offer its readers the possibility of "self-actualisation" (and thus a restoration of their masculinity) through its non-fiction articles and through the goods and services its advertisements offered, the fiction presented in the magazine – geared as it was to a masculine audience – often engaged with this same problem of individuation and conformity directly. Schlesinger's essay makes a strange pairing with Truman Capote's *Breakfast at Tiffany's*, a novella that would lead Norman Mailer to declare its author "the most perfect writer of my generation."[69] Of course the story acts, in Schlesinger's equation, as one of the "techniques of liberation" for men (in this case, art), but at the same time Capote's tale describes a set of gender dynamics that critiques *Esquire*'s hegemonic masculinity project.

Breakfast at Tiffany's may seem, at a glance, like an obvious fit for *Esquire*, inasmuch as it depicts an urbane New York lifestyle, similar to the one advertised in 1930s *Esquire* and the contemporaneous, newly published *Playboy*. Both the bachelor existence of the narrator, Fred, and the upscale, socialite materialism of Holly Golightly resonate with the magazine's lifestyle pages. Moreover, Capote's novelette shares with *Esquire* an interest in consumption, lifestyle, and identity, and with Schlesinger an attention to 1950s conformity. Both points are clarified by Thomas Fahy's pertinent discussion of *Breakfast at Tiffany's* in *Understanding Truman Capote*. In an analysis equally relevant to *Esquire*, Fahy compares Capote's story to the recently launched *Playboy*, to demonstrate how both Golightly and *Playboy* saw identity as something that could be remodelled through developing a cultivated consumer lifestyle.[70] Fahy's focus is Golightly, who has left the South and her husband behind, and in coming to New York has disguised her accent, lost weight, and changed her name, all in the hopes of creating a new identity for herself. Fahy argues that Capote stages Golightly's commitment to "lifestyle" – in other words, to her own "lineaments of personality" – in order for the author "to raise questions about the investment American culture places on outward appearances."[71] For Capote, people most often make consumerist lifestyle choices to conform, putting him in direct opposition to Schlesinger. Indeed, *Breakfast at Tiffany's* can be read as a pointed rejoinder to "The Crisis of American Masculinity." Their shared place of publication, in a single issue of *Esquire*, invites such a reading. Whereas Schlesinger calls for cultivated consumption as the cure to a masculine crisis caused by conformity, Capote uses Golightly to criticize a culture "that encourages – even requires – superficial transformations for social acceptance."[72]

The relationship between Capote's story and *Esquire* becomes even more complex when *Breakfast at Tiffany's* depiction of gender and sexuality is taken into consideration. As Tison Pugh has argued, despite foregrounding Golightly's liberated heterosexuality, *Breakfast at Tiffany's* contains queer themes and homosexual characters, including the narrator.[73] Both Fred's homosexuality and Golightly's progressive sexual attitudes contrast with the conservative sexual mores and strict gender roles of the 1950s. However, as Fahy points out, conformity ultimately wins out in the end, since Fred and Golightly can only "pursue their own desires so long as they look and behave according to certain social stands … [revealing] a rigid class hierarchy in America that limits personal and social freedom."[74] The novella therefore challenges the very bases of *Esquire*'s hegemonic masculinity project, criticizing both its fixation of superficial lifestyle choices and compulsory heterosexuality. The point here is not just to focus on the contradiction, but to read the tension between the magazine and the fiction it published as part of an ongoing process through which masculinity is contested and negotiated.

In addition to satire, art, and politics, *Esquire* also offers men a lifestyle flush with leisure and consumption. As is usually the case with the magazine, there is an obvious relationship between the issue's

advertisements and editorial content. The most obvious example is
the regular travel column: Richard Joseph's "Travel Notes: Mexico" is
interrupted by two large advertisements, one from the Government
of Mexico Tourist Department and another from Aeronaves de Mexico.[75] The relationship is not always so direct; more often, the articles
and advertisements suggest the same type of products and lifestyle.
For example, this issue features an article on Guinness and a photo essay on cognac, while the pages of the magazine are rife with advertisements for alcohol such as Ballantine's scotch, Cutty Sark whisky, and
Cinzano vermouth, to name but a few.[76] The magazine features both
a men's fashion spread, produced by the magazine, and paid advertising for clothing brands, companies, and products, such as Winthrop
shoes, Jockey Underwear, and the California Sportwear Company.[77]

Added to these advertisements and Capote and Schlesinger's contributions are articles on hunting and Broadway musicals – altogether
a collection of masculine interests that point to both the central role
of consumer choices in the performance of gender identity and the
multiplicity of masculinities available in a capitalist society. Without
offering one absolute message to readers, the editorial content and
the advertising are sufficiently synchronized that the issue can be
thought of as a loosely unified ideological package, but one with occasional inconsistencies and contradictory messages that point to the
always unstable, always contested nature of masculinity. Taken as a
whole, *Esquire*'s November 1958 issue demonstrates the "historically
mobile relation" of hegemonic masculinity and how "the defence of
patriarchy" is managed and made intelligible in the magazine's pages.
In *Leading with the Chin*, this gender project is analysed, critiqued, and
complicated.

Chapter Breakdown

Part One, "Recovering Masculinity in the 1960s," focuses on a decade
in which *Esquire* negotiated African American civil strife and the aforementioned post-War "crisis of masculinity" for its male readership.
Chapter 1 examines Norman Mailer's *An American Dream*, which was
originally published in *Esquire* in a series of instalments throughout
1964. Shortly after its publication, feminist critics, including Judith
Fetterley, Kate Millett, and Mary Ellmann, decried the novel as misogynist, and in subsequent years even its defenders had to comment
on the published novel's superficial sexism. Examining the *Esquire*

version of *An American Dream*, and noting its differences from the Dial Press version that was the first collected printing of the novel's instalments, I argue that the magazine version provides openings through which a reading of a more radical gender project is possible. In particular, I focus on the novel's different introductions to demonstrate how the *Esquire* version offers possibilities for identification with feminine role models and subordinated, specifically queer, masculinities, while also highlighting the role of homophobia in the construction of dominant forms of masculinity. The *Esquire* version therefore troubles its protagonist's heterosexual performance, and demonstrates the instability central to hegemonic masculinity projects, especially within polyvalent cultural discourse, captured so well in the form of the magazine.

The second chapter turns to the nonfiction writing of James Baldwin. *Esquire* may have published Baldwin as a voice of the Civil Rights movement and as a commentator on the so-called "Negro problem," but, as fitting the focus of the magazine, he continually framed his discussion of race as a discussion of masculinity. I argue that aspects of Baldwin's critique of hegemonic masculinity – especially the role it plays in enforcing and maintaining racism – are present throughout Baldwin's *Esquire* articles, in particular in two early essays from the 1960s: "Fifth Avenue, Uptown" and "The Black Boy Looks at the White Boy." Making this argument in the pages of *Esquire*, Baldwin indicts those complicit with the contemporary construction of the gender order and encourages a radical change to conceptions of American masculinity. Furthermore, I closely analyse Baldwin's writing in the material context of the July 1968 issue of *Esquire* magazine, to demonstrate the ways the magazine attempted to diminish his counter-hegemonic critique through racially charged textual strategies that reinforce the dominant form of white masculinity and reinscribe the marginalization of black masculinity.

In Part Two, "'The Richness of Life Itself' in the 1970s," the study turns from the politically charged gender and racial projects of the previous section to the relationship between masculinity and consumerism, specifically as presented in the works of Raymond Carver and Truman Capote. The works of both authors fixate on consumer items, though they reflect on men of completely different economic strata: Carver focuses on working-class men, while Capote turns his attention to the jet-set elite. In fact, though Carver's characters are economically inferior to *Esquire*'s ideal readership, Capote's jet-set group is probably superior. Together, Carver and Capote speak to the interrelationship of economic and masculine domination – and this is an aspect of the magazine as well, as it attempts to sell masculinity as a function of consumerism. In chapter 3, I argue that Carver's protagonists represent the increasingly alienated lower-middle and working classes, who do not live the good life promised in *Esquire* and cannot afford to consume the cultural codes and meanings advertised. If *Esquire* posits consumption as one of the few avenues available for practicing a hegemonic masculinity project, then Carver posits that those men who cannot afford to consume the "right" things logically feel their economic constraint as a constrained masculinity. In the context of the magazine, Carver's work can be read both as warning men against buying into a consumer-based hegemonic masculinity project and as confirming *Esquire*'s project by demonstrating what life would be like without purchasing the products advertised, thus presenting the slippery and at-risk nature of the magazine's capitalist masculinity project.

Complementing Carver's focus on the role of consumption in the practice of hegemonic masculinity is Truman Capote's *Answered Prayers*, a novel that follows the exploits of a jet-set gigolo. In chapter 4, I argue that while Carver's working-class protagonists cannot afford to practice the hegemonic masculinity project offered by *Esquire*, and therefore suffer subordination, Capote's characters are able to escape domination and launch their own masculinity projects in two related ways: first, by commodifying themselves, and becoming objects of exchange in the marketplace, and second, by entering extremely affluent social spheres (gender regimes) in which masculine domination holds little sway. In both chapters, men are understood as consuming subjects who renegotiate their place in the gender order via consumption, thus highlighting the ways in which masculinity is a cultural product advertised and sold in the marketplace.

The 1970s, and the concern with consumerism that characterized its fiction, give way to the 1980s, which saw the election of Ronald Reagan and a cultural retrenchment of masculine domination. In Part Three, "Cold Warriors of the 1980s," I turn to the work of Tim O'Brien and Don DeLillo. Chapter 5 reads O'Brien's *The Nuclear Age* as a reaction to what Susan Jeffords calls the "remasculinization of America." The novel delineates and criticizes the way hegemonic masculinity mobilizes conservative, ideologically charged symbols (i.e., exemplars of masculinity and emphasized femininities) and creates social spaces (i.e., the bomb shelter) that buttress institutional authority and masculine domination. The novel's protagonist, William, questions his sanity because he finds himself alienated from patriarchy: though practicing a complicit form of masculinity, he is continually denied what he considers his fair share of the patriarchal dividend. The novel presents these problems as contributing factors to his insanity, since William has been culturally indoctrinated to believe that patriarchy is natural and that as a man he has certain rights and privileges that guarantee his dominant place in society, especially over women. Instead, he feels his patriarchal authority is constantly threatened, resulting in his own feelings of obsession and paranoia. William's dilemma clearly takes on wider cultural significance when measured against the masculine project of *Esquire*, which itself struggles with culturally conservative notions of patriarchy while trying to articulate its own version of dominant masculinity.

This study's sixth and final chapter turns to Don DeLillo's *Libra*. *Libra* demonstrates the ways in which, in the American cultural consciousness, Kennedy's assassination is a privileged site wherein hegemonic masculinity is reshaped, contested, and potentially fragmented. Moreover, by reading *Libra* along with the excerpts published in *Esquire* magazine, and by viewing the novel alongside DeLillo's previous *Esquire* publications, it becomes clear that the role of the author is implicated, by *Esquire*, as an exemplar of masculinity, perhaps the most exemplary masculinity for the postmodern era, since only the author has the capacity to control and make sense of the world. With *Libra*, DeLillo provides an entire masculinist metanarrative, one that diagnoses the problems of twentieth century American manhood. Subsequently, *Esquire* – in a way that DeLillo might distrust, but implicitly authorizes – prescribes a type of remedy to those problems in the figure of the author himself.

I end my study by suggesting a renewed interest in the intersection of masculinity and capitalism. Current theorists of neoliberalism have argued that so-called identity politics have hindered leftist analyses of capitalism; indeed, it has been suggested that our attention to diversity has had the effect of turning our attention away from issues of economic inequality. In response to this, I argue that *Leading with the Chin* demonstrates the still-salient connection between economic and masculine domination. I further argue that a certain brand of toxic masculinity drives our neoliberal economic

practices, and that our current neoliberal moment is perhaps setting the stage for a return of patriarchy as a governing ideology.
The study's conclusion therefore turns to recent issues of *Esquire*
magazine to demonstrate the ongoing, fraught relationship between masculinity and the marketplace.

PART ONE

Recovering Masculinity in the 1960s

1

American Dreams, Gendered Nightmares

"Nobody was born a man," he once wrote. "Manhood was earned provided you were good enough, bold enough." He also wrote that "there are two kinds of brave men: those who are brave by the grace of nature, and those who are brave by an act of will." He was writing about Hemingway, whom he placed in the second category, but he was also writing about himself, as he always did.

– Tom Junod[1]

For by now Mailer is as much a cultural phenomenon as a man of letters, fulfilling his enormous ambition to exert a direct effect on the consciousness of his time. What he offers for our edification is the spectacle of his dilemma, the plight of a man whose powerful intellectual comprehension of what is most dangerous in the masculine sensibility is exceeded only by his attachment to the malaise.

– Kate Millett[2]

Norman Mailer may well have been America's most outspoken figure on the subject of masculinity. Certainly he fixated on the concept with an intensity that approached neurosis. As Junod and Millett suggest, few major mid-century novelists were as single-mindedly focused as he was on the pressures – historic, existential, or otherwise – supposedly facing American men. Presenting himself to the world as a kind of urbanite, latter-day Hemingway, Mailer sought to articulate in his writing, fictional or otherwise, a straight, white masculine identity fit for the twentieth century.[3]

Given this preoccupation, it should come as no surprise that Mailer was a frequent contributor to *Esquire* magazine throughout the early

1960s. Here was a publication whose interests matched his. Like Hemingway before him, Mailer used *Esquire* as a platform for his own celebrity; in his column, "The Big Bite," which ran regularly from November 1962 to December 1963, he held court on such topics as Marilyn Monroe, boxing, and Cold War politics. Prior to this, Mailer had published his short story "The Language of Men"[4] in *Esquire*, as well as the seminal essay on John F. Kennedy, "Superman Comes to the Supermart."[5] Perhaps no single item better exemplified Mailer's masculine posturing than the graphic accompanying his July 1963 article, "Norman Mailer Versus Nine Writers": the black and white photograph shows Mailer standing in the corner of a boxing ring at Wiley's Gym in Harlem where just that day, the next page informs readers, Sugar Ray Robinson had been training. The caption accompanying the photograph reads "On the Next Page: Norman Mailer vs.," followed by a list of nine contemporary authors whom Mailer would take on in "nine literary bouts."[6] Here, we are presented with the spectacle of American literature as a boxing match, with Mailer as heavyweight champion.

Despite the synchronicity of masculine interests, the relationship between Mailer and *Esquire* was not uncomplicated. In fact, at times it was fraught and acrimonious. Mailer had originally titled his piece on Kennedy "Superman Comes to the Supermarket." When the editors changed the last word to "Supermart," Mailer sent a letter snidely stating that he would no longer work for them.[7] The separation didn't last long, and by mid-1962 his contributions returned to print. Even after author and magazine reconciled, the association was never an easy one: for example, in December 1963, *Esquire* published an article by Calder Willingham, written in response to Mailer's "Norman Mailer versus Nine Writers." Willingham takes Mailer to task for his confrontational article, charging the author with "status-grubbing" and "egotistical caterwauling" before dismissing him as an object to be pitied.[8] Mailer lent *Esquire* prestige, and the magazine gave him a place to polish his masculine persona, but that didn't mean that they wouldn't criticize him when his performance was found wanting.

In his final "Big Bite" column, published in the last month of 1963 (in the same issue as Willingham's criticism), Mailer announced his intention to write a serial novel in the pages of the magazine. The column begins with Mailer discussing the March on Washington for Jobs and Freedom. Though he never mentions Martin Luther King, Jr's "I Have a Dream" speech, he quotes at length from a *Village Voice* article by Robert Levin that reads, in part, "If the Negro energy is going to make a revolution that would achieve something more than the dubious right to dream the American Dream too ... then violence must be risked."[9] Mailer comments in detail on the role that violence should or shouldn't play in the Civil Rights Movement, before changing the topic to his upcoming novel. He ends the article with what, considering the context, can only be read as a provocation: he will be titling his new work *An American Dream.*

Though Mailer may be writing in the spirit of the unrest, civil strife, and turbulence of the times, no one could mistake *An American Dream* for a Civil Rights novel. The novel focuses on Stephen Richard Rojack, a white, New York academic and minor celebrity. The almost mythic narrative charts Rojack's movement from a conforming, "square" member of the Establishment to a fully free, individualized agent. To accomplish this emancipation from Cold-War conformity, Mailer has Rojack murder his wife in the novel's opening chapter. Subsequently, Rojack engages in a series of violent and sexual encounters with the denizens of a noir-style New York cityscape. In Rojack, Mailer offers readers a hegemonic masculinity project, quite different from the one prescribed by *Esquire*: rather than suggesting that hegemony can be maintained through consumption, *An American Dream* sees masculinity as gaining dominance through the direct, violent domination of women and other(ed) men.

Though seemingly all of Mailer's writing fixated on the issue of being a man in America, *An American Dream* represents his clearest and definitive statement on the subject. Originally published in 1964, *An American Dream* ran as a serial in *Esquire* from January to August before Dial printed a fully revised version the following year. Because Rojack is thoroughly invested in his masculinity project, critics such as Mary Ellmann, Kate Millett, and Judith Fetterley have decried *An American Dream* as misogynist since its first publication by *Esquire*. For Ellmann, Mailer and *An American Dream* are examples that demonstrate the need for a feminist criticism.[10] Millett pithily summarizes the novel as "an exercise in how to kill your wife and be happy ever after."[11] Indeed, Fetterley neatly sums up the feminist consensus on the novel when she calls it "sexism gone berserk in a metaphoric frenzy."[12] To be sure, both Mailer and *An American Dream* are obvious (and deserving) targets of feminist criticism and anger.

More recent criticism of the novel has seen scholars divided over whether it promotes or deconstructs hegemonic masculinity. For example, Mike Meloy's 2009 essay, "Tales of 'The Great Bitch,'" situates the novel in a Cold War discourse of masculinity that sought to counter conformity with hypermasculinity (as I do, below). In doing so, Meloy argues that Rojack acts as a role model for men who want to rise above the "feminine and potentially homosexual American public."[13] In contrast, Justin Shaw's 2014 article argues that Mailer represents misogyny only to critically compare Rojack's sexual conquests with the exploitative processes of late capitalism.[14] Finally, Maggie McKinley's 2015 monograph, *Masculinity and the Paradox of Violence in American Fiction, 1950–75*, sets itself against the tendency to "rehearse" the previously published criticisms of misogyny in that text, and instead examines Mailer's masculinity project in relation to French existentialism – in particular, the work of Simone de Beauvoir and Jean-Paul Sartre – through Mailer's fixation on the tension and identification between self and other (in this case, gendered or racialized others).[15] Moreover, McKinley suggests that *An American Dream* (and Mailer's work more generally) "offers significant insight into prevalent issues of conflicted gendered identity in American culture."[16] Each critic situates the novel in the 1950s discourse of masculinity in crisis, and each reads it in relation to Mailer's 1957 essay, "The White Negro," but each of them comes to a very different conclusion about the results of Mailer's masculinity project.

None of its most recent critics read the novel as it was originally published in the pages of *Esquire*, which was a notably different text. In fact, Hershel Parker is the only critic who has explicitly discussed the serialized *Esquire* version. Parker's principal concern is not with the novel's portrayal of gender, but with changes between the *Esquire* and Dial versions that, in his eyes, lessen the overall impact of the novel.[17] However, Parker does address gender when he identifies the original version as a courageous exploration of masculinity.[18] Accordingly, Parker suggests that it is through studying *An American Dream* in *Esquire* that a more complex and significant analysis of American masculinity can take place.

Aside from local, stylistic revisions, Parker highlights the major omissions from the Dial version. These include three of Rojack's memories of Harvard (Parker suggests that they may have been too autobiographical), a set of passages that deal with Rojack's fears, and episodes that relate Rojack's thoughts on homosexuality.[19] Provocatively, he wonders whether "Mailer's retrenchments for the Dial version prove that growing up in macho U.S.A. is a burden to the best male literary minds around as much as it is to every little boy who dreads being called a sissy."[20] This is to suggest that Mailer made revisions out of fear of how his own masculinity would be judged because of his similarity to Rojack. If this is the case, then comparing the Dial and *Esquire* versions of the novel reveals an act of textual homophobia, and the original, unrevised version is all the more important because it provides readers with an image of the state of American masculinity that is deeply complex and contradictory.

Parker does not address the completely revised introduction; the *Esquire* version included a roll call of nonconformist individuals and an extended description of Rojack's relationship with John F. Kennedy. Combined, the omissions noted by Parker and the original introduction demonstrate the ways the *Esquire* version presents a more contradictory and complicated masculinity than the one studied by subsequent scholars.

My contention, in this chapter, is that situating *An American Dream* in the context of its publication in *Esquire*, and noting the changes made to the novel and its larger material context as presented in the magazine, greatly strengthens studies such as Shaw's that find in the novel a possible subversion of hegemonic masculinity. In particular, I argue that the serialized novel provides openings through which a more radical gender project is possible, and that the *Esquire* version of the novel subtly offers possibilities for identification with feminine role models and "other," specifically queer, masculinities, while also highlighting the role of homophobia in the construction of dominant forms of masculinity, two openings in the text that were closed off by Mailer in his subsequent revisions. To do so, I first contextualize the novel in the popular discourse of the supposed "crisis of masculinity" in the 1950s, and explain how such crisis discourse is mobilized to retrench hegemonic masculinity. Next, I discuss how *An American Dream*, especially in its Dial version, responds to – and potentially complicates – this crisis discourse. Finally, I turn to the *Esquire* version to analyse the ways it troubles Rojack's rigidly heterosexual performance, and calls into question the legitimacy of hegemonic masculinity.

1. The Crisis of Masculinity and the Problem of Conformity

Given Mailer's sometimes myopic interests, it was inevitable that *An American Dream* would fixate on masculinity, regardless of its original place of publication; however, it is hard to imagine a more suitable locale for its first print run than *Esquire* magazine. As I argue in the introduction, *Esquire* is one place that registers the historic pressures shaping masculinity. In its pages, one can find evidence of the historical labour that goes into negotiating hegemonic masculinity for a straight, white, professional audience. As such, it is hardly surprising that *Esquire* in the 1950s expressed an anxiety about man's changing social status in an economy increasingly dependent on white-collar work. Outside the pages of the magazine, a number of books articulated this anxiety, including David Riesman's *The Lonely Crowd* (1950), C. Wright Mills's *White Collar* (1955), and William H. Whyte's *The Organization Man* (1956), each of which contributed to the notion that professional-managerial labour fundamentally changed man's relationship to patriarchal authority. The Organization Man came to be the paradigm for "square" society, a figure more-or-less emasculated by his need to conform. As previously mentioned, *Esquire* responded most directly to this particular articulation of masculinity in crisis with the publication of Arthur Schlesinger, Jr's "The Crisis of American Masculinity" in 1957. Rather than arguing for a return to patriarchal sex roles that would subordinate women to men, Schlesinger prescribes satire, politics, and art as the remedy for masculine malaise. In other words, the *Esquire* reader could become a kind of conforming nonconformist, or what Barbara Ehrenreich called a "gray flannel rebel." These "rebels" "cultivated an acute awareness of the problem of conformity – much as everyone else did – and achieved, through their awareness, a kind of higher, more reflective conformity."[21] *Esquire*'s ideal reader individuated himself through lifestyle rather than counter-cultural activity.

By 1964, the year it published *An American Dream, Esquire* had begun to turn its attention away from the pressures of conformity. Publisher Arnold Gingrich tackles this issue directly in January of that year:

Conformity was king in the days of the melting pot, when the open doors of unlimited immigration made all the new arrivals eager to melt into the uniform grey pattern of American existence, and try earnestly to be or to pretend to be like everybody else, in an age when efficiency was worshiped and the prevailing trinity was mass production, standardization, and interchangeability of parts.

Today, those centripetal stirrings of the melting pot have been reversed, and we see a centrifugal force of fragmentation splitting our culture up into a bewildering variety of subcultures, instead of the uniform amalgam of the past.[22]

According to Gingrich, in the 1960s, advanced consumerism and leisure press for "diversity" in much the same way that 1950s culture used to press for conformity – the urge this time, however, is to stand out, rather than get lost in the masses. He goes on to argue that "today's mass customer has almost an embarrassment of choice ... yet in spite of today's multitudinous incentives to buy – or because of them – his behavior, in the mass, was never less predictable."[23] A reader might infer from Gingrich's article that, as a "mass customer" with "an embarrassment of choice," he needs to read *Esquire* to know best what to do. In any case, Gingrich's article highlights the recent threat of conformity and implies exactly how the magazine might be of service to its masculine readership.

Instead of conformity, in the sixties *Esquire* focused on the related fears of "the Establishment." As Timothy Melley explains, post-war American culture was characterized by agency panic, which he defines as "a pervasive set of anxieties about the way technologies, social organization, and communication systems may have reduced human autonomy and uniqueness."[24] The Establishment is one popular focal point of agency panic: it is the "square" society against which the counter-culture rages, the institutionalized face of conformity, and the sometimes-hidden source of the power that supposedly shapes our lives (and so threatens our agency). Like the figure of the Organization Man, the Establishment is a powerful force for the status quo.

"The Establishment," as a pejorative and "popular capsule description of the established societal hierarchy ... those institutions, bureaucracies, and individuals that exercise control of any sort of population," played a recurring role in the pages of *Esquire* throughout the decade. The *Encyclopedia of Cold War Politics* credits the popularity of the term to Richard H. Rovere's essay "The American Establishment,"[25] which was published in *Esquire* in 1962.[26] Though the essay speaks to the prevailing sense of "agency panic" noted by Melley, it does so with a tongue-in-cheek style that subsequent discussions of the Establishment lacked.

Rovere described America's historical situation in this way:

Summing up the situation at the present moment, it can, I think, be said that the Establishment maintains effective control over the Executive and Judicial branches of government; that it dominates most of American education and intellectual life; that it has very nearly unchallenged power in deciding what is and what is not respectable opinion in this country. Its authority is enormous in organized religion (Roman Catholics and fundamentalist Protestants to one side), in science, and, indeed, in all the learned professions except medicine. It is absolutely unrivaled in the great new world created by the philanthropic foundations – a fact which goes most of the way toward explaining why so little is known about the Establishment and its workings. Not one thin dime of Rockefeller, Carnegie, or Ford money has been spent to further Establishment studies.[27]

Seeking to illustrate the Establishment's structure and workings for *Esquire*'s readers, Rovere paints a portrait of a vast cabal of politicians, academics, and captains of industry, loosely organized but nevertheless led by an Executive Committee and a Chairman whose very existence is kept secret from America-at-large.

Not all readers reacted to Rovere's essay as satire. John Gentile of Upper Darby, PA, lauded the article in his letter to the editor, stating that "This article proves that former Maj. Gen. Edwin A. Walker was right when he spoke of America's no-win policy-makers. Without a doubt, he had the Establishment in mind." Gentile claims that "a deep analysis" of the Establishment's membership "would indicate this assemblage to be fiery and dangerous Pink," before concluding: "*Esquire* has raked the coals; America thanks you."[28] Gentile's letter seems to unintentionally represent the type of thinking that Rovere mocked, demonstrating the centrality of the Establishment to the cultural imagination.

"The American Establishment" was the first in a series of articles that became a semi-regular feature for *Esquire*. Often forgetting the sardonic tone of the original, subsequent features sought to demystify the workings of a number of lesser, more specific Establishments, including Rust Hills's "The Structure of the American Literary Establishment" (July 1963), Karl E. Meyer's "The Washington Press Establishment" (April 1964), Bill Veeck's "The Baseball Establishment" (August 1964), Harold Rosenberg's "The Art Establishment" (January 1965), William Worthy's "The Black Power Establishment" (November 1967), and James L. Goddard's "The Drug Establishment" (March 1969). Most of these articles came with a two-page, coloured chart that supposedly visualized for its readers the structure of the particular Establishment under analysis. Whether satirical or seemingly written in earnest, each article adds to the idea that hierarchical power structures wielded real control over American society and limited the agency and potential of the individual.

Significantly, Mailer's name is not absent from *Esquire*'s discussions of the Establishment. Noting that "The Establishment has in its top councils some people who appear to the unsophisticated to be oppositionists," Rovere claims that "Norman Mailer, the self-styled 'hipster' novelist ... enjoy[s] close relations with leading figures of the Executive Committee."[29] In the chart accompanying Hills's article on the Literary Establishment, Mailer's name appears four times. I would argue that Mailer's obsession with a nonconforming, radical individual is motivated in some ways by the cultural position he occupies – that is, Mailer is someone who positions himself as a hipster and outsider, while at the same time his position as a mainstream public intellectual and writer makes him part of the very Establishment he seemingly loathes. Rojack is a fantasy figure constructed specifically for this historical situation.

In the post-war era, *Esquire* identified two supposed dangers to American masculinity: the Organization and the Establishment. Though the two concepts differ, both are particularly threatening to *Esquire*'s nominally straight, white, professional-managerial male readers. Both the Organization and the Establishment threaten masculine agency and individuality: the former does so by demanding conformity, the latter by redirecting power and agency elsewhere, through either covert machinations or amassed, entrenched, and unassailable privilege. It is to these exact threats that Mailer's *An American Dream* seemingly responds.

In 1957, the same year Schlesinger prescribed *Esquire* readers consumption as the remedy for masculine crisis, Mailer offered a more radical solution in his essay "The White Negro," published in the pages of *Dissent* magazine. On the one hand, *Esquire* is robustly capitalist, and in its first issue promised to be "all things to all men";[30] on the other, *Dissent* is ardently socialist, and in its first issue declared itself against "the bleak atmosphere of conformism that pervades the political and intellectual life of the United States."[31] The differences between the two articles, and the two responses to masculine malaise proffered by the authors, speak to the differences between the two magazines and Mailer's positioning of himself as a marginal intellectual.

Echoing Whyte, Reisman, and Mills, and staying true to *Dissent's* mission statement, Mailer saw the 1950s as an era of stultifying conformity:

> One could hardly maintain the courage to be individual, to speak with one's own voice, for the years in which one could complacently accept oneself as part of an elite by being a radical were forever gone. A man knew that when he dissented, he gave a note upon his life which could be called in any year of overt crisis. No wonder then that these have been the years of conformity and depression. A stench of fear has come out of every pore of American life, and we suffer from a collective failure of nerve. The only courage, with rare exceptions, that we have been witness to, has been the isolated courage of isolated people.[32]

Typical of the author's pugilistic pose, Mailer sees conformity as a type of cowardice. Throughout the '50s and '60s, Mailer would frequently argue that manhood was measured in bravery: for example, just two years after "The White Negro," in 1959, he wrote that "being a man is the continuing battle of one's life, and one loses a bit of manhood with every stale compromise to the authority of any power in which one does not believe,"[33] and many similar statements followed. In "The White Negro," Mailer defines the identity necessary for breaking the stultifying bonds of social conformity, which he associates with the figure of the "square." Mailer makes the dichotomy clear, stating that "One is Hip or one Is Square ... one is a rebel or one conforms, one is a frontiersman in the Wild West of American night life, or else a Square cell, trapped in the totalitarian tissues of American society, doomed willy-nilly to conform if one is to succeed."[34] Set up against this square, conforming figure is Mailer's hero, the hipster, an "American existentialist."[35]

Whereas Schlesinger suggested that men strengthen their "lineaments of personality" through culture, Mailer argues that white American masculinity can be revivified through "the art of the primitive,"[36] which he associates with African Americans. Mailer finds a suitable model for modern (white) man in a racist caricature: versus the Organization Man, this stereotyped black man is ruggedly primitive, lives in the present, and is situated in the body. Mailer sees this one-dimensional black identity as something that can be co-opted by white men, whom he calls hipsters.

The prescription Mailer offers men in "The White Negro," to liberate them from conformity, may seem substantially more radical than

Schlesinger's directions to engage in satire, art, and politics, but the logic is strikingly similar. Schlesinger offers consumption as a means to self-actualization, and so, in a sense, does Mailer, even if the self-actualized man of the former would be a sophisticate, the latter a psychopath. In this one-dimensional fiction of African American identity, Mailer finds certain practices, attitudes, and performances which can be co-opted or mimicked by white men as a set of lifestyle choices: hence the "White Negro." The "White Negro" as lifestyle is especially obvious when one considers Mailer's focus in the essay on the significance of jazz musicians and orgasms to the hipster's identity,[37] no different than a magazine's focus on music and sex in its attempt to rescue masculinity (in, for example, *Esquire* or *Playboy*).

Furthermore, Mailer's identification of the hipster as a "philosophical psychopath"[38] clearly points to the fact that freedom from conformity comes less from a new way of being and more from a new way of thinking. Even if Mailer intended his "White Negro" to be more of a revolutionary than the typical *Esquire* reader, this attitude he describes is something that a white, professional male audience could actually adopt "without going to the extremes of countercultural disengagement"[39] – the same promise implicitly made by the magazine. As Lee Konstantinou has argued, the mid-century hipster was defined by "his mastery of codes of consumption," and that "All hipsters, of whatever class position, saw power as a function of knowledge, curated taste, and strategic consumption. Hip was a theory of power."[40] Like Mailer, *Esquire* offered imaginary nonconformity through advertising individuality as lifestyle: how a man dressed, and how he spent his leisure time, made him an individual. Furthermore, *Esquire* readers could counter conformity through consuming the right types of writing and fiction, such as the writing offered by Mailer and Schlesinger.

2. Hegemonic Masculinity in *An American Dream*

An American Dream is a novel focused on this conflict between the individual and the Establishment, the hipster and the square. The novel's protagonist takes up a masculinity project meant to propose a "solution" to this supposed "problem" of conformity. This is to say that the "White Negro," as promulgated in Mailer's essay of the same name, is a masculinity project that Rojack later puts into practice. The "White Negro" is, to use Connell's terms, an attempt to configure a "gender practice" meant to "answer to the problem of the legitimacy of patriarchy."[41] In this case, the "problem" of legitimacy is the one outlined in the discourse of masculinity in crisis: that men have lost agency – been effeminized – via their connections to institutions and conformity. Rojack attempts to remasculinize his own version of masculinity through his "White Negro" project. In doing so, he not only commits all of the problems inherent in hegemonic masculinity (in particular, his practice of masculinity depends on the domination of women), but also discovers that such projects cannot succeed without institutional support.

Mailer's novel narrates a movement away from "squareness," away from a subject position that is fully imbricated in a number of institutions, to a "rootless" position, which is achieved through violent encounters with the Establishment. As Nigel Leigh argues, the novel conceives of American society as nothing more than the Establishment.[42] Like the popular discourse of a "crisis of masculinity," the novel is rife with "agency panic."[43] At the start of the novel Rojack situates himself, and his subjectivity, within square society, explaining that, after nine years of marriage to Deborah, he had "learned to speak in a world which believed in the *New York Times*: Experts Divided on Fluoridation, Diplomat Attacks Council Text, Self-Rule Near for Bantu Province, Chancellor Outlines Purpose of Talks, New Drive for Health Care for Aged."[44] Rojack sees himself as not only a member of square society, but also as actually speaking the language of institutionalized squareness.

As well as being generally associated with squareness and the Establishment at the novel's outset, Rojack is also particularly identified with various institutions. Institutions apply and circulate power within a society, and they also, as discussed in this study's introduction, propagate social hierarchies within the gender order. As Stephen Whitehead notes, "key structural entities such as the state, education, the media, religion, political institutions and business, being historically numerically dominated by men, all serve the project of male dominance through their capacity to promote and validate the ideologies underpinning hegemonic masculinity."[45] Rojack's relationship with institutions highlights the paradox at the centre of the 1950s "crisis of masculinity": while institutions are seen as effeminizing, it is also Rojack's connection to institutions that first prove his masculine credentials.

Rojack's ascendency to power and prominence – the position from which his adventure begins – starts with his role as a soldier in World War II; subsequently, Rojack moves from war hero to congressman, and then to minor celebrity as a popular academic and television personality. Even in this late stage of his fame, he is planning a return to politics. So, before the main events of the novel even begin, Rojack is firmly associated with most of America's major institutions, moving from what Louis Althusser would call "Repressive State Apparatuses," which ultimately function by violence, to "Ideological State Apparatuses," which function by ideology.[46] The Repressive State Apparatuses to which Rojack initially belongs include the military and the government; following his role in these institutions, he moves to the Ideological State Apparatuses of academia and the media. This movement is significant, because Rojack's masculinity project involves confronting, often violently, other hegemonic formulations of masculinity, most of which are associated with institutions and all of which (except in the final instance of Barney Kelly) function by overt violence. Rojack's journey, then, implies a re-masculinization through physical conflict – the type of physical conflict that typified his time in the military.[47]

Rojack's murder of Deborah, in this reading, serves as a symbolic (and mental) severance between Rojack and square society. The novel immediately introduces Deborah as having a long connection with institutional power: "She was Deborah Caughlin Mangaravidi Kelly, of the Caughlins first, English-Irish bankers, financiers and priests; the Mangaravidis, a Sicilian issue from the Bourbons and the Hapsburgs; Kelly's family was just Kelly; but he had made a million two hundred times. So there was a vision of treasure, far-off blood, and fear" (1). Unpacking her multiple family names, Mailer connects Deborah to the world of finance, the Church, European industry, and big business. Since Rojack was depending on Deborah's family connections for his return to politics (17), his future in government dies with her. Rojack feels effeminized by his reliance on Deborah's institutional connections, in much the same way that Mills, Riesman, and Whyte see the Establishment as an emasculating force. Significantly, Rojack murders Deborah when she mocks his masculinity and claims to be performing an undescribed sexual act on other men (23–32). Having murdered the supposed source of his emasculation, much of the rest of the novel sees Rojack practicing a nonconforming, violent, physicalized masculinity.[48]

The connection between Rojack's project of radical individuation and the "White Negro" can be seen in several key ways. In the most general sense, Rojack's goals are the goals of the "White Negro": he

radically breaks from "square" society and moves towards a deracinated subject position. Moreover, there are several specific connections between Rojack's character and the project outlined in "The
White Negro." Most obviously, Rojack's narrative begins when he
"encourage[s] the psychopath"[49] in himself by murdering his wife and
proceeding to fight against all aspects of "square" society. Furthermore, Rojack demonstrates a seemingly supernatural sense of smell[50]
and apparent (or possibly imagined) psychic powers.[51] In addition,
Rojack describes a heavenly city that he sees several times during the
novel: first, when he murders Deborah (31); next, when he climaxes
with Ruta (46); and again, when he makes love to Cherry (128). In
"The White Negro," Mailer explains that "the hipster moves through
his life on a constant search with glimpses of Mecca in many a turn
of his experience (Mecca being the apocalyptic orgasm)."[52] Gabriel
Miller makes Rojack's connection to the "White Negro" clear when
describing Rojack as "a prototype of the heroic new individualist who
will emerge in modern America to assault the repressive state."[53] Rojack is therefore an exemplar of masculinity for "gray flannel rebels"
and other professional, white-collar readers who somehow fear the
castrating conformity of "square" culture.

Exemplars of masculinity, transmitted through the symbolic order
and valorized by institutions, establish and solidify hegemonic masculinity, since "To be culturally exalted, [hegemonic masculinity] must
have exemplars who are celebrated as heroes."[54] Furthermore,

> exemplary masculinities may be constructed (e.g. in commercial sport)
> which do not correspond closely to the lives of the majority of men,
> or even correspond closely to the actual lives of the richest and most
> powerful men, but which in various ways express ideals, fantasies and
> desires, provide models of relations with women and solutions to gen-
> der problems and above all 'naturalize' gender difference and gender
> hierarchy.[55]

Though exemplars of masculinity are often real men constructed
in specific gender regimes, they become symbols when taken up as
exemplars of masculinity – they are "models of admired masculine
conduct" circulated by the media and exalted by masculinist institutions such as *Esquire*.

Moreover, exemplars of masculinity are not necessarily like most,
or the richest, men, and men from marginalized and subordinated

groups can even be held up as exemplary. Connell calls this latter process "authorization"; examining the American context, she provides the example of wealthy black athletes, who are held up as exemplary but whose statuses do nothing to benefit the social status of black men more generally.[56] That is to say that exemplars of masculinity benefit hegemonic masculinity as symbols of masculine superiority: they tend to embody an aspect of hegemonic masculinity which can be used to symbolically buttress men's statuses more generally.

Not only is Rojack an exemplar of masculinity for the professional-managerial class, but he is also forced to prove his masculinity against inferior, institutionalized exemplars. *An American Dream* dramatizes Rojack's dissociation from the Establishment, and attempts to prove the superiority of his masculinity project, by continually putting him into conflict with exemplars of masculinity indicative of highly institutionalized gender regimes. As Philip Bufithis argues, minor characters in the novel stand in for larger institutions.[57] Suspected of murder, Rojack must fight against the police, especially in the form of Detective Roberts. He also immediately comes into contact with organized crime, in the form of mafioso Eddie Ganucci. Because the discourse of the crisis of masculinity views conformity as emasculating, it is important that Rojack has institutionalized versions of masculinity to face and best, to prove the superiority of his nonconformist masculinity project. As Barry Leeds has noted, while the men standing in for institutions are tough, their strength is based on their connection with the Establishment, resulting in the corruption of conformity.[58] Rojack must prove the superiority of his masculinity, and so the men he faces must be suitably tough and physically threatening, or else his victories would be too easy and prove nothing; however, because these competing forms of hegemonic masculinity are committed "to a corrupt system," they can never quite contend. Rojack's encounters with the Establishment must include intermediaries or representative figures with whom he can do battle, either physically, or at the level of manly nerves. However he faces them, it is important that there is an embodied, male enemy whom he can best.

In addition to Roberts and Ganucci, Rojack's opponents include the boxer Romeo and the jazz singer Shago Martin. Though not representative of state apparatuses (repressive or ideological), the two nonetheless represent institutions central to American culture – sport and music respectively. Both men are physical threats to Rojack, but both are also regime-specific exemplars of hegemonic masculinity. In

particular, Romeo is representative of masculinity's culturally held association between masculinity and violence, which sport institution-
alizes,[59] and Shago (as his name implies) demonstrates dominance
over women via sexual prowess.[60] Besting both men, Rojack proves
the superiority of the "White Negro" masculinity project.

Each of these encounters develops towards a final showdown with
Deborah's father, Barney Oswald Kelly. Kelly represents a final major
institution – business – but also much, much more. In the final chapters of the novel, the reader learns that Kelly sits at the head of the
Establishment: the mob, the CIA, and the government, all answer, in
some way, to Kelly. Mailer's Establishment is institutional and totalizing, a paranoid image of society.[61] Rojack's confrontation with Kelly
is not only a battle against a diabolic father figure, but against the
ultimate Organization Man.

The narrative of the novel, then, works to move Rojack from an
institutionalized position bereft of courage, wit, ambition, and hope
to one of absolute individualism and masculine violence, able to best
men with fists or with his nerves, capable of bedding any woman he
wants, and gifted with seemingly supernatural senses. Such a separation between Rojack and the organizations that maintain power – and
thus patriarchy – should have the potential to make Rojack a counter-
hegemonic figure. However, this is not the case, since Rojack's journey
towards individuality is, at every step, a chauvinist, masculinist quest.
Rojack is able to move from conformity to autonomy only through
the use of violence, the exercise of his sexual virility, and acts of "courage." Rojack's journey involves defeating competing versions of masculinity, but in their place he can only offer a masculinity project that
is more violent, more physical, and more toxic. In breaking out of the
Establishment, Rojack nonetheless reinforces patriarchy, by acting as
an exemplar of masculinity who demonstrates masculinity's privileged
connection to domination through violence.

A critical response to An American Dream needs to question why
Rojack's journey of self-actualization must necessarily be expressed
in such a misogynistic fashion, especially considering Mailer's admission that "Hip" seems to be connected with bisexuality, which could
open the door for alternate configurations of masculinity and a possible subversion of a rigid, heteronormative gender hierarchy.[62] Indeed, Mailer unequivocally notes that "many hipsters are bisexual,"[63]
while more ambiguously stating that "the condition of psychopathy"
is present in "promiscuous homosexuals,"[64] and that "the Negro ...

discovered and elaborated a morality of the bottom" through, among other things, "perversion, promiscuity, pimpery."[65] The important difference between the hipster and Rojack, then, is that while the hipster might be sexually ambiguous – or, more specifically, bisexual or "perverted" – Rojack's enactment of the "White Negro" takes an oppressively heterosexual form.[66] This is not to say that he is unproblematically heterosexual – as further discussion will make clear, Rojack's heterosexuality is inflated with heterosexism, and possibly functions to efface what is obliquely represented as his own barely sublimated homosexuality – but that Rojack's actions, and the narrative of the novel, are strictly, rigidly heterosexual. This important difference between Mailer's hipster and the novel's protagonist has a major effect: it ensures that Rojack, in his new, "rootless" state, nonetheless reasserts masculine hegemony. Making Rojack too "straight," Mailer subverts his most radical potentialities. Rojack reinscribes patriarchy in the potentially free liminal space he finds outside of "the Organization," of "square society," usually as a response to masculinity challenges prompted or exacerbated by homophobia. Attempting to describe the creation of a "rootless" hero, Mailer recreates a social situation based on patriarchy and masculine domination.

Though Rojack's journey involves separating himself from the institutions that confine and define him, the one "institution" or construct he continually *refuses* to challenge is gender. Indeed, in the novel version of *An American Dream*, gender – especially masculinity – is viewed by Rojack not as a construct, but as a ground or base upon which other constructs – false constructs – have been erected. This is what Mailer means when he refers to the "White Negro" as a primitive: he sees society as something that has gotten in the way of "natural," "primitive" man, and the "White Negro" is an attempt to return to this primitive state. Holding such a view of a "primitive" man, Rojack fails to see that masculinity is an institution, much like the other institutions that he seeks to avoid. Thus privileging masculinity, Rojack cannot help but pathologically reconstitute patriarchy, even as he attempts to break down society.

Rojack reconstitutes patriarchy in his supposed rootlessness by taking advantage of the perceived privileged relationship between masculinity and violence. Simply put, men are supposed to fight, hurt, and dominate, or, at the very least, they have access to these actions in a way that women do not.[67] Rojack murders his wife (31–2), engages in seemingly consensual rough sex with Ruta that

nonetheless is presented in terms of a violent rape (especially in relation to the seemingly forced anal penetration) (41–6), and brutally
beats Shago Martin (192–3), and in every instance he gains from
these experiences. Rojack's continuous use of violence enacts this
system of domination – to which white, heterosexual men have the
easiest, most "justifiable" access – while at the same time revealing
the fraudulence of the gendered order: patriarchy and male privilege are only maintained through violent acts, giving the lie to any
notion that the hierarchy it enforces is "natural" or that it should
even be seen as stable or naturalized. Perhaps Millett is correct to
argue that "*An American Dream* is a rallying cry for a sexual politics
in which diplomacy has failed and war is the last political resort of a
ruling caste that feels its position in deadly peril";[68] the novel implies
that it is not masculinity that is in crisis, but patriarchy itself.

Rojack himself gains some small insight into the flaws in his masculinity project. In the final chapter, when he meets Kelly at the Waldorf,
Rojack begins to realize that the violent, physical domination he has
practiced corresponds with the institutional violence with which he
struggled. Shaw directs attention to the following passage from this
section, in which Rojack ponders his surroundings:

> Aristocrats, slave owners, manufacturers and popes had coveted these
> furnishings … a field of force was on me here, an air rich with surfeit
> and the long whisper of corridors, the echo of a banquet hall where red
> burgundy and wild boar went down. That same field of force had come
> on me as I left Deborah's body on the floor and started down the stairs
> to the room where Ruta was waiting. (235)

As his surroundings demonstrate, Kelly is the embodiment of the
Establishment, as represented not only by his wealth and social position, but also by his privileged place within a history of institutional
oppression. Rojack recognizes in Kelly's chambers – a place he identifies as an "antechamber of hell" (234) – a legacy of institutional power
and domination in which he has unwittingly participated. Shaw calls
this "Rojack's epiphanic meditation on the history of American power
and oppression."[69] Rojack now recognizes his own complicity in hegemonic masculinity and, further, he realizes that the patriarchal dividend for which he has fought is available to him only because of the
institutions of domination against which he has set himself. In other
words, Rojack has realized that masculine domination is not natural

but historical, that the historical forces that maintain patriarchy are the institutions from which he has tried to uproot himself, and that, in practicing a masculinity project intent on nonconformity, this practice has nonetheless extended, rather than countered, the supposed logic of hegemonic masculinity. Here, Rojack comes to understand the futility of trying to escape institutions while trying to reinvigorate masculinity: his nonconformist masculinity has simply reinforced the status quo.

Rojack's enactment of the "White Negro" results in a masculinist fantasy, in which Rojack "regains" masculine privilege and agency by radically uprooting himself from the Establishment. However, "hegemony is likely to be established only if there is some correspondence between cultural ideal and institutional power, collective if not individual."[70] Rojack – a rootless, deracinated individual – cannot be, in the final instance, properly hegemonic, since he is so drastically opposed to – and alienated from – institutional power. Rojack reinforces hegemonic masculinity despite the fact that he appears to be challenging the institutions that maintain male domination. The "White Negro" provides a masculine fantasy of agency in a world dominated by the Establishment, but the Establishment itself is most likely to be the home of actual masculine hegemony. A truly radical figure could pose a threat to this hegemony, but *An American Dream* does not – and it fails to do so because of Rojack's gender performance.

3. *An American Dream* and *Esquire* Magazine

Though Mailer's Rojack – and the "White Negro" – is not properly hegemonic, because of his radical nonconformity, he nevertheless helps to maintain, and perhaps even renegotiate, hegemonic masculinity. He does so by acting as an exemplar of masculinity for his readers – in the first instance, the white-collar (gray flannel rebel) reader of *Esquire*. When *Esquire*'s ideal reader consumes Mailer's work, hegemonic masculinity is renegotiated in the marketplace.

Unlike Rojack or the "White Negro," *Esquire*'s ideal reader is not likely going to do anything that is actually radical. These men are not going to live the type of adventure narrated by Rojack; they can, however, read about this radicalism from the safety of their home or office. At the end of the 1950s, and throughout the 1960s, *Esquire* in particular allowed its readers to engage in a counter-cultural discourse, not on the frontlines, but through the activity of consumption. *An American Dream* makes intelligible the particular masculine malaise that men felt, or were told to feel, and provided a fantasy of liberation from this dissatisfaction. Men were not so much suffering from a genuine loss of agency, but a *perceived* one, and *An American Dream* (and *Esquire*) offered a safe, culturally authorized way to feel that they had broken free from conformity while remaining in their white-collar jobs. The anti-establishment thrust of *An American Dream*'s angst can be stripped of its radical potential, and the desire for individualism and agency can be displaced onto the desire for consumer goods, which the magazine could offer. In this way, the political is transubstantiated into the aesthetic, and the politically resistant is transformed into the economically normative. White-collar readers might not attempt to absorb the "existential synapses" of African Americans[71] by defeating a jazz singer in unarmed combat, but they might consume their language and culture;[72] they might not become hipsters by embracing their inner psychopath, but they might consume the experimental literature of Beat writers such as William Burroughs or Gregory Corso. Institutionalized, hegemonic masculinities are thus propped up, and patriarchy as a whole bolstered, since potential sites of resistance are re-enfranchised through the creation of a consumer lifestyle.

Perhaps the most obvious example in the magazine of the process that repurposes individualism as lifestyle can be found in the July 1964 feature entitled "The New Sentimentality," published in the same issue as the seventh instalment of *An American Dream*. Drawing a distinction between what they see as "Old" and "New" sentimentality, authors David Newman and Robert Benton delineate the tenets of a new masculinity, one that embraces individualism through consumption. Consider this section of the introduction:

> The changeover came in the Fifties. Eisenhower was a key figure, perhaps the last bloom of Old Sentimentality. It was seen that the masses loved him as a father or maybe Gramps …
>
> Suddenly it was 1960 and John Kennedy was there, and the wise, the intellectual and the taste-making people did him homage. They didn't think he was a father or Gramps. They liked him because he was tough, because he was all pro, because he was a man who knew what he wanted and grabbed it. They loved that in him as furiously as the crowds loved Ike. They sentimentalized every power grab. And that was when the New Sentimentality came out in the open.[73]

The article may just as well refer to "Old Sentimentality" as "square" sentimentality. "Old Sentimentality" belongs to the "masses," while the "New Sentimentality" refers to *Esquire*'s ideal readers: intellectual, "taste-making" people who find in JFK a number of masculine features (toughness, professionalism, and agency) to love.

The article continues, in a tongue-in-cheek manner, to contrast these two different views. On the one hand, the "Old Sentimentality" had "values," enumerated as "Patriotism, Love, Religion, Mom, the Girl."[74] On the other hand, the "New Sentimentality," had a list of tenets, including "Sharpness," "self-indulgence," and the "ability to change." Most interesting, though, is the discussion of "New Sentimentality's" abiding motivation, personal interest:

> In the Old way you had ideals, causes, goals that were in some way beneficent to all. In the New, your primary objective is to make your life fit your style. There is Professionalism above all. For example, the Old concept of "selling out," which used to drive good men crazy, causing them to cry in their beer and bemoan their wasted talent (writing ad copy, for instance), has disappeared. Now we glory in what pros we are, and a man loves himself for writing the best jingle in the market.[75]

The "New Sentimentality," then, outlines a new masculine project, one that distinguishes itself from square society ("Old Sentimentality") and that is able to adjust to the Establishment so that individuality and agency comes through lifestyle, through distinction, through excelling in the corporate world. In fact, the "New Sentimentality" is not sentimentality at all, but self-interest.[76] The New Sentimentalist is most assuredly an individual – not a Hipster, no, not something so potentially counter-cultural – but a taste-maker, one who can appreciate the sort of counter-cultural art *Esquire* provides as an object for consumption, and is thus someone who has begun to negotiate himself out of the "square" versus Hip dilemma. These New Sentimentalists (to keep using *Esquire*'s term) seem to be those who, in some way, responded to Schlesinger's original call back in 1958 to develop their "lineaments of personality" not through radical means, but through the act of consumption. From the early days of 1950s "agency panic" to the publication of *An American Dream, Esquire* can be seen as negotiating this "New Sentimentality" for its readers. In this way, the "White Negro" and *An American Dream* can be seen as objects consumed by white-collar readers for just this purpose, and so act to renegotiate hegemonic masculinity for a new cultural context, while at the same time losing any radical political potential.

However, though *Esquire* encourages consumption as a process that renegotiates hegemonic masculinity, it is in the pages of the magazine that *An American Dream* offers the potential for a more radical gender project. Consider, for example, the opening paragraphs of the two versions of the novel. The first lines, as subsequently published in novel form, read, "I met Jack Kennedy in November, 1946. We were both war heroes, and both of us had just been elected to Congress. We went out one night on a double date and it turned out to be a fair evening for me. I seduced a girl who would have been bored by a diamond as big as the Ritz" (1). Compare this opening to *An American Dream* as it was originally published in the January 1964 edition of *Esquire* magazine:

> Every one of you finds yourself lonely, but you discover your loneliness by living a life which is like the life of everyone else; you are understood perfectly; it is just that nobody wants to listen. Still, you hear of men and women who have a life which proves to be their own; history records their name because they found no place. Ernest Hemingway is the first who comes to mind, and Marilyn Monroe. So too does Patterson, Floyd Patterson, and Liston; Edith Piaf and Dr. Stephen Ward; Christine Jorgensen, Porfirio Rubirosa, Luis Miguel Dominguin. So too do I – to myself at least. For I take from this second species of loneliness a property which is peculiar to us: we believe in coincidences and take our memory from meetings. I know I measure my life by such a rule. I met Jack Kennedy, for instance, in 1946. We were both war heroes and were both Freshmen in Congress. Congressman John Fitzgerald Kennedy, Democrat from Massachusetts, and Congressman Stephen Richards Rojack, Democrat from New York. We even spent part of one night together on a long double date and it promised to be a good night for me. I stole his girl.[77]

The original opening begins by addressing "you." This is not the first time that the magazine directly addresses the reader. Indeed, advertisements constantly hail the reader of *Esquire*: "Reduce the Size of *Your* Waistline,"[78] "*You* Can Have a HE-MAN Voice!"[79] and "I'll Make *You* a Mental Wizard in One Evening!"[80] Combined with the advertisements, the story's opening lines work to interpellate[81] the individual reader into *Esquire*'s imagined ideal reader. The "you" of the story's opening lines is the same as this imagined reader, who suffers from the conditions of the modern world, which leave him less an individual and more a simple member of the crowd, since he lives "a life which is like the life of everyone else." In short, the original opening acts as a diagnosis of the "agency panic" associated with the figures of the Organization Man, the Establishment, and the "square," and the discourse of constrained masculinity with which they are associated.

This imbrication continues as Mailer's narrator holds up, by way of contrast, examples of individuals who can act as role models, "who have a life which proves to be their own," two of whom are *Esquire*'s favoured exemplars of masculinity: Ernest Hemingway and JFK. Others fit archetypal, and largely hegemonic, masculine types: the war hero, the politician, and the boxer. Rojack, the narrator, then includes himself in this list, clearly identifying himself – in a way that is never made as explicit in the novel version – as an exemplar of masculinity, as a fantasy figure capable of breaking from the masculine malaise of the 1950s and '60s.

The original, longer introduction does two further things that the revised version does not. First, it highlights the degree to which the novel focuses on the competition between Rojack and other men – specifically a competition over women. Second, the original introduction acknowledges feminine role models such as Monroe and Piaf and, perhaps more transgressively, Christine Jorgensen. Feminine power and agency is deemphasized throughout the novel, and part of that de-emphasis is the result of the erasure of these feminine role models from the beginning of the novel. As previously mentioned, and as this aspect of the introduction indicates, the *Esquire* version of the novel creates a greater potential for a more radical gender project.

Rojack's implied competition with JFK over Deborah inaugurates one of the novel's most enduring patterns: the repeated conflict between Rojack and other men over women, which is ostensibly a repeated battle meant to "prove" Rojack's superior masculinity.[82] The original introduction makes clear that Rojack was in competition over Deborah with none other than JFK: not only did he compete with the future (and, at the time of publication, recently assassinated) president, but this was a competition he won.[83] This contest further connects the figure of Rojack to Mailer, who, in writing *The Presidential Papers*, had been in a sort of one-sided contest with the president.[84] It also proves Rojack's masculine credentials, right from the outset. This anecdote clearly states what is at stake in contests between men:

women. This initial masculine contest sets the tone for the rest of
the novel, wherein Rojack's masculinity project takes shape through
a series of masculinity challenges, and he understands his masculinity
only in relation to other versions of masculinity.

The episodes omitted from the novel version emphasize this pattern of masculinity challenges. One of the more disturbing excised
passages takes place on the streets outside of Deborah's apartment.
When Roberts insists that they – Rojack and the other policemen – go
to the precinct, Rojack has a startling thought:

> As they stood up, I was aware of a mood which came up from them. It
> was the smell of hunters seated in an overheated hut at dawn waiting for
> the sun to come out, drunk from drinking through the night. I was game
> to them at this moment, but in about the way a naked whore would be
> game if she were dragged into their hut on the dawn and they took her
> one by one rather than ripping overpowered charges of Magnum into
> ducks sitting on the water fifteen yards away. As I stood up to go with
> them, I felt a weakness go through me, and no adrenalin followed.[85]

Rojack's comparison of the police officers to hunters remains in the
Dial version, but the metaphor comparing Rojack to a "naked whore"
is omitted. The Dial version puts the police in the masculine role of
the hunter, and implies that Rojack is prey, perhaps even drawing an
implicit comparison that questions Rojack's masculinity, while the
Esquire version explicitly illustrates that Rojack views the police in a
sexually threatening way, one that renders him not only feminine, but
also a passive female victim of their violent sexual advances. Rojack
feels feminized particularly by the presence of other, dominant men.
Moreover, in this passage Rojack views male sexuality as predatory, at
least in others. In his metaphor, the hunters have sex with the "naked
whore" in place of killing ducks, which they would have done not for
meat or for trophies, as the ducks would be destroyed by "overpow-
ered charges of Magnum," but for the sheer pleasure of destruction.
In this omitted passage, Rojack recognizes the violence that can un-
dergird sexual relations between women and men who practice hegemonic masculinity.

In another example of what I'm calling textual homophobia, the
Dial version omits a further passage from the same section of the narrative, one that similarly involves Rojack reconceptualizing his masculinity in relation to different situations and different men. In the

novel, when faced with the possibility of being tried and convicted
for Deborah's murder, and locked up in a prison, Rojack ponders
the future: "I would lie in a cell at night with nothing to do but walk
a stone square floor" (87). As it was originally published, the same
sentence includes an important mention of Rojack's desires: "I would
lie in a cell at night with nothing to do but walk a stone square floor
and dream through heats of desire for one of the girls in the men's
wing of the prison, one of those girls with all but a woman's body (and
a man's organs) and I would die through endless stupors and expired
plans."[86] The figure of the prison "queen" points to performativity,
seeing gender ("one of those girls") as disassociated from sex ("with
all but a woman's body"), complicating Rojack's seemingly essentialist
view of gender. Unlike the passage with the hunters, in which Rojack views himself as the passive, effeminized victim, here he imagines himself as active and masculine. When confronted with a more
aggressive, more physical version of masculinity – as is the case with
the police officers, representatives of a Repressive State Apparatus –
Rojack fears emasculation, while when in the marginal institution of
the prison, Rojack would attempt to reassert his dominance in the
gender hierarchy. As Stephen Donaldson has argued, "manhood"
in prison is "always subject to being 'lost' to another, more powerful
or aggressive, Man,"[87] and queens are subordinated in the prison's
sexual hierarchy. By taking up with a queen, Rojack would be reassert-
ing the superiority of his masculinity within the gender regime of the
prison. However, Rojack's desire for a queen nonetheless complicates
his masculinity by focusing on a nonnormative object of desire.

These two omitted passages demonstrate the degree to which Rojack views masculinity as something that is given by (or taken from)
other men. Moreover, Rojack only understands masculinity as a project of dominance. This is most clear in how Rojack views women. As
Kimmel argues, in the homosocial construction of masculinity, the
"conquest" of women improves men's social standings in relation to
other men.[88] Rojack's murder of Deborah, and his sex with Ruta (who
calls him a "genius") and Cherry (who has her first orgasm), gain new
significance when viewed as instances of an ongoing competition with
Barney Oswald Kelly. In this way, the women in the novel are less important as objects of masculine desire than, as Kimmel puts it, a sort
of currency in a homosocial economy.

Echoing, among others, Eve Sedgwick, Kimmel insists that "Manhood is demonstrated for other men's approval. It is other men who

evaluate the performance."[89] Kimmel's contention is that masculinity
is a homosocial construct: men choose and shape its rules and judge
how each man measures up. Kimmel goes on to explain the important role of fear in the construction of masculinity. This fear has, at
its root, homophobia, "the fear that other men will unmask us, emas-
culate us, reveal to us and the world that we do not measure up, that
we are not real men."[90] Because gender is ordered hierarchically, and
this hierarchy is historical and malleable, one's position in that hierarchy is always contestable. Men have to continually reassert masculinity,
and marginalization is always a possibility, even for men previously
practicing some form of hegemonic masculinity.

Significantly, Parker has noted that most of the major differences
between the *Esquire* version of *An American Dream* and the subsequent
Dial version deal with fear.[91] Fear still plays a major role in the novel
version, but the *Esquire* version gives it greater prominence. All told,
Mailer deleted roughly three dozen references to Rojack's fear,[92] thus
weakening the correlation between masculinity and homophobia
present in the *Esquire* version.

Rojack's homophobia is brought on not only by the presence of
men, but also the presence of women, as demonstrated in another
omitted section of the *Esquire* version, in which Rojack confides
in Cherry:

> "I'm always afraid of a woman," I said. It was not altogether true. It had
> certainly not been true with Ruta, and many a time I had not felt a thing,
> but for a hundred fifty of some two hundred women there had first been a
> quarter hour of dread which arrived when I found myself alone with them
> and left me afterward familiar with the intimate feel of my cowardice, nor-
> mally sealed in as deep upon itself as the moldering center of a vegetable.[93]

Discussing this line as it was published in the novel – "I'm always
afraid" (118) – Stanley Gutman sees it as "the undirected fear that
grows out of a man's sense of his own mortality."[94] As it was originally
published, it is clear that Rojack's fear is in fact specifically focused on
women. Here, it is not the proximity of men that provokes homophobia, but the presence of women. When Rojack initiates sex with most
women, he experiences an intimate feeling of cowardice that he believes is normally "sealed" deep inside of him. His fear of failing in
bed is a fear of failing in his performance of heterosexual masculinity,
or an anxiety about his own suitability for this performance.

In addition, in the same passage, Rojack's (eventually omitted) admission that he had slept with "some two hundred women" brings to mind Judith Halberstam's contention that "excessive masculinity turns into a parody or exposure of the norm."[95] The excesses of Rojack's masculinity are seen not only in this number of sexual conquests and the exaggerated reaction women have to him, but also in the many masculine roles he wears at different points in the story: super-soldier, boxer, public intellectual, and so on. In this passage, Rojack's hypermasculine exterior is exposed as having, at its centre, a "moldering center" of cowardice and homophobia. Rojack's masculine actions mean to reassure him (and other men) that he is, indeed, an "authentic" man: acts of sex and acts of violence (not always clearly differentiated) are a direct result of Rojack's homophobia.

Indeed, Rojack's excessive masculinity – combined with the unending, overwrought nature of his similes, which are the primary feature of his narrative voice – open up the possibility that *An American Dream* can be read as a criticism of such a hegemonic masculinity project. While the supposedly straight (i.e., obvious and heterosexual) reading that the novel demands is reinforced by its placement in *Esquire*, as a site of cultural (and masculine) hegemony, the magazine also opens up the possibility of resistant readings. It is therefore possible to see the novel as masculinist camp. Indeed, whether it is intentional or not, Mailer's novel presents elements that share an articulation with camp, pointing to the slippery and unstable nature of hegemonic masculinity as such.

As George Chauncey argues in his study of "the making of the gay male world," camp was a "cultural *style* and a cultural *strategy*" that "helped gay men make sense of, respond to, and undermine the social categories of gender and sexuality that served to marginalize them." It did this through "irony, incongruity, theatricality, and humour … sometimes exaggerating convention to the point of burlesquing it."[96] Rojack's ability to outperform all other men, his ability to bed any woman he wants, comes off as exaggeration verging on parody, and when combined with the previously noted critiques of masculinity found in the novel (e.g., the connection between masculinity, violence, and the Establishment), suggests that *An American Dream* might fruitfully be read as a multifaceted criticism of hegemonic masculinity, especially as it was originally published in *Esquire*.

Chauncey's analysis of camp as a culture and a strategy specific to gay men supports the arguments of Michael Snyder, Howard

Silverstein, and Andrew Gordon, who argue that Rojack is compensating for his unacknowledged homosexuality.[97] The *Esquire* version adds further credence to this claim. In the same passage in which Rojack admits to fearing women, he explains to Cherry that he had been a breech birth: "They had to go in with forceps and pull me out. It must be that my preference then was to die in the womb rather than enter life. I must have been more attached to where I had been before than to where I was going now."[98] Pertinent to this passage is the belief in psychiatry, widely held at the time of Mailer's writing, that male children who identified too much with their mother risked becoming effeminate or homosexual.[99] When he discusses his birth, Rojack admits to a powerful connection with his own mother – a figure who is otherwise totally absent from the novel. The implication is that Rojack himself might be gay – at least according to his own understanding of psychology.[100]

While the theme of homosocial competition and homophobia remains present in the novel form of *An American Dream*, the omissions from the *Esquire* version – in particular, the repeated references to fear and the blatant references to homosexual panic – greatly reduce this aspect of the novel, resulting in a less problematic portrayal of masculinity. The result of reading the original text of the novel is that fault lines appear in the masculine fantasy of Mailer's fiction, and even in the masculine project of *Esquire* itself. Despite the fact that, as I have argued, *An American Dream* can reinforce patriarchy and, especially in the pages of *Esquire*, serves to renegotiate hegemonic masculinity in an era of increased consumption and white-collar work, the exposure of these fault lines allows for the possibility of unmasking masculinity as camp, as a homosocial construct, created by men and foisted upon both men and women in a ruthless self-generating hierarchy. As Gutman explains, the notion that Rojack's actions are no more than homophobic *re*actions undermines the supposedly "existential" or counter-cultural elements of his journey.[101] The quest for masculinity in *An American Dream* (and, by implication, in general) is the pathological drive to enact masculine signifiers despite knowing that those signifiers are not natural, only learned performances, but that a failure to enact them results in the potential disenfranchisement of the male individual from the system of masculinity, and this is attended by homophobic panic.

This reading of *An American Dream* leaves masculinity, especially hegemonic masculinity, an incongruent mess. The novel seems to exalt

hegemonic masculinity *and* parody it, see violence as masculine privilege *and* symptomatic of patriarchy's illegitimacy, and offer the "White
Negro" as an exemplary masculinity *and* mock those who would seek
to emulate such a version of masculinity. I would argue that the novel's contradictory representation of masculinity is not a weakness, but
a way of narrating the complexity and sometimes incoherence of hegemonic masculinity. Moreover, the *Esquire* version of the novel gives
alternate gender identities greater prominence, hinting at the possibility of liberation from this pathological gender regime. As it was
written in *Esquire* magazine, *An American Dream* begins with a roll call,
with a list of "men *and women* who have a life which proves to be their
own; history records their name because they found no place."[102]
That Mailer (as Rojack) includes the names of women in this roll call
of heroes opens up the possibility of an alternative to Mailer's masculine nightmare.

Perhaps the most transgressive name on Rojack's list is Christine
Jorgensen: in 1952, Jorgensen, an ex-G.I., became the first person
to gain fame for undertaking sex-reassignment surgery.[103] As James
Gilbert explains in his study of masculinity in the 1950s, Jorgensen's
widely discussed case "vividly challenged the biological stability of
gender and gender definitions by introducing the possibility of trans-
sexuality."[104] Whereas I have argued that Rojack's main fault in his
enactment of the "White Negro" is his inability – or unwillingness –
to view gender as a cultural institution, akin to the other organizations in which he is caught, and to instead view it as a ground upon
which cultural institutions are constructed, Jorgensen clearly provides an example of a figure who can destabilize this "ground." As
Gilbert explains further, the popular discussion around Jorgensen's
transition

> suggested the prospect of a radical rupture between biology and sociol-
> ogy, between organic sexual characteristics and psychological identity in
> a way that reverberated through some of the decade's most controversial
> cultural productions. The recognition of ambiguity ... profoundly desta-
> bilized the assumed continuities of biology and personality upon which
> the gender crisis and its most facile resolution rested.[105]

Jorgensen, then, provides some similarities to another excised figure from the *Esquire* version of the novel, the jailhouse "punk" whom
Rojack fears he will long for.[106] In both instances, the rigidity of

gender is called into question, and it is explicitly shown that there is a disconnect between biological sex and cultural ideas of gender. Both figures, too, choose femininity over masculinity, thumbing their noses at hegemony and its corresponding homophobia; this is an especially provocative gesture in the case of Jorgensen who, as an ex-G.I., once embodied a hegemonic gender position.

Joanne Meyerowitz picks up on the way that contemporary accounts of Jorgensen focused on the performance of her gender as the most important aspect of her gender identity: "The stories on Jorgensen ... ultimately undermined the attempt to restabilize gender. It could provoke anxieties about the failure of boundaries dividing female and male, and it could also invite fantasies about the possibility of traveling across the suddenly permeable border that separated women from men."[107] Jorgensen, and the public discourse surrounding her, proved that gender could be destabilized, and that biological sex was in no way an ultimate "ground" for experience. When Meyerowitz notes that Jorgensen could provoke anxieties about the boundaries between male and female, she seems to be pointing to Jorgensen as a potential cause of the type of homophobic panic continually on display in *An American Dream*. However, by listing Jorgensen as someone who managed to live a life that was her own, who found no place within the Establishment, Mailer seems to be endorsing her status as someone who actually destabilizes gender.

Inviting fantasies about gender instability, Jorgensen can be seen as a fantasy gendered-figure – not, obviously, an "exemplary masculinity," but instead a figure who seeks to problematize hegemonic masculinity rather than support it. Mailer's invocation of her name in the novel's original introduction, and the points of similarity between Jorgensen and Rojack, supports her potentially exemplary status. Like Rojack, Jorgensen served in the American army in World War II, and while she never entered politics or the academy, like Rojack she transitioned from soldier to television celebrity. Just as Rojack came to practice an exaggerated, hypermasculine role, so too did Jorgensen take up the role of fantastic female figures: as David Serlin explains, Jorgensen's Las Vegas cabaret show "culminated with Jorgensen parading around on stage dressed in a Wonder Woman costume and knee-high boots while holding ignited sparklers."[108] Like Rojack, Jorgensen's gender performance suggests camp, specifically as a "recognition of the artificiality of social roles."[109]

Also listed in Rojack's roll-call of heroes is Marilyn Monroe, who almost ten years later would be the subject of another of Mailer's books, *Marilyn*. Marilyn makes a surprising appearance in the novel's epilogue, when Rojack, seemingly insane, phones up Cherry in the afterlife. The call is brief, and only Cherry speaks: "Why, hello, hon, I thought you'd never call. It's kind of cool right now, and the girls are swell. Marilyn says to say hello. We get along, which is odd, you know, because girls don't swing. But toodle-oo, old baby-boy, and keep the dice for free, the moon is out and she's a mother to me" (269). The omission of Marilyn from the beginning of the novel makes her return even more abrupt; as it was published in *Esquire*, Marilyn helps to bookend the story. More importantly, Marilyn's identification in the original introduction as a role model worthy of emulation, combined with her association with the moon, highlights the way the moon is not just a focus of Rojack's pathology, but an important female symbol.

One aspect of the novel this chapter has not yet touched on is Rojack's relationship to the moon: in the early stages of the novel, he admits to communicating with the moon (the first chapter is entitled "The Harbors of the Moon"). Furthermore, Rojack's murder of Deborah is preceded by Rojack rejecting the moon's command to kill himself (12–13). Rojack refers to the moon as "the Lady" (12), and after rejecting her command feels as though he "had disappointed a lady and now must eat the cold tapeworm of her displeasure" (13). After noting this feeling, he acknowledges that "Nothing noble seemed to remain of me" (13). In some ways, Rojack's consequent chauvinist actions can be seen as a result of this denial of the feminine (12–13). Rojack's relationship with the moon is emblematic of his problematic relationship with femininity, and an almost singular instance of the novel presenting femininity in favourable terms. When Cherry seems to indicate that she is not in heaven, but on the moon with Marilyn and "the girls," the moon – and the heavenly city that Rojack keeps seeing – becomes a positive symbol not only associated with femininity, but from which Rojack is explicitly excluded. The connection between Marilyn and the moon helps to emphasize the notion that the moon is not just a site of abject, exterior femininity, but is actually a desirable female enclave, a space disconnected from the Establishment and yet off limits to Rojack.

Further deletions weaken the notion of female empowerment, which is, admittedly, only present in nascent form in the *Esquire* version. Found in *Esquire*, in the nightclub scene where Rojack fires mind bullets at his enemies, is the figure of a sorceress:

> Exhibit: The old widow with the queer was (in defense) mounting curses all about her. A hint of iridescence was in the light above her head. The thought came to attack her. For nothing. For no more than to see the technical grace of one's weapons, or was it that one's confidence had been damaged by the judge. So an arrow was shot into her largest curse (one huge luminous jelly fish shimmering in the air), her curse burst and sent needles back into my skin, ten thousand needles which pricked on my face like the touch of Deborah's hand.[110]

Certainly this scene seems to reinforce patriarchy: the widow's feminine curses (shapeless, luminous jelly fish instead of solid, manly bullets) are no match for Rojack's masculine powers of the mind. However, this omission follows the pattern of Mailer's other deletions: female power, even if it is described as no real threat to masculine domination, is erased. Rojack may not come off any the worse for this encounter, but this is still an instance of him being harmed – no matter how insignificantly – by a female source. Unlike Deborah and Ruta, the widow's transgression remains unpunished: somehow, she stands outside the pattern of trespass and punishment running throughout the novel. The widow may be no substantial threat, but she and "the queer" present an alternative gender configuration, one that does not so easily fall into Rojack's rigid gender hierarchy, and so, in the novel version, she is totally deleted.

4. Conclusion

Jorgensen, Marilyn, and the widow all represent, in some way, a threat to hegemonic masculinity, and so Mailer's deletions of their presence in the novel drastically reduces the possibility of a more radical gender project coming out of the novel. Instead, *An American Dream*, as it was published in novel form, presents masculinity in a less problematic way (since homophobia is de-emphasized), and omits most of the possibilities of feminine agency present in the *Esquire* version. As the novel was published in *Esquire*, there exists a greater chance for a counter-patriarchal discourse, since the pursuit of masculinity can be read as camp, or as a pathological exercise in homophobia, undermining the legitimacy of the gender hierarchy, and also because liberatory feminine figures exist as signifiers of existing fault lines in a rigidly constructed conception of gender.

The *Esquire* version of the novel therefore asks us to revisit those historical moments in which a narrative of "crisis" emerges, and to imagine them as moments in which the previous justification for patriarchy is no longer tenable: these are times during which hegemonic formulations of masculinity need to be renegotiated. Examining *An American Dream* as it was originally published, we can see how it is at these moments, before a new hegemonic formulation is established, that the contradictory and fragmented nature of masculinities is most obvious, and the possibilities for new, less toxic versions of masculinity appear.

Finally, even though the *Esquire* version provides a stronger criticism of patriarchy and provides the reader with instances of feminine power, it nevertheless reproduces many of the problems inherent in hegemonic masculinity. The novel's most blatant remaining weakness is its treatment of its African American characters. Most obviously, the novel still portrays black men, as represented in the figure of Shago Martin, as hypersexualized fetish objects for white masculinity. Certainly the novel does not repudiate the racist premise of "The White Negro," a figure to which James Baldwin directly responded in the pages of *Esquire*. As we shall see in the next chapter, Baldwin, largely in response to Mailer, used *Esquire* to launch a critique of hegemonic masculinity, focusing specifically on how white hegemonic masculinity projects construct harmful versions of black masculinity. In so doing, Baldwin offered *Esquire*'s readers an analysis of masculinity more powerful than anything Mailer could imagine.

2

Cooling It with James Baldwin

The American ideal, then, of sexuality appears to be rooted in the American ideal of masculinity. This ideal has created cowboys and Indians, good guys and bad guys, punks and studs, tough guys and softies, butch and faggot, black and white. It is an ideal so paralytically infantile that it is virtually forbidden – as an unpatriotic act – that the American boy evolve into the complexity of manhood.

– James Baldwin[1]

Originally titled "Freaks and the American Ideal of Manhood" and published in *Playboy* in 1985, James Baldwin's essay "Here Be Dragons" is perhaps his most sustained and direct criticism of American masculinity.[2] The shape of this particular attack on American masculinity, launched late in his career, was not new, nor was his strategy of criticizing masculinity in a publication devoted to valorizing it. Indeed, one can trace strands of Baldwin's critique of masculinity-as-ideology throughout his career, often as a direct response to white constructions of black masculinity, such as Norman Mailer's "The White Negro." Building on the considerable scholarship devoted to an analysis of Baldwin's critique of masculinity,[3] I argue that his critique forms a crucial part of his 1960s contributions to *Esquire* magazine. Baldwin may have been in *Esquire* as a voice of the Civil Rights movement and as a commentator on the so-called "Negro problem," but, as fitting the focus of the magazine, he continually framed his discussion of race as a discussion of masculinity.

In the quotation that forms the epigraph to this chapter, one could replace Baldwin's reference to "the American ideal of masculinity"

with Raewyn Connell's term "hegemonic masculinity" to clarify how
Baldwin is indicting the type of gender order Connell outlines.
In that passage, Baldwin identifies masculinity as a kind of master
code for identity. In other words, if the characteristics that make
up most hegemonic formulations of masculinity are the culturally
favoured identities in a series of binaries – rich not poor, straight
not gay, white not black, young not old, and so on – then why is Connell's (and Baldwin's) major focus on *masculinity*, rather than, for
example, hegemonic whiteness, or hegemonic youth? Baldwin clari-
fies this emphasis. In a patriarchal society, masculinity is the dominant identity category, the characteristic that supersedes all others.
Baldwin directly and powerfully addresses the American ideology of
masculinity and thus provides a significant analysis of the intersec-
tions of masculinity, race, and power. Baldwin therefore critiques
the problematic hegemonic masculinity projects offered by Norman
Mailer ("The White Negro") and *Esquire* itself. Baldwin's critique of
masculinity is more focused and direct than the other writers in this
study, and he illustrates how masculinity, as a dominant category,
intersects in illuminating ways with other forms of identity. Furthermore, even in his critique, Baldwin demonstrates how patriarchy's
assumption of its own centrality, and not necessarily its *actual* centrality, results in masculinity being understood as *the* master code
for identity. This is why, as seen in the first chapter of this study,
and as I will demonstrate in the following chapters, male characters are consistently represented as feeling that any failing in (or
threat against) any aspect of their identities are failings in (or threats
against) their masculinity. Furthermore, it is through what Kimmel[4]
calls the homosocial enactment of masculinity – the fact that masculinity is demonstrated for and evaluated by other men[5] – that men
are codified into an uneven gender hierarchy. Baldwin's point, in
the passage above, is that it is when each man's performance of masculinity is judged against a (largely symbolic) hegemonic form that
some become "faggots" and some become "studs," and, in the most
crucial part of Baldwin's argument, it is also only through this act of
masculine evaluation that some become "black" and some become
"white." It is the larger gender order, policed by (regime-specific)
hegemonic concepts of masculinity, that creates, naturalizes, and reinforces racial categories.

As I will demonstrate, Baldwin's critique of American masculinity is central to his fiction, beginning as early as *Giovanni's Room* and

intensifying throughout his fiction of the 1960s. Significantly, Baldwin articulated parts of his critique of hegemonic masculinity in the pages of *Esquire* magazine, a panopticon-like field with its own hegemonic masculinity project, wherein constructions of masculinity are nego- tiated and reinforced.[6] I argue that aspects of Baldwin's critique of hegemonic masculinity – especially the role it plays in enforcing and maintaining racism – are present throughout Baldwin's *Esquire* arti- cles, in particular in two early essays from the 1960s, later republished in *Nobody Knows My Name*: "Fifth Avenue, Uptown" and "The Black Boy Looks at the White Boy." The criticisms Baldwin makes in these essays provide a foundation for his more provocative attacks against hegemonic masculinity in his subsequent fictional works of the 1960s, in particular "Going to Meet the Man" and *Blues for Mister Charlie*. Making his argument in the pages of *Esquire*, Baldwin indicts those complicit with the contemporary construction of the gender order and encourages a radical change to conceptions of American mascu- linity, and he does so through the more direct method of nonfiction rather than through the medium of fiction, which could be dismissed as purely aesthetic. Furthermore, I closely analyse one issue of *Esquire* magazine from the late 1960s to demonstrate how the magazine at- tempted to diminish his counter-hegemonic critique through racially charged textual strategies that reinforce the dominance of white, pro- fessional/managerial masculinities, and reinscribe the subordination of black masculinity.

1. Baldwin's Critique of Hegemonic Masculinity

Baldwin's critique of hegemonic masculinity was situated within a series of important, overlapping historical contexts. Baldwin began publishing with *Esquire* in 1960, the first year of a decade that saw mas- sive political and social change for African Americans. The decade witnessed the passing of the Civil Rights Act (1964) and the Voting Rights Act (1965), the foundation of the Black Panther Party (1966), and the assassinations of Malcolm X (1965) and Martin Luther King, Jr (1968), to name only a few noteworthy events. Baldwin became, if not a leader of the Civil Rights Movement, then one of its most famous spokesmen. As a socially conscious black author, Baldwin was placed in an African American literary tradition – following the dominance of the Harlem Renaissance and the social protest novel, and seeing the emergence of the nascent Black Arts Movement – and at the centre of the rise of Black Nationalism and Civil Rights, all of which proffered competing conceptions of black and white masculinity.

As several scholars have argued, configurations of masculinity were central to articulations of blackness during this period. In particular, several African American activists promoted a discourse of aggressive, heterosexual black masculinity to oppose an insufficient white masculinity. Baldwin's critique significantly overlaps with Black Nationalism and Black Arts Movement critiques in several places, though it just as significantly differs. As Darieck Scott argues, Black Power and Black Arts Movement writers saw sexuality "as one of the primary means by which black subjugation was achieved and ... as one of the primary arenas in which black liberation was to be won."[7] Consequently, Black Nationalism and the Black Arts Movement, which was one of its analogues in literature, often framed its attacks on institutional whiteness in terms of masculinity. For instance, when Larry Neal discusses theatre in his 1968 essay "The Black Arts Movement," he refers to Edward Albee's *Who's Afraid of Virginia Woolf?* as "very American: sick white lives in a homosexual hell hole."[8] For comparison, when Neal describes LeRoi Jones's [Amiri Baraka's] 1964 play *The Dutchman*, in which the African American man Clay is murdered by the white woman Lula, he foregrounds the contestation of masculinity in matters of race, arguing that "the relationship between Clay (Black America) and Lula (white America) is rooted in the historical castration of black manhood."[9] Accordingly, one of the implicit goals of the Black Arts Movement was to articulate new, revolutionary formulations of masculinity, resulting in numerous critics leveling charges of misogyny against the movement.

Those black writers concerned with masculinity were responding, in no small part, to the demonization of black masculinity, especially the white caricature of black men known as the "black beast," a central stereotype of segregation that characterized black men as animalistic, hypersexual predators of white women. As a stereotype, the "black beast" was central to the sexual policing of African Americans by white men.[10] As Richard Schmitt explains, this white, masculine fear of black masculinity's sexuality came into being during the social and cultural changes in the post-Civil-War south. Schmitt argues that the stereotype was mobilized as a reaction to the Populists, a multiracial group of small farmers. To re-establish the subordination of black men and white women, white men "mounted a concerted campaign to persuade Whites that Black men were a constant and serious threat to the honor and safety of White women, because Black men had huge genitals and an insatiable sexual appetite, particularly for White women."[11] Schmitt is here describing the renegotiation of hegemonic masculinity in the post-Civil-War south. This renegotiation happened, in part, because of stoked-up fears of the exaggerated sexuality of the "black beast," and in particular through the dissemination of the supposedly threatening image of the black man's "huge genitals." Furthermore, in what is typical of the functioning of hegemonic masculinity, Schmitt argues that this renegotiation has, as its primary goal, the maintenance of men's control over women.[12] This supports Toby Ditz's claim that "the gender order pivots on men's access to women, its differential distribution, and challenges to it,"[13] demonstrating that one of the primary ways gendered power plays out in a system of hegemonic masculinity is through policing which men have access to which women.

As will be discussed shortly, this synecdochal reduction of the "black beast," and therefore black masculinity, to the image of the "huge black penis," is a technique of domination that Baldwin specifically identities and speaks out against. Other black male artists were not so critical of its implications. As Schmitt argues, to understand the fixation on "the giant Black penis," one needs to situate it in a phallocentric world view, one in which "all men, White and Black, think of themselves as embodied in their sexual organ."[14] Revised articulations of black masculinity often fell into the trap of arguing against white masculinity while simultaneously being stuck in the old discourse of hegemonic masculinity. As Anne Pochmara explains, though black articulations of masculinity have a radical quality, inasmuch as they counter white stereotyping, they inevitably reproduce the sexism of those very same stereotypes.[15] Black writers and revolutionaries were invested in rearticulating black masculinity in such a way that it would escape the emasculating effects of living in a white, heterosexist society; however, a "remasculinization" of black masculinity threatened to reinscribe heterosexist and patriarchal discourse. bell hooks speaks to this conundrum:

> The discourse of black resistance has almost always equated freedom with manhood, the economic and material domination of black men with castration, emasculation. Accepting these sexual metaphors forged a bond between oppressed black men and their white male oppressors.

They shared the patriarchal belief that revolutionary struggle was really about the erect phallus.[16]

Similarly, William J. Spurlin notes that Eldridge Cleaver's *Soul on Ice* follows this pattern, writing that Cleaver's criticism of Baldwin "reduces black power to the phallus and leaves one asking about the role of black women in the politics of liberationist struggle."[17] What hooks and Spurlin identify here as a major problem in the discourse of black resistance is the way it seeks to renegotiate hegemonic masculinity so as to allow for greater access to the patriarchal dividend for black men. Such an alliance would benefit only black men: women would remain subjected to a system of masculine domination.

During the 1960s, Baldwin's writing about race and masculinity attempted to escape the trap identified by hooks and Pochmara: while fixating on castration, emasculation, and manhood in much the same way as the writers hooks castigates, Baldwin's sophisticated critique nevertheless attempted to resist sexist, patriarchal sympathies with white masculinity. Instead, Baldwin saw masculinity, and the feelings of castration and emasculation that come with it, as ideology, as the very tool by which white America subordinated and marginalized African Americans. Baldwin's fiction therefore articulates his critique of racism as a critique of hegemonic masculinity.

Baldwin perhaps most clearly expresses this critique in his controversial 1956 novel *Giovanni's Room*. Set in Paris, the novel follows the love affair between David, a young white American, and Giovanni, a young Italian man. Though the novel presents no black characters, it is nevertheless critically concerned with the intersection of race and masculinity – indeed, writing about the novel, Marlon Ross argues that "Baldwin makes the central problem of the twentieth century the strange meaning of being white, as a structure of feeling within the self and within history."[18] As Robert Reid-Pharr has noted,[19] the discussion of race begins on the very first page, as David describes himself: "My reflection is tall, perhaps rather like an arrow, my blond hair gleams. My face is like a face you have seen many times. My ancestors conquered a continent, pushing across death-laden plains, until they came to an ocean which faced away from Europe into a darker past."[20] Reading this with Lacan's theory of the "Mirror Stage" in mind,[21] here David identifies in his *imago* an idealized version of himself: "ideal" to the extent that his reflection is a kind of exemplary masculinity, arrow-like and blonde, immediately recognized and immediately recognizable in relation to a history of colonialism and genocide. Against this ideal, colonial masculinity, David must compare his "real," homosexual self. It is the conflict between these two versions of David that dominates his characterization.

David's investment in his whiteness – as demonstrated in this early, formative reference to his ancestors – helps to explain, when read through Connell's concept of hegemonic masculinity, why he continually relates heterosexuality with whiteness and homosexuality with blackness.[22] David, the narrator, cannot describe the appearance of homosexual characters, or even their lodgings, without associating them with blackness. David's description in the opening passage is an example of hegemonic masculinity – or in Baldwin's terms "the American ideal of masculinity" – and his narration makes clear its workings. Gay masculinity, like black masculinity, is subordinated or marginalized within the American gender order, the gender order that educated David and that he has internalized. In addition, both are abject, to the extent that a series of oppositions (in this case, white, not black; straight, not gay) define hegemonic masculinity. Hegemonic masculinity "denies" or marginalizes both kinds of masculinity, and the slippage, in David's perception, between blackness and homosexuality only emphasizes the ways both marginalized identities are categories created by the ideology of hegemonic masculinity itself.

While *Giovanni's Room* establishes Baldwin's critique of hegemonic masculinity, his later fiction develops this critique, though it has as its focus a different aspect of the racist conflation of race and gender. Indeed, Baldwin's fiction of the 1960s repeatedly turns to a white obsession with African American male sexuality – in particular, the fetishization of black penises – and to the literal act of the emasculation of black men by white men. While Baldwin touches on this theme in novels of the 1960s, especially *Another Country*,[23] the two works which most horrifically foreground this theme are the play *Blues for Mister Charlie* (1964) and the short story "Going to Meet the Man," published in a collection of the same name (1965). Both feature the murders of African American men, and both explicitly connect racial hatred with the fetishization of black masculinity.

Blues for Mister Charlie, dedicated to Medgar Evers and loosely based on the murder of Emmett Till, takes place in the segregated location of Plaguetown, U.S.A. Plaguetown, divided between "Whitetown" and "Blacktown," is the setting of the murder of Richard Henry, a young

African American man, at the hands of the white store-owner Lyle Britten. The play begins with Richard already dead, and continues to depict the trial of Lyle, in the present, and a series of flashbacks recounting Richard's actions, leading up to his murder. As the plot unfolds, Baldwin makes it clear that at the root of the racial tension in the town, and the conflict between Lyle and Richard, is white, male conceptions of black masculinity. This is most obvious in a discussion between the denizens of Whitetown:

> ELLIS: Mrs. Britten, you're married and all the women in this room are married and I know you've seen your husband without no clothes on – but have you seen a nigger without no clothes on? No, I guess you haven't. Well, he ain't like a white man, Mrs. Britten.
> GEORGE: That's right.
> ELLIS: Mrs. Britten, if you was to be raped by an orang-outang out of the jungle or a stallion, couldn't do you no worse than a nigger. You wouldn't be no more good for nobody. I've seen it.
> GEORGE: That's right.
> RALPH: That's why we men have got to be so vigilant.[24]

In this passage, Ellis and George, as symptomatic white men, clearly express that the justification for racism is the fear of black men's exaggerated sexuality. Ellis and George invoke for Mrs Britten the figure of the "black beast." Some of Richard's last words to Lyle reflect his acknowledgment, if not his understanding, of the psychosexual predicament in which he has been caught: "Why have you spent so much time trying to kill me? Why are you always trying to cut off my cock? You worried about it? Why?"[25] In addition, Lyle's acquittal depends on white fears of black men's sexuality. While on the witness stand, Jo Britten, Lyle's wife, concocts a story about Richard assaulting her sexually, and the State repeatedly refers to Richard's ownership of photographs of naked white women.[26] *Blues for Mister Charlie* therefore demonstrates the degree to which racist ideology relies on the construct of the "black beast" for the policing and segregation of black masculinity, as well as the instability of a white masculinity that, in creating so many "Others" (black, homosexual, and so forth) has created so many cracks in its own edifice. If black masculinity, like white masculinity, is a product of patriarchy, of the development of patriarchal gender regimes, then the policing of black masculinity is in fact the policing of white masculinity.

In "Going to Meet the Man," Baldwin returns to this theme, with an unforgettably brutal description of a lynching. It is in this story that Baldwin asserts that, by creating the "black beast" stereotype to police racial segregation, (racist) white men have created a fetish. Citing the dreams and fantasies of his white patients, Frantz Fanon claims that "One is no longer aware of the Negro, but only of a penis: The Negro is eclipsed. He is turned into a penis."[27] This synecdochal effacement of black masculinity by the fantasy of the penis allows for not only the dehumanization of black men, but also its symbolic appropriation, whether in Fanon's France or Baldwin's America. Lynne Segal argues that this racist stereotyping of black masculinity is not only common among traditional racists, but also supposedly liberal, equality minded progressives. She provides the examples of Jack Kerouac (*On the Road*) and Mailer (178–9), both of whom Baldwin criticizes in "The Black Boy Looks at the White Boy." Segal cites the example of "The White Negro" to support her claim that Mailer is invested in this myth of black sexuality; a similarly apt example is *An American Dream*, especially the point at which Rojack is given Shago Martin's phallic umbrella after savagely beating him.[28] If the myth of the black man as hypermasculine has resulted in the black penis as a mythological symbol of virility, then it functions both as threat and object of desire. The black penis (in the white-supremacist, patriarchal imagination) becomes the locus of a number of white conceptions of black masculinity.

"Going to Meet the Man" begins in bed, where Jesse, a white Southern sheriff, is unable to get an erection. His impotence is only cured by remembering a lynching he witnessed as a youth. The description of this lynching is both horrifically violent and sexually charged:

> The man with the knife took the nigger's privates in his hand, one hand, still smiling, as though he were weighing them. In the cradle of the one white hand, the nigger's privates seemed as remote as meat being weighed in the scales; but seemed heavier, too, much heavier, and Jesse felt his scrotum tighten; and huge, huge, much bigger than his father's, flaccid, hairless, the largest thing he had ever seen till then, and the blackest. The white hand stretched them, cradled them, caressed them. Then the dying man's eyes looked straight into Jesse's eyes – it could not have been as long as a second, but it seemed longer than a year. Then Jesse screamed, and the crowd screamed as the knife flashed, first up, then down, cutting the dreadful thing away, and the blood came roaring

down. Then the crowd rushed forward, tearing at the body with their hands, with knives, with rocks, with stones, howling and cursing. Jesse's head, of its own weight, fell downward toward his father's head. Someone stepped forward and drenched the body with kerosene. Where the man had been, a great sheet of flame appeared. Jesse's father lowered him to the ground.

"Well, I told you," said his father, "you wasn't never going to forget this picnic." His father's face was full of sweat, his eyes were very peaceful. At that moment Jesse loved his father more than he had ever loved him. He felt that his father had carried him through a mighty test, had revealed to him a great secret which would be the key to his life forever.[29]

The young Jesse, his father, and the lyncher all find sexual arousal in the victim's masculinity and emasculation. The lyncher cradling and caressing the black man's genitals connotes sensuousness seemingly out of place with the violent murder. Jesse's immediate reaction is to feel his "scrotum tighten," and the description of Jesse's father after the lynching – face full of sweat, eyes peaceful – seems to evoke a post-orgasmic state. Reading this same passage, Sara Taylor argues that it demonstrates "white patriarchy's false construction of a hyper-sexualized black masculinity, as well as its subsequent attempts to repress and destroy that construction."[30] The racist formulation of black masculinity depicted in "Going to Meet the Man" reveals white men's investment in an uneven gender hierarchy, at the same time that it demonstrates the instability of that very hierarchy.

The last sentence of the above passage is perhaps the most troubling, but also the most revealing. The "great secret" that the white men share seems to be the degree to which their own identities require the violent subordination of black masculinity. Taylor comes to a similar conclusion, arguing that the story reveals that "true white manhood, in a heteronormative, sexist, and racist paradigm, can be achieved only by destroying the masculinity of the black male, while the tenets of socially constructed black masculinity are dictated by this selfsame white patriarchy. Baldwin, then, suggests that the system of creating masculinities for both blacks and whites is a system of destruction of all."[31] Taylor is right that Baldwin identifies "the system of creating masculinities" as the root cause of domination and inequality for both black and white alike; however, I would argue that "destroying the masculinity of the black male" is not as central as Taylor claims. Though Baldwin provides numerous examples where destruction is the obvious result, the homoeroticism of the lynching scene offers an alternative never taken – the possibility for a sensual, not a violent, relationship. In this case, then, heterosexism actually trumps racism as the mechanism that causes racial segregation and the subordination of racialized masculinities. As Lee Edelman explains, systems of domination are

> systems that generate a "racial" discourse suffused with homophobia insofar as it plays out the incoherences of a heterosexual masculinity that cannot afford to acknowledge, as it cannot afford to deny, the centrality of its narcissistic investment in, and hence the intensity of its desire for, the culturally institutionalized authority of the phallus that never fully distinguishes itself from the anatomical penis.[32]

If masculinity is the primary signifier of power in a patriarchal order, then all differentiations of power come with a sexual dimension, and even racism is another form, or at least motivated by another form, of heterosexism. Homophobia polices the possibility of overcoming racism between men, and the types of domination found in a society overlap and reinforce one another.

Baldwin has constructed a multifaceted critique of hegemonic masculinity, seeing the American ideal of heteronormative masculinity as the foundation for every other system of domination – especially racial. The specific way black masculinity is subordinated – through its hypermasculinization and the myth of the "black beast" – simultaneously denies and fetishizes black masculinity (specifically the black man's penis) while denying black men the "patriarchal dividend." Black men remain estranged from masculinity – and yet, they are still invested in it, since their gender presumably justifies their access to patriarchal authority. It is precisely this system which Baldwin critiques, and, significantly, when the opportunity arises, he does so in the pages of a magazine dedicated to white hegemonic masculinity.

2. Baldwin's Queer Critique of Race in *Esquire*

Though Baldwin wrote several essays for *Esquire* during the 1960s, of special significance are "Fifth Avenue, Uptown" and "The Black Boy Looks at the White Boy." For the first of these essays, *Esquire* had agreed to publish an article on Harlem, as part of its July 1960 magazine focused exclusively on New York City. Baldwin had recently returned to

America from Paris, and this particular *Esquire* article drew Baldwin's attention to civil rights and the ongoing struggle.[33] The issue in which it was published featured the work of other noted literary authors – in particular Truman Capote and John Cheever. While most of the rest of the magazine paid homage to the Big Apple, Baldwin's piece was a condemnation of Harlem's housing projects and, more generally, a denunciation of the white American society that had allowed the projects to exist in the first place.

Baldwin's critique of Harlem in many ways parallels his critique of hegemonic masculinity. In particular, Baldwin sees Harlem's projects as ideological constructs meant to restrict African Americans to a subordinate position within the larger American society (and in particular the larger American gender order, as I argue below). As Baldwin states, "The projects in Harlem are hated. They are hated almost as much as policemen, and this is saying a great deal. And they are hated for the same reason: both reveal, unbearably, the real attitude of the white world, no matter how many liberal speeches are made, no matter how many lofty editorials are written, no matter how many civil-rights commissions are set up."[34] I would argue that Baldwin sees the housing projects as a representation of what Slavoj Žižek calls "objective violence."[35] The housing projects, like policemen, are not only Repressive State Apparatuses, in Louis Althusser's expression, but are also symbolic of the state violence that marginalizes African Americans. This kind of violence – the looming projects, the patrolling policemen – creates the "zero-level standard" of supposed non-violence. Street-level violence, from assault to the aforementioned rioting, is only visible against the otherwise non-violent background of Harlem.

Baldwin considers the questions that will arise when just such a demonstration of subjective violence occurs: "One day, to everyone's astonishment, someone drops a match in the powder keg and everything blows up. Before the dust has settled or the blood congealed, editorials, speeches, and civil-rights commissions are loud in the land, demanding to know what happened."[36] It is following this quotation that Baldwin explicitly links the subordination of African Americans to masculinity. In answer to the hypothetical situation of riots taking place in Harlem, and the presumed question regarding "what happened," Baldwin explains that "What happened is that Negroes want to be treated like men"[37] Repeating this line in the next paragraph, Baldwin continues:

Negroes want to be treated like men: a perfectly straightforward statement, containing only seven words. People who have mastered Kant,
Hegel, Shakespeare, Marx, Freud, and the Bible find this statement ut-
terly impenetrable. The idea seems to threaten profound, barely conscious assumptions. A kind of panic paralyzes their features, as though
they found themselves trapped on the edge of a steep place.[38]

Baldwin understands African American men as primarily feeling their
subordination as a form of emasculation. African Americans feel the
containment to the slums, in the first instance, as a containment of
their masculinity, and the violence that will eventually result therefore
stems from the emasculation of the African American male.

Not only do African American men primarily feel their disempower-
ment as emasculation, but also that emasculation – their segregation
from, and the inaccessibility of, the patriarchal dividend – is seen as
the root of racial segregation. As Roderick Ferguson argues, Baldwin's
work "suggests that racial regulation emerges from heteronormative
exclusion … [W]hite racial dominance 'others' African Americans as
'queer' subjects, as people who exist somewhere outside of proper
heterosexual interaction."[39] African Americans are only "queer" inasmuch as white, patriarchal society understands their assumed
heterosexuality as nonnormative. As Ferguson further explains, the
"black beast" stereotype serves to label African American sexuality as
irrational and so external to (presumptively white) citizenship.[40] Accordingly, Baldwin most clearly understands masculinity as a system
of domination.

Importantly, Baldwin is not arguing for a renegotiation of hegemonic masculinity, one that would at best incorporate African Americans into the hegemonic bloc, or at worst increasingly authorize black
exemplars of masculinity in the symbolic realm. (*Esquire* takes up this
second stance, as will be discussed below.) Such a renegotiation may
improve, however slightly, the position of African American men, but
it would leave in place the unequal power hierarchy. The system that
subordinates African Americans is the same system that authorizes
them. On the contrary, Baldwin is arguing for the destruction of the
existing gender order in a manner similar to his argument against
the existence of slums: "The people of Harlem know they are living
there because white people do not think they are good enough to
live anywhere else. No amount of 'improvement' can sweeten this
fact. Whatever money is now being earmarked to improve this, or any

other ghetto, might as well be burnt. A ghetto can be improved in one way only: out of existence."[41] The projects are ideological constructs – they are meant to keep African Americans marginalized. Even if they are improved, their function remains the same. As Baldwin advances his critique of hegemonic masculinity, he makes a similar argument: that "blackness" is a category invented to marginalize African Americans, and that the only way to counter this situation is to overturn the gender order that finds hegemonic masculinity at its pinnacle.

Though Baldwin's critique aims to dismantle hegemonic masculinity, one could easily charge him with forwarding a patriarchal point of view, one that simply effaces women from the picture. Such a critique is not without merit; however, I will demonstrate that Baldwin's argument has larger implications that include women, albeit implicitly, and that his critique is more sophisticated than has yet been established. Though Baldwin does not expressly make this claim, his critique of masculinity allies nonetheless with a feminist critique of patriarchy, inasmuch as he wishes to dismantle a system that ultimately subordinates women, even if his focus is on that system's effect on subordinated and marginalized versions of masculinity. This critique of the system itself is not limited to Baldwin's magazine articles, but is present in his novels as well. As Hélène Christol argues, Baldwin's fiction argues that all systems of dominance and oppression will continue to operate as long as America maintains its ideal of masculinity. Until hegemonic masculinity is re-examined and ultimately abandoned, relations among men and between men and women will be exercises in power and violence.[42] It is important to add to Christol's assertion that Baldwin saw the American ideal of masculinity not only as the centre of systems of oppression based on gender, but also at the centre of racial discrimination. Still, the fact that Baldwin seemingly ignores women in his nonfiction writing is problematic, and could allow his critique to bolster the system of masculine domination that it hopes to diminish.

Baldwin develops his critique in "The Black Boy Looks at the White Boy," a May 1961 *Esquire* article about his troubled relationship with Norman Mailer. As *Esquire* historian Carol Polsgrove explains, the two writers and their relationship were an important part of *Esquire* in the 1960s. Indeed, Polsgrove claims that both Mailer and Baldwin were crucial to *Esquire*'s construction of masculinity.[43] It is not surprising, then, that the crux of the dispute between the two men, as articulated by Baldwin in "Black Boy," represents Mailer's embrace of idealized

white masculinity and his fetishization of black masculinity. The un-
ease at the centre of the article, and at the centre of the two authors'
relationship, stems from Mailer's "The White Negro," an essay that,
as demonstrated in the last chapter, forms the basis for *An American
Dream*, and articulates the contemporary renegotiation of hegemonic
masculinity for the era of white collar, conformist masculinity. As Leeming argues, "The Black Boy Looks at the White Boy" reveals Mailer as
a "representative of the white man's naïve and arrogant perversion
of black culture – a culture centered in pain and deprivation – for
bourgeois 'hip' purposes."[44] Baldwin's article consequently highlights
exactly how white men marginalized and fetishized black masculinity
in the same period.

As Baldwin describes it, Mailer's arrogant perversion of black culture is a symptom of his position as a man trapped in his role as a
masculine author. Baldwin refers to Mailer "striding through the soft
Paris nights like a gladiator," states that Mailer's novels, *The Naked
and the Dead* and *Barbary Shore*, "are written in a lean, spare, muscular prose," and that at a party, Mailer's "shoulders hunched, seeming, really, to roll like a boxer's, and his hands moving as though he
were dealing with a sparring partner."[45] In these instances, and elsewhere, Baldwin repeatedly emphasizes Mailer's exaggerated performance of masculinity. The point of Baldwin's critique is not just to
caricature Mailer's masculine ego, but to articulate the ways Mailer's
practice of masculinity is intimately connected to the fetishization of
African American masculinity – that hegemonic forms of masculinity
are predicated on the subordination of all other forms of masculinity, and therefore reinforce not only inequalities based on gender,
but also every other type of inequality. In this way, Mailer's ostensibly
liberal, urbane, white-collar masculinity is revealed to be similar to
the Southern, working-class masculinities of "Going to Meet the Man"
and *Blues for Mister Charlie*. This is a rather pointed message to make in
the pages of a magazine invested in the promotion and consumption
of hegemonic masculinity for a white male readership.

Baldwin not only highlights Mailer's roleplaying, but also his own.
Arguing that both writers played the role of the "toughest kid on the
block," Baldwin goes on to state that "the roles that we construct are
constructed because we feel that they will help us to survive and also,
of course, because they fulfill something in our personalities; and one
does not, therefore, cease playing a role simply because one has begun to understand it. All roles are dangerous. The world tends to

trap and immobilize you in the role you play." "The toughest kid on a block" is a role, but so are Mailer's and Baldwin's racialized gender identities, as presented by Baldwin: "I am a black boy from the Harlem streets, and Norman is a middle-class Jew."[46] While here Baldwin may seem guilty of essentializing these roles, he is rather, as Douglas Taylor sees this, distinguishing between naturalness and situatedness.[47] This is to say that a "black boy" from the lower-classes and a "Jew" from the middle-classes are not depicting subjects but subject-positions: "black" and "lower-class" can be added to "homosexual" in a series of coordinates that situate Baldwin within the larger gender order. Just because these different identities are historical, not essential, does not mean that they are not real; rather, they are discursive, and thus open to reinterpretation and renegotiation. This is what Baldwin means when he says that one cannot "cease playing a role simply because one has begun to understand it," since one is not situated in that position by choice but by a system of domination; thus, "All roles are dangerous."

Baldwin goes on to demonstrate that he is, indeed, aware of his role, and it is because of his particular situatedness that he is able to critique hegemonic masculinity. In the essay's most pointed passage, Baldwin states:

> I think that I know something about American masculinity which most men of my generation do not know because they have not been menaced by it in the way that I have been. It is still true, alas, that to be an American Negro male is also to be a kind of walking phallic symbol: which means that one pays, in one's own personality, for the sexual insecurity of others. The relationship, therefore, of a black boy to a white boy is a very complex thing.[48]

In this passage Baldwin claims that his outsider status allows him to see the reality of American masculinity and heteronormativity, and from this vantage point he is better able to critique it.[49] From this fringe position, Baldwin is able to see not only the structures that shape Mailer's perception of African Americans, but also the mechanisms that marginalize them. As the passage continues, Baldwin clearly returns to the criticism articulated in *Blues for Mister Charlie* and "Going to Meet the Man": African Americans are denied masculinity by the very mechanism which makes them "hypermasculine" in the eyes of white America. Reduced to only a phallus, black men are more readily made into "tools" for hegemonic masculinity.

By writing for *Esquire* magazine, Baldwin was taking part in the renegotiation of American masculinity for the 1960s.[50] His voice, though
strong and reasoned, nonetheless came from a subordinate position
in the gender hierarchy, and so his influence was, understandably,
not as considerable as Mailer's. However, in articles such as "Fifth Avenue, Uptown," and "The Black Boy Looks at the White Boy," Baldwin
repeatedly brought in a consideration of masculinity when discussing
the effects of racism. In a publication that continually explains to its
readers "How to Be a Man," Baldwin's answer was to indict the very
notion of masculinity, and to make clear the connections between racism and masculine domination.

3. "James Baldwin Tells Us All How to Cool It This Summer"

Throughout the 1960s, *Esquire* continued to assume a white, male
readership, while also invoking fear of black radicalism. In each issue, African Americans are largely absent as implied readers, and are
never hailed as the subject of interpellation. Take, for example, the
January 1967 issue. Advertisements depicting the type of fashionable,
leisure-based lifestyle thought desirable by advertisers exclude any
representation of African Americans. Advertisements for the '67 Plymouth Barracuda (depicting sexy, stylish couples)[51] and Haig blended
scotch whiskey (again depicting stylish people, identified as "under-
water worldlies," "young fashionables," "comers in the combos," "elite
equestrians in St. Moritz," "the big game set," and "Nomads of the
international set")[52] feature only white models. An entire section of
the issue, entitled "New Year's Eve with Elegance," consists of several
photo spreads of luxurious, formal, black-tie gatherings, made up entirely of white people.[53] No African Americans are photographed to
accompany such articles as "A Sportsman's Tip Sheet on the West Indies"[54] or "How to Fly to Europe Without Buying a Ticket."[55] *Esquire*
assumed a white audience, and its portrayal of a desirable, ideal life
took no consideration of African American subjects.

   That is not to say that African American masculinity is entirely absent from the magazine. On the contrary, the issue features an article on Black Rights leader Stokely Carmichael. As a radical Black
Power leader, Carmichael represents a threat to the (white) way of
life depicted in *Esquire*. The article's author, Bernard Weinraub, almost immediately describes Carmichael as "six-feet-one and [having]
the build of a basketball guard: a solid chest, slender waist, powerful

legs."[56] Emphasizing Carmichael's physicality makes him more of a threat, in much the same way that the "black beast" stereotype did. Instead of the "black beast," the author's rhetorical comparison to a black athlete brings to mind a traditional form of exemplary masculinity that would be familiar to *Esquire*'s readers. Such readers would find the only other black figures in the magazine in the "Dubious Achievement Awards" section, including Cassius Clay (named "Mealymouth of the Year") and Adam Clayton Powell, Jr ("Poor Mouth of the Year").[57] Black masculinity is authorized only to the extent that it can be used to reinforce hegemonic masculinity; challenges to hegemony are always represented as potentially threatening or are ridiculed by the magazine.

When the potential threat of black masculinity could not be subverted, *Esquire* was not above resorting to fear mongering. The November 1967 issue features an exposé on "Black Power," predominantly written by William Worthy. The articles that make up the section include Worthy's "The American Negro is Dead," described as a showcase of "Negroes who have been in touch one way or another with the N.L.F.[58] and other non-white revolutionaries,"[59] and "The Black Power Establishment," a diagram that seeks to visualize the power structure of Black Power.[60] The former article is accompanied by the following description: "Don't look now, honky, but some of his best friends are Vietcong."[61] The short description manages to both note the racial identity of the assumed reader ("honky") and to other the Black Power Movement by associating it with foreign, communist influence. Here, the article presents Black Power as powerful and frightening, giving white masculinities something to rally against. Furthermore, the March 1968 issue features a lengthy article by Gary Wills entitled "The Second Civil War," its first page promising "This time it's simpler: black and white."[62] Wills later revised the article into a book. These few examples gesture to a larger fear of Black Nationalism, Black Power, and Civil Rights promoted by the magazine throughout the decade.

Esquire's July 1968 issue hit the stands just two months after the assassination of Martin Luther King, Jr, in the wake of the consequent riots and ongoing racial tension. The issue plays a strange game of slight-of-hand: *Esquire* seemingly brings in Baldwin, a long-time contributor, to explain how African Americans can "cool it" that summer, a message that would no doubt go over well with white society. In the table of contents, though, the description accompanying the Baldwin feature betrays, however sarcastically, a degree of white condescension, and perhaps even fear, when it asks "Comes [sic] summer, what will Whitey give up?"

Baldwin *had* been deliberately attacked by *Esquire* before. Polsgrove explains how Harold Hayes, *Esquire*'s then-editor, assigned Bob Adelman to profile Baldwin for the August 1964 issue.[63] The article opened with what Polsgrove describes as "an unflattering photograph of Baldwin, his eyes popping at a host of hands extended toward him," while the profile's author, Marvin Elkoff, "laid out a sequence of scenes featuring a needy, exhibitionist Baldwin."[64] Polsgrove suggests that *Esquire* editor Hayes did indeed intend the profile to "get" Baldwin, since he viewed Baldwin's attacks on white liberals as hypocritical (he suggested that white liberals made up "the better part of Baldwin's audience"), and thought that his "recent work" (1964) showed a "virulent strain." Baldwin subsequently did not appear in the magazine for several years.[65] When he did appear in *Esquire* again, it was for the interview under discussion.

In the July interview, Baldwin steadfastly refuses to play the role that the magazine has assigned him, instead pointing to a large variety of ideological problems that underpin the violence in the streets. Baldwin continually declines to have his position (and that of the black rioters) defined by the white interviewer, for instance, by avoiding the rhetorical trap of referring to African Americans involved in the riots as "looters." The interviewer begins by proposing that police have been more "permissive" by refraining from shooting "looters," and, when Baldwin objects, insists that the label is accurate, asking what Baldwin would call someone "who smashes in the window of a television store and takes what he wants." Baldwin uses this opening to launch an attack on systemic racism: latching onto the word "looters," Baldwin queries the interviewer, "how would you define somebody who puts a cat where he is and takes all the money out of the ghetto where he makes it? Who is looting whom?" Furthermore, he insists that the interviewer is "accusing a captive population who has been robbed of everything of looting. I think it's obscene."[66] The act of labelling African Americans "looters" is an act of what Althusser calls interpellation, a hail which Baldwin refuses, and it is similar to the act of labelling African Americans as "Negroes" or "Sambo," attempting to hail them into a subordinate position. For Baldwin, it is not the action of "Negroes" but the creation of "Negroes" that is the criminal act.

Baldwin further attacks the systemic violence of subordination and marginalization when he explains "whiteness" and "blackness" as ideological categories:

> BALDWIN: White by the way is not a color, it's an attitude. You're as white as you think you are. It's your choice.
> Q. Then black is a state of mind too?
> BALDWIN: No, black is a condition.[67]

Here, though he obviously uses a terminology of his own, Baldwin details a racial ideology propagated by the system of hegemonic masculinity later identified by Connell. In this interview, Baldwin does not directly and consistently reference masculinity (and gender) as a root cause of racial problems; however, the critique of hegemonic masculinity previously established and, I argue, central to all of Baldwin's discussions of race clearly informs his argument. Baldwin's answers suggest that "whiteness" is the choice of complicity, the attitude of investing in the gender order as it is stratified by hegemonic masculinity. "Blackness," on the other hand, is a "condition," to the extent that it is a subject position enforced on African Americans by those invested in the gender order: the "condition" of blackness is the effect of an act of subordination.

In keeping with Baldwin's long-standing critique of American masculinity, he continually frames his discussion in gendered terms, arguing that "The price in this country to survive at all still is to become a white man. More and more people are refusing to become a white man." Baldwin's gendered pronoun is not idly chosen: freedom remains solely in the purview of men. Furthermore, when Baldwin speaks of truly free African Americans, he shifts his gendered pronoun from "man" to "male," stating that "The American white man does not really want to have an autonomous Negro male anywhere near him."[68] The "white *man*" occupies a constructed subject position within the current gender order; the "autonomous Negro *male*" represents a figure outside of a system of hegemonic masculinity. However, African American men do not exist outside of this system; this is one reason why African American men understand colour divisions as a form of emasculation.

Baldwin's discussion of Carmichael references both this form of emasculation and the perceived threat of black men to hegemonic masculinity: "Stokely is a leader for a great many people. Stokely is even more than that, Stokely is a symbol for a great many people. A great many emasculated black boys turn to Stokely because he's fighting against their emasculation."[69] Michele Wallace, a scholar of black masculinity, supports Baldwin's assessment of Carmichael. In addition, she discusses Carmichael's perceived threat in terms of masculinity, stating, "Here was a black man with an erect phallus, and he was pushing it up in America's face." Moreover, Wallace calls Carmichael "the nightmare America had been dreading – the black man seizing his manhood, the black man as sexual, virile, tough and dangerous."[70] Here is a figure that claims the masculinity otherwise denied African Americans – here is a figure embodying Baldwin's claim from 1960, that when violence occurs in Harlem, and white society asks what happened, "What happened is that Negroes want to be treated like men."[71] Carmichael, a "black man seizing his manhood," is the leader implicitly foretold by Baldwin, and a predictable leader for a subordinated group of men wishing to escape their emasculation. Carmichael's version of black masculinity – at least as it has here been articulated – certainly has obvious parallels with the "black beast" archetype, and with the jazz musicians and "hipsters" of Mailer's (and *Esquire's*) naive fantasies. However, Carmichael's masculinity cannot be as easily appropriated based on both his education (supposedly incommensurate with a hypermasculine black man) and his Black Nationalism, which proposes a systemic assault against white privilege. Still, Baldwin does admit to "disagreements" with Carmichael, and his reticence to clearly identify Carmichael as a leader is not surprising, given that Carmichael's investment in masculinity puts him at odds with Baldwin's critique of hegemonic masculinity.

Baldwin's argument, in the published interview, boils down to an assault on the gender order itself. He cites the "nightmarish" black, masculine figure of Carmichael in his objection to integration:

> I think Stokely's right when he says that integration is another word, you know, the latest kind of euphemism for white supremacy. No, I don't want to be integrated into this house or any other house, especially not this burning house. I don't want to become ... like you. You, the white people. I'd rather die than become what most white people in this country have become.[72]

What Baldwin offers as a true remedy to the "Negro problem" is not the integration of African Americans into white society – that is, in

Connell's terms, Baldwin is not arguing for a renegotiation of hegemonic masculinity so as to include African Americans in a hegemonic bloc – but the dismantling of the system that creates "Negro problems." In fact, Baldwin argues that the "Negro" is actually the creation of a Fordist society, stating that "Labor unions along with the bosses created the Negro as a kind of threat to the white worker."[73] Therefore, for African Americans to improve their position, the system of hegemonic masculinity will need to be overthrown altogether, and those complicit masculinities invested in its continuation will have to sacrifice their access to the patriarchal dividend: "It means in short that if the American Negro, the American black man, is going to become a free person in this country, the people of this country have to give up something."[74] For Baldwin, freeing African Americans will involve the destruction of hegemonic masculinity itself, and consequently the end of subordinated, marginalized, and complicit masculinities, and the patriarchal dividend.

It is near the end of the interview that Baldwin forwards his most articulate critique of hegemonic masculinity. In response to the interviewer's question "You would say, then, that we have a lot to answer for," Baldwin argues that the overthrow of hegemonic masculinity (though not, obviously, in those terms) will not only require the work of white men, but also result in a freer society for all:

BALDWIN: I'm not trying to accuse you, you know. That's not the point. But you have an awful lot to face. I don't envy any white man in this century, because I wouldn't like to have to face what you have to face. If you don't face it, though, it's a matter of *your* life or death. Everyone's deluded if they think it's a matter of Sambo's life or death. It isn't a matter of Sambo's life or death, and it can't be, for they have been slaughtering Sambos too long. It's a matter of whether or not *you* want to live. And you may think that my death or diminution, or my disappearance will save you, but it won't. It can't save you. All that can save you now is your confrontation with your own history ... which is not your past, but your present. Nobody cares what happened in the past. One can't afford to care what happened in the past. But your history has led you to this moment, and you can only begin to change yourself by looking at what you are doing in the name of your history, in the name of your gods, in the name of your language. And what has happened is as though I, having always been outside it – more outside it than victimized by it, but mainly *outside* it – can see it better than you

can see it. Because I cannot afford to let you fool me. If I let you fool
me, then I die. But I've fooled *you* for a long time. That's why you keep
saying, what does the Negro want? It's a summation of your own delusions, the lies you've told yourself. You know *exactly* what I want![75]

Baldwin's claim that he is "outside" of "what has happened" parallels
his statement, in "The Black Boy Looks at the White Boy," that he
"know[s] something about the American masculinity which most men
of my generation do not know because they have not been menaced
by it in the way that I have been."[76] Here, Baldwin argues that his
blackness and his homosexuality have led him to be able to perceive
the system of domination as a whole, from a doubly marginalized position. Furthermore, the white man's history, which Baldwin references,
is the history of hegemonic forms of masculinity – it is the history that
"has created cowboys and Indians, good guys and bad guys, punks and
studs, tough guys and softies, butch and faggot, *black and white*."[77] It is
this history that white men must face, come to understand, and then
overcome, if a freer world – for white and black, men and women – is
to be established. Such a criticism is hard for men to accept, since,
as Connell argues, all men, the vast majority of whom are not hegemonic, profit from a patriarchal dividend; however, Baldwin's argument is that men need to recognize that this patriarchal dividend is
predicated on the system of marginalization and subordination that
negatively impacts the vast majority of men and all women. Perhaps
it is precisely the ideal readers of *Esquire* magazine – readers so interested and invested in "how to be a man" – who not only need to hear
this message, but also are equipped, however insufficiently, to understand it, given that very interest.

The possibility that readers might read and understand Baldwin's
critique is met, however, with a variety of textual manoeuvres in the
published magazine that subvert or undermine Baldwin's message.
The first and most obvious instance of this subversion is the cover itself.[78] The cover image, and the choice of language, seeks to sabotage
Baldwin's argument, diffusing his anger and his critique of ideology
by providing for its white readers more easily recognizable and assimilable images of black masculinity. The men on the cover imply a
different connotation of "cooling it" – not "calming down" the riots
following King's assassination, but the type of "cool" associated with
jazz music ("cool jazz") and African American slang.[79] Furthermore,
the men on the cover are clearly adopting what Richard Majors and

Janet Mancini Billson call the "cool pose," which they define as "a strategy that many black males use in making sense of their everyday lives."[80] These figures are significant for two reasons. First, they represent easily recognizable stock images of black masculinity; in particular, they represent the character of the "cool cat," whom Majors and Billson describe as "an exceptional artist of expressiveness and flamboyant style."[81] The cool cats on the cover are reminiscent of Shago Martin in Mailer's *An American Dream*, and, as discussed in chapter 1, they are figures whose particular masculine performance can be fetishized and appropriated by hegemonic forms of masculinity, especially given that they lack the threatening nature of Carmichael's Black Nationalist masculinity.

Second, African American men adopt the strategy of the "cool pose" as a coping mechanism for the emasculating effects of being a black man in a white-dominated American society.[82] The "cool pose" is, according to Majors and Billson, sometimes the only way that African American men can distinguish themselves and their masculinity in a culture that deprives them of the material symbols to do so.[83] As such, "The ironclad façade of cool pose is a signature of true masculinity, but it is one-dimensional. If it fails, masculinity fails."[84] The "cool pose" is only necessary because of the opportunities denied African American men through a gender order that subordinates them. The ideal readers of *Esquire* are Ehrenreich's "gray flannel rebels" (discussed in the previous chapter), a type of masculinity complicit not only in the gender order that subordinates African American men, but also in the appropriation of signifiers of African American masculinity, done to shore up or renegotiate white patriarchy. All of which is to say that a version of black masculinity both one-dimensional and easily consumable by *Esquire*'s white audience threatens to occlude Baldwin's nuanced and radical criticism of race and masculinity in America. It is as though by using such a pat phrase and such easily recognizable images of black masculinity, *Esquire* hopes to force Baldwin into a subject position more easily digestible for the magazine's consumers. A reader could be forgiven for believing that the magazine offered advice from Baldwin regarding style and music, rather than an uncomfortable discussion of race riots.

Though the subversion of Baldwin's message begins on the cover, it certainly does not end there. "Cool it," a phrase first appearing on the cover, repeats throughout the magazine and is used to weaken Baldwin's argument. The phrase features prominently in the rather unwieldy subtitle of the Baldwin interview: "Q. How can we get the

black people to cool it?/James Baldwin: It is not for us to cool it./Q.
But aren't you the ones who are getting hurt the most?/ James Baldwin: No, we are only the ones who are dying fastest." The interviewer
uses the phrase "cool it" (or some version thereof) in six questions;
though Baldwin repeats the phrase, he makes clear his distaste for the
term, stating "I am not the one to be cooled" and "I suggest that the
mayor of every city and the President of this nation go on the air and
address the white people for a change. Tell *them* to cool it." While in
this usage "cooling it" refers to relaxing racial tensions (the onus being placed on African Americans to do so), this rather serious matter
is further discredited by an accompanying feature: "Advice for Summer Drinkers: Cool It." Here, "cool it" becomes a suggestion for how
to prepare drinks.[85] The accompanying pictures show wealthy white
people imbibing various beverages in a tropical location; the captions
identify Miss Cheryl Del Vecchio, for instance, and James Kimberly,[86]
but the only African American represented goes unidentified, and
is one of the wait staff, dressed in uniform and holding a drink. The
idea of "cooling it" – that is, easing racial tension – is deflated, and
Baldwin's example of a radical version of black masculinity is replaced
by literally subordinated examples.

Other features in the magazine work to further undermine Baldwin's subject position, and thus his critique. Finding resonance with
Baldwin's claim, made in the same issue, that "black is a condition,"
Lawrence Lasker's article "A White Shade of Black" discusses derma-
tological treatments for the skin disorder vitiligo, treatments that can
lighten the skin colour of African American sufferers of this ailment.
The accompanying description has the same tone of white condescension as the previously cited description of the Baldwin interview: for
the Lasker article, it states that "An ointment has turned fifty-five Negroes white, and there may soon be a pill that can do the job more
effectively – presuming, of course, that by then there is still some advantage in *being* white."[87] While the ointment is a treatment for vitiligo, the article makes clear that the real "skin condition" that needs
curing is the condition of blackness. During dinner out with Lasker,
Dr Robert Stolar, one of the interviewed practitioners of the treatment, gestures to the African American waiter and says, "You see, he
shouldn't have to be black, if he doesn't want to be. He doesn't have
to be."[88] The same tone of contempt found in the article's description
is taken up by the author of the article, who describes one derma-
tologist, Dr Aaron Lerner, as "doing research [into skin lightening]

which would make him *the most important man* in the history of race relations";[89] this is a rather poor joke, if it is indeed intended as a joke, given the article's close placement to the Baldwin interview (it starts less than ten pages after the first break in the interview) and, even more significantly, the recent assassination of King, two black men who could actually be identified as "important" in the history of Civil Rights.

Despite the tone of the article and the nature of the doctors' treatments, both Stolar and Lerner make statements that betray an understanding of the social dimension of blackness. Lerner, for instance, states that "It would be quite a blow to people who think of Negroes as inferior to have a Negro able to switch colors with them," indicating that the perception of racial inferiority is only that, a perception. Further, Stolar "claims that each of his fifty-five patients changed social status. Many were able to get better jobs."[90] Though it is impossible to forgive the article's racism and the misguided interest of the dermatologists, the physicians' statements nonetheless reveal an understanding that race is, in fact, only "skin deep." This understanding is nevertheless drastically different from Baldwin's, who sees black not as a skin colour, but as a label or position imposed on people of a certain skin colour by the ideology of hegemonic masculinity. African Americans do not need to get rid of their black skin; rather, white America needs to get rid of its perceptions of what black skin supposedly signifies.

In keeping with my methodology throughout this study, I am not arguing over editorial intention; that is to say, I am not arguing that the placement of these different representations of blackness and black masculinity is necessarily deliberate. Rather, I am arguing that in pursuing its own hegemonic masculinity project, the magazine was published with patterns that detract from Baldwin's message by foregrounding other versions of masculinity and downplaying the importance of racial discrimination. This particular issue of *Esquire* thus applies a number of strategies typical of the magazine as a whole to disrupt Baldwin's message. These strategies appear in the content authored by *Esquire*'s writers and editors, and include the representation of more easily assimilable versions of black masculinity, the degradation of black skin colour, and the repetition of the phrase "cool it," as previously outlined. Representations of black masculinity that appear in the advertisements – and which are therefore *not* produced by the magazine itself – are more complicated. For example, an advertisement for the NAACP Legal Defense & Educational Fund features a stark black and white photograph of a young African American man raising a Molotov cocktail in a threatening manner. The advertisement, directed at *Esquire*'s white, middle-class male readership, asks "Does he make you mad? Scared? Guilty?" The tone of the advertisement is much more in keeping with Baldwin's approach to civil rights: as well as challenging white perceptions of black masculinity, it baldly states that "White America traps the Negro in a cycle of prejudice and poverty that denies him humanity and destroys his dignity."[91] The magazine therefore does not omit challenges to white masculinity, though it does present them in a package that threatens to dull their critical edge.

4. Conclusion

In "The New Lost Generation," published in *Esquire*, Baldwin speaks about those individuals who, like David in *Giovanni's Room*, fled America for Europe, leaving behind not only the country, but the ideological apparatus that gives it meaning. He argues that "many expatriates vanish into the lives of their adopted country ... This applies especially, of course, to women, who, given the pressures of raising a family, rarely have time to be homesick, or guilty about 'escaping' the problems of American life. Their first loyalties, thank heaven, are to the men they married and the children they must raise."[92] Here, then, Baldwin highlights an important limit – not to his critique, but to his own historical perception. Theoretically, Baldwin's attack on the American gender order would, if successful, benefit women most of all – hegemonic masculinity is predicated, in all instances, on the domination of women by men. Certainly masculinities are subordinated or marginalized based on sexuality and skin colour, but in every instance, in a patriarchal society, these "lesser" masculinities still find themselves in a higher position than women, by virtue of their masculinity. The overthrow of the gender order would have as its primary benefactors the 50 per cent of the population that is female. However, Baldwin seems unable to fully grasp this; despite his radical critique of masculinity, he continues to see women in traditional gender roles. This shortcoming highlights Baldwin's own historical situatedness, but does not undermine the possibilities implicit in his critique. Even if he does not valorize phallic masculinity, he still falls into a trap akin to those highlighted by Pochmara and hooks; perhaps he avoids allying black men with white men against women, but he fails by omitting a consideration of the place of women from his analysis of hegemonic masculinity.

Central to my argument throughout this study is the idea that *Esquire* magazine is a site where the renegotiation of hegemonic masculinity plays out. With its ideal readership of white, middle-class professionals, *Esquire* is directed towards a culturally significant and economically influential group of consumers, a group powerfully invested in the changing definition of masculinity. The magazine is therefore an ideal place for Baldwin to make his critique of hegemonic masculinity, to reveal the ways those who are complicit in the maintenance and articulation of hegemonic masculinity are also complicit in the maintenance of racial inequality. He is also an ideal author for *Esquire* to recruit, not only because his literary *gravitas* makes him suitably distinguished, but also because their hegemonic masculinity project is always a work in progress, and must work through various possible definitions of masculinity. The 1960s were a time when the alliances that constituted hegemony were in a state of flux, and Baldwin, at least at the beginning of the decade, presented the kind of figure through which certain alliances could be made. Though Baldwin's articles rarely explicitly focus on masculinity, his critique is always present, and even highlighted by the context of the magazine that published them. Baldwin's contributions to the magazine therefore have the potential to provide a more radical impetus to the renegotiation of masculinity, and to challenge readers to critique their own valuations of the very concept. However, while a publication focused on masculinity is therefore a pivotal place in which to make such a contribution, it is also a place invested in patriarchy, in the valorization of masculinity and the maintenance of hegemonic masculinity; it is therefore simultaneously a place open to, and resistant of, such a radical critique.

For Baldwin, the treatment of black masculinity as a commodity is a major contributing factor to its subordination and marginalization; in the 1970s, the continued commodification of masculinity would increasingly become the focus of American fiction published in *Esquire*. For Carver, the commodification of masculinity will be seen as a limitation even to complicit forms of white masculinity; for Capote, this commodification is a necessary first step to a type of mobility previously unavailable to queer masculinities.

PART TWO

"The Richness of Life Itself" in the 1970s

3
Low-Rent Tragedies of Beset Manhood

Raymond Carver, perhaps the most well-known American short story writer of the mid-twentieth-century, is famous for the spare form of his prose, but also his recurring themes, including an attention to consumer goods, a fixation on alcohol and drinking,[1] and cuckoldry. Carver's fiction, which began to reach a larger audience in the 1970s, came to prominence in the 1980s, part of a vanguard of new, realistic fiction that emphasized unadorned prose and working-class lives. In particular, Carver's fiction depicts everyday situations in working-class life, focusing on what one reviewer called "people who read *Popular Mechanics* and *Field and Stream*, people who ... work at shopping centers, sell books, have milk routes, or try, drunkenly, to manage a motel."[2] Carver's early protagonists represent the working class of the 1970s, a decade during which a struggling economy resulted in an increased gap between the rich and the poor.[3] In the new American economy of undervalued labour and increased consumerism, Carver's protagonists, usually male, are down on their luck, often out of work, and struggling just to get by, suffering through what Robert Towers calls "Low-Rent Tragedies."[4]

The 1970s would see several social and economic changes that would challenge the hegemonic formulation of masculinity. As I will discuss in further detail next chapter, *Esquire*'s masculinity project changed, in limited ways, to reflect these historic pressures, even if its overall message was inevitably the same: that men could keep apace of change through consumption. If Norman Mailer's protagonist Stephen Rojack seemed a suitable figure for the 1960s, then his heroic masculinity seemed completely incompatible with the America of the 1970s. Indeed, *Esquire* even highlighted this very issue in its March

1972 feature "In the Absence of a Hero for the Seventies," a satirical piece that suggests that heroic masculinity was missing during the decade. Its authors lamented the men of the period: "*What a piece of clay is modern man! how crippled in reason! how infinite in frailties! in action how like a pansy! in apprehension how like a clod!*"[5] After declaring it an "unheroic age," the authors conclude that "*Heroic heroes have gone the way of God, James Bond and the buffalo. Charisma is buried beneath an eternal flame in Arlington.*"[6] *Esquire* even dropped the subtitle "The Magazine for Men" from its cover in August 1975, de-emphasizing masculinity as a focus of the magazine.[7]

Moreover, the emphasis on race and conformity, central to the discourse on masculinity in the 1960s, shifts in the 1970s to the relationship between men and the economy.[8] Carver's men are not, in any way, living the good life advertised in *Esquire* magazine, which was the first national, popular magazine to publish his work, and established his relationship with long-time collaborator Gordon Lish. Carver's men are illustrative of the disparity between, on the one hand, the world of sophistication and commodities offered by the magazine, and on the other, the life of those male readers whose access to patriarchal power is limited by their distance from obtaining the goods on display in the magazine's glossy pages. *Esquire* advertised a particular hegemonic masculinity project as a lifestyle, one that was at least ostensibly available to the members of the professional-managerial class, who make up the magazine's target audience. Carver's protagonists, however, represent the increasingly alienated lower-middle and working classes, who not only do not live the good life promised in *Esquire*, but also simply cannot afford to consume the cultural codes and meanings advertised. For them, practicing hegemonic masculinity becomes a practice of cruel optimism. If men understand consumption as one of the few avenues available for self-fashioning masculinity and accessing patriarchal authority, then Carver posits that those men who cannot afford to consume the "right" things logically feel their economic constraint as a constrained masculinity.[9]

For Paul Skenazy, "The trademark Carver tale is a kind of mundane ghost story in which these people are haunted by the presence of some lost, almost forgotten, not-really-expected possibility."[10] In this chapter, I suggest that the "presence" haunting these characters is the commodity form and the realm of advertising that is its primary vehicle. To do so, I argue that Carver writes a form of "capitalist realism" I call "consumer realism," in which his characters are troubled by the unbridgeable distance between their own lives and the lifestyles promised them by the world of consumerism, as exemplified in the magazine's articles and advertisements. Read in the context of the publication in which they appeared, Carver's *Esquire* stories narrate the increasingly detrimental effects of reification on blue-collar and working-class masculinities. Here, I am using reification in the Marxist sense (fraught though the term may be). *A Dictionary of Marxist Thought* offers a succinct definition:

> The act (or result of the act) of transforming human properties, relations and actions into properties, relations and actions of man-produced things which have become independent (and which are imagined as originally independent) of man and govern his life. Also transformation of human beings into thing-like beings which do not behave in a human way but according to the laws of the thing-world."[11]

As understood by Georg Lukács and those who have developed his thinking, reification is a central feature of capitalism and is closely related to Marx's commodity fetishism. As presented in *Esquire*, Carver's "Neighbors," "What is it?," and "Collectors" – all subsequently published in Carver's first collection, *Will You Please Be Quiet, Please?* – reveal reification as an inevitable aspect of life under neoliberalism, which is a life structured by the commodity form and the aesthetics of advertising.

1. "The Market Represents": *Esquire*, Carver, and Consumer Realism

Carver's literary career was marked by an author-editor relationship with Gordon Lish, *Esquire*'s fiction editor for most of the 1970s. Carver's style – influenced by Lish[12] – is viewed as paradigmatic of his aesthetic "school" and has gone by many names: "Kmart realism," "dirty realism," and "minimalism."[13] Philip Simmons argues that minimalism is "a plain style response that seeks to grab the moral and epistemological high ground with its claim to a more faithful representation of the speech and experience of 'ordinary' men and women."[14] This description highlights the connection between Carver's style and the genre of realism: by being more "faithful" to representation, Carver's fiction presents a realism characterized by the perceived absence of a barrier between readers and *things*. This is to suggest that what is "faithful" about Carver's representation is its close association with the commodity form. Moreover, readers can only understand Carver's style as "unmediated" in a society where the commodity has become naturalized, in which the eye has been so thoroughly trained that it no longer *sees* reification as a mediating experience.

In other words, Carver's realism is a particular form of "capitalist realism." The term "capitalist realism" has its roots in visual art and advertising, and has recently been picked up by literary scholars, most notably Richard Godden, Alison Shonkwiler, and Leigh Claire La Berge. In the introduction to *Reading Capitalist Realism*, Shonkwiler and La Berge set out to provide a working definition and theory of capitalist realism.[15] The authors see capitalist realism as necessarily articulating the "lived economic, social, and affective" experience of life in "an inequitable, winner-take-all system of casino capitalism [that] has seemingly achieved popular consent."[16] Most importantly, the authors explain how capitalist realism operates as both an ideological formation describing "the pervasive logic of capitalism" and a mode demonstrating the colonization of the real by the process of commodification.[17] The process of reification is therefore central, as capitalist realism depicts "the real world" using typical realist practices, but from a totally reified perspective, wherein "human experience takes on the quality of things"[18] and society has learned to "satisfy all its needs in terms of commodity exchange."[19]

Furthermore, Shonkwiler and La Berge argue that capitalist realism "shares an articulation" with neoliberalism. Dating the rise of the neoliberal era as the early to mid-1970s – the time at which Carver begins publishing with *Esquire* – the authors define neoliberalism as "an economic and political paradigm in which freedom is conceived almost entirely in market terms."[20] Similarly, capitalist realism is a mode that represents via "market terms." In other words, the economic and cultural shift to neoliberalism coexists with a complementary aesthetic shift in realist fiction. As Shonkwiler and La Berge elegantly put it, "in liberalism the market was represented; in neoliberalism, the market represents."[21] The market, the central metaphor of a neoliberal society, therefore shapes all forms of representation.

If the market speaks, it speaks through advertisements. As Robert Goldman explains, advertising is "a key social and economic institution in producing and reproducing the material and ideological supremacy of commodity relations."[22] A focus on advertising brings the discussion of capitalist realism back to its earliest uses. First, the coinage of "capitalist realism" comes from the "German Pop Art" group, whose aesthetics were largely connected to consumer culture. Their art show "Living with Pop – A Demonstration on Behalf of Capitalist Realism" took place in a furniture store. The store was part of the show.[23] In its original use, capitalist realist art therefore demonstrated "the point at which realism simultaneously records and undergoes the economic processes of commodification."[24] Furthermore, Michael Schudson developed the most thoroughgoing discussion of capitalist realism in his book *Advertising, the Uneasy Persuasion.* Seeing capitalist realism as a response to socialist realism,[25] Schudson argues that the crucial difference is that socialist realist art idealizes the producer, capitalist realist art the consumer.[26] The earliest articulations of capitalist realism therefore conceived the term in relation to the aesthetics of advertising.

Shonkwiler and La Berge's more recent discussion of capitalist realism suggests a wide range of possibilities for the term and the mode. For example, the authors argue that capitalist realism "demands an engagement with specific economic forms such as the commodity, money, and finance, as well as organized economic processes such as production and consumption."[27] Capitalist realism's characteristics are therefore well-defined, yet general enough that we might speak of multiple capitalist realisms. Consequently, I would like to introduce the term "consumer realism" as a category of capitalist realism, one that specifically focuses on the role of the consumer, rather than, for example, the producer, the labourer, or the investor. Furthermore, it is the commodity form rather than the financialization of capital that shapes consumer realism. Consumer realism does not just comment on capitalism, per se, but on consumerism more specifically, where the individual is not merely alienated from the product of his or her labour, but is in fact hollowed out, replaced with consumer product-identification.[28]

Flipping through *Esquire* magazine is a trip through the world of consumer realism. It offers a fully reified perspective, presenting both the "good life" and masculinity as commodities. Not only is each magazine rife with advertisements, but *Esquire* itself is a form of advertising, and the regular articles on books, film, and culture function in much the same way as these "proper" ads. As Schudson argues, the most significant effect of advertising results not from the individual ad, but from the cumulative effect of the constant inundation from advertising. Though the primary goal of a given ad is to convince consumers to purchase a particular item, the overall effect of advertising is the gradual acceptance that consumption itself is a remedy for inadequacy, and that this "belief in a larger sense" comes to dominate "the assumptions and attitudes of people surrounded by ads."[29] *Esquire* may convince readers to go out and purchase one of the advertised brands of scotch, or it may more generally convince readers that the advertised objects are material manifestations of the good life.

In *Esquire*, the "good life" is specifically associated with masculinity, through both its third-party advertisements and its editorial content. The advertisements that promote the "good life" do so while presenting their audience with idealized images of gender. The magazine's system of advertisements demonstrates the imbrication of capitalist and gender ideology, not only within each particular advertisement but in society more generally. As Sut Jhally has argued,

> Advertising draws us into *our* reality. As hyper-ritualistic images, commercials offer an extremely concentrated form of communication about sex and gender. The essence of gender is represented in advertisements ... Furthermore, we cannot deny them [advertisements] because we define ourselves at our deepest level through the reality of advertising.[30]

Gender is cultural, and advertising is the most effective and pervasive form of communicating cultural forms. If advertising's primary function is to promote the consumption of commodities, then gender itself is "essentialized" and commodified through advertising.

In her analysis of *Esquire*, Denise Kervin argues that the magazine's advertisements guide male readers to associate "stereotypical masculine characteristics and having money, consumer goods, and leisure ... In addition, and also continuing today, compensation reinforcing traditional masculine behavior comes from its association with the admiration of women – a goad to achieve greater success."[31] Examples of what Kervin here describes can be found throughout the pages of *Esquire*. For example, a fashion spread in the August 1975 issue demonstrates the connection between masculine traits and the good life. A male model dominates the frame in each image, his clothes connoting not only style and sophistication, but the financial success required for such a sartorial display. He obviously lives the good life, his clothing demonstrating his access to wealth and leisure. In each picture the female model is relegated to the edge of the image, leaning on the male model or touching, connoting his strength – she needs his support – but also relegating her to the role of accoutrement. Significantly, she is always desirously looking at the male model, while the male model looks out at us, confident in his display of goods, almost challenging the assumed male reader's presumably inferior masculinity. The model's superior clothing signifies his superior social position, and his reward is the admiration of women.[32]

Because consumer realism as a mode is a combination of realist practices and commodity aesthetics, it is less related to the world of finance than it is to the realm of advertising. The critical edge found in consumer realism is that it frames a reality in which articulations of values alternative to capitalism are repressed or absent; writers can only describe reality itself in terms influenced by the commodity aesthetics of advertising.[33] Consumerism is an area of cultural production not limited to advertising but dominated by its aesthetics. That is to say that consumer realism represents a fully reified world, a world of signs.[34] Moreover, it is during the neoliberal era that user-centred advertising replaced product-focused advertising,[35] thereby situating the subject, rather than the commodity, at the centre of the market. Consumer realism is thus a mode that represents the world through an eye educated by advertising. Consequently, Carver's consumer realist stories emphasize the perception of the consumer thus situated, as well as the affective experience associated with this new social reality. In particular, I argue that situating Carver's stories in *Esquire* highlights their use of consumer realism, and that these stories reveal the social and affective instabilities specific to working-class masculinities in the 1970s.

The third-party advertising found in *Esquire* displays a similar logic. For example, an advertisement for suits states that "The man on the way up chooses a suit of Hart Schaffner & Marx Viracle … when a man's on the way up, his suit shows it. A Hart Schaffner & Marx Viracle Suit will keep you looking great – all the way to the top."[36] The men are in poses similar to the male model's from the last example, eyes staring out at the reader, connoting confidence and a possible challenge to the reader. The repetition of "man on the way up" emphasizes a connection between clothing and success in business (and with virility, since the doubling of "up" suggests an erection).

One connotation of both the advertisement and the fashion spread is that masculinity itself is a commodity. This is made explicit in a Stetson shoe advertisement, which claims "No ordinary man can wear these shoes, Because no man who steps into Stetson remains ordinary."[37] Though the explicit statement of the ad is that the shoes augment their wearer's masculinity, the implication is that masculinity resides in the item itself. While I have focused here on clothing, *Esquire* advertised other commodities in a similar fashion, such as cars, alcohol, and cigarettes – the kinds of items upon which Carver's characters often fixate. The advertisements and editorial content of *Esquire* speak to a larger cultural myth that views consumer items as emblematic of both success and masculinity.

2. Carver's First *Esquire* Story: "Neighbors" and the "Space" of Advertising

It is fitting that Carver's first publication with *Esquire* is the frequently anthologized "Neighbors."[38] Perhaps no story by Carver better illustrates the idea of consumer realism. The story is simple enough: when Jim and Harriet Stone leave to visit relatives, they ask their neighbours, Bill and Arlene Miller, to look after their apartment. This mundane domestic agreement has a dramatic effect on the neighbours, who become obsessed with the Stones' residence. By situating Carver's story within the realm of consumer realism, I will demonstrate how the Stones' apartment functions as an advertisement, and that the Millers' interactions with the apartment mimic the relationship between consumers and advertisements, much like the relationship readers have with the magazine itself.

"Neighbors" presents the Millers as a couple whose attitudes reflect the "belief in a larger sense" in consumerism. Carver's example of the Millers suggests, as Schudson argues, that those surrounded by ads have internalized the perspective of advertising itself.[39] Playing the role of consumers, the Millers view the Stones' life with eyes shaped by reification. Their own life has taken on the quality of things: they understand "lives" to be made up of things, and they see the Stones' lives as made up of superior things.

The additional material that *Esquire* included with the story augments this focus on reification. For instance, under the title, the magazine included a description of the story: "a cup of sugar, an egg, a stick of butter, and thou."[40] Carver biographer Carol Sklenicka suggests that this hints at sexuality, in a way typical of the magazine,[41] but it also foregrounds the story's aesthetics of reification, in the sense that it illustrates the process identified by Goldman as "equivalence."[42] The grocery list-like blurb presents "thou," indicating a relationship between people, in the same fashion as a number of consumer items, first implying that the relationship takes on the character of a thing, and then suggesting equality between relationships – whether between people or people and objects.

Moreover, *Esquire* included with the story Jean Lagarrigue's illustration of a couple roughly split in half at the hips; their upper bodies head towards one apartment, while their legs head to another. As Sklenicka argues, the illustration foregrounds for *Esquire* readers one interpretation of the story: "a modern couple, divided and walking away from themselves."[43] As Richard Westerman explains, developing the argument made by Georg Lukács, as a result of reification, the proletariat suffer "an absolutely sundered double existence – as both object (the daily reality of his existence) and subject (the abstract vendor of labor power, ostensibly the 'cause' of the objectification of labour power)."[44] The Millers roughly fit the definition of the proletariat: they are labourers, even if their labour is white-collar (Bill a bookkeeper, Arlene a secretary), and their last name is associated with a trade. Whatever its intent, the illustration depicts the division of the subject, one of the effects of reification, a process which is central, I argue, to the story – in fact, this illustration could be seen as a commodification of the story itself.

Carver introduces the Millers as feeling that "they alone among their circle had been passed by somehow."[45] They can only feel "passed by" in comparison to others; in this particular case, they compare themselves to the Stones, who they feel "lived a fuller and brighter life." They feel that "The Stones were always going out for dinner, or entertaining at home, or traveling about the country somewhere."[46] In the Millers' eyes, the Stones live a lifestyle closer to the "good life" depicted in advertisements. Carver describes their apartment like a catalogue, a collection of things:

> He opened all the cupboards and examined the canned goods, the cereals, the packaged foods, the cocktail and wine glasses, the china, the pots and pans. He opened the refrigerator. He sniffed some celery, took two bites of cheddar cheese, and chewed on an apple as he walked into the bedroom. The bed seemed enormous, with a fluffy white bedspread draped to the floor. He pulled out a nightstand drawer, found a half-empty package of cigarets [*sic*] and stuffed them into his pocket ... He looked out the window, and then he moved slowly through each room considering everything that fell under his gaze, carefully, one object at a

time. He saw ashtrays, items of furniture, kitchen utensils, the clock. He saw everything.[47]

Bill wanders through the apartment like a reader flipping through advertisements, gazing at "one object at a time," in a casual, meandering sort of way. Of course, it is not the listing of objects in and of itself that makes this a work of consumer realism; rather, it is the association between these objects and the supposed promise of satisfaction that they seem to make.

Stuart Ewen and Elizabeth Ewen offer a context for understanding the Stones' appeal to Bill: "the appeal of advertising, for example, must be understood in a cultural context in which ... survival is to a large extent a matter of appearance and surface impressions."[48] In Carver's consumer realism, the Stones' apartment functions as an advertisement. Consequently, within the apartment, Bill acts out the role of the consumer. As Ewing Campbell notes,[49] Bill's behaviour in the Stones' apartment falls into two related categories: he inserts himself into their spaces and their belongings (e.g., the rooms of their apartment, their clothing), and he ingests their belongings (e.g., air, cigarettes, pills, alcohol, food). He even samples the Stones' Chivas Regal, a scotch prominently advertised in the very issue in which "Neighbors" was published. All of which is to say that Bill acts like an *Esquire* reader, perusing the display of goods, the selling of a lifestyle. Bill is not hoping to find the Stones' "good life" among their display of goods; rather, conflating life and lifestyle, Bill hopes to understand the relationship between the Stones' goods and their seemingly superior social standing. However, the Millers' apartment does not reflect the type of superior goods that *Esquire* associates with a superior lifestyle. Bill will not unlock the mystery by examining these ordinary goods – they are not exceptional items, nor is their quality or brand even worth noting. He sees with eyes trained by advertising, but the training misleads him. The goods, and their production, do not matter at all: what really matters is one's position within the cycle of advertising and consuming.

That Bill is attracted to this advertised lifestyle is obvious from his frequent, lengthy trips to the apartment, and by the fact that Carver describes the apartment in attractive terms when compared to the Millers' apartment: as well as seeming cooler, the air is described as "vaguely sweet."[50] Bill's trips to the apartment, and his behaviours there, literalize Goldman's description of the function of advertising, which invites us "to step into the 'space' of the ad to try on the social self we might become if we were the product image."[51] When Bill and later Arlene walk through the door into the Stones' apartment, they are, in a sense, walking through the pages of *Esquire* magazine; not into the sophisticated world it promises, but into the world of advertisements for items, for things that offer this promise.

The result of the apartment's seduction is increased sexual activity: in the six-page story (two full pages in the magazine), Bill and Arlene have sex three times, and, as Campbell notes, Bill masturbates ("He lay for a while with his eyes closed, and then he moved his hand under his belt") and it is implied that Arlene does as well ("He noticed white lint clinging to the back of her sweater, and the color was high in her cheeks").[52] Campbell equates Bill's "browsing" of the Stones' lives with "voyeurism," which leads to "excitement that has been absent from his life."[53] Indeed, reading advertising amounts to a type of voyeurism since, as Haug notes, "commodities cast amorous glances at potential buyers."[54] It is not surprising, then, that Bill and Arlene find themselves aroused by the world of commodities the Stones' apartment represents: they are, in fact, responding to advertising in the very way advertisers hope.

However, not all critics see the reinvigoration of the Millers' sex lives as entirely positive. Arthur Bethea astutely notes that Carver's description of these sexual moments subtly detracts from the notion that these are generative experiences. For example, a sexual encounter begins with Bill "awkwardly" grabbing at Arlene and responding to her question "What's gotten into you?" with "Nothing." Afterwards, the two order food and eat "without speaking."[55] As Bethea notes, both "nothing" and "awkwardly" have potentially negative connotations, and it is not emotional closeness but disconnection the follows the sexual act.[56] In a later example, Bill explains his long absence in the Stones' apartment by stating that he "had to go to the toilet." Following this statement, the narrator states that "they made love again."[57] Here, Bethea notes that the juxtaposition of references to defecating and copulating undercuts any potential emotional intimacy of the sexual encounter.[58] Bethea's observations aid in developing a reading of the story as an example of consumer realism: importantly, the Millers' sex is affectless because it takes place in this same realm of reification and commodity aesthetics. This is not the lovemaking of producers – neither the Stones nor the Millers have children – but the sex of consumers, which produces nothing. Rather than children, or joy, both couples have *things*.

The story moves towards its conclusion with Arlene and Bill planning to enter the apartment together. As the Millers cross the hall towards the apartment, Arlene hopes aloud, "Maybe they won't come back." She seems to give voice to Bill's desires as well; he responds, "It could happen ... Anything could happen."[59] Here, their desire to step into the Stones' lives shows how completely they have been seduced by the belief that the lifestyle advertised in their apartment could be the cure for their own marriage, their own lives.

However, this cure is not to be had. Arlene locks the keys in the Stones' apartment, effectively "banishing" the two from this consumer realm:

> He tried the knob. It was locked. Then she tried the knob. It would not turn. Her lips were parted, and her breathing was hard, expectant. He opened his arms and she moved into them.
> "Don't worry," he said into her ear. "For God's sake, don't worry."
> They stayed there. They held each other. They leaned into the door as if against a wind, and braced themselves.[60]

Bill and Arlene's response seems totally incommensurate with the actual event; they are only locked out of the Stones' apartment, denied only things to which they had no access only days ago. I would suggest that the deprivation perceived by the Millers is a reminder of inadequacy, identified by Schudson as a function of advertising. Having been immersed in the realm of commodities, they find themselves confronted with the inadequacy of their own lives. As Schudson argues, when art "begins to take everyday life as the subject of its idealization ... the art enchants and tantalizes the audience with the possibility that it is not false. If it can play on this ambiguity, art becomes less an imitation of life and turns life into a disappointing approximation of art."[61] The inadequacy that the Millers felt at the beginning of the story has now been amplified, and is now accompanied by the anxiety brought on by reification.

"Neighbors" could be read as a complement to *Esquire*'s ads, as the Miller's story depicts the consequences of failure (a form of negative reinforcement), while the ads depict the rewards of success (positive reinforcement). Ostensibly, then, the stories do not challenge consumerism at all, depicting, as it does, characters entranced by commodities. However, while the story reproduces commodity aesthetics, it also allows enough critical distance for a critique of such a reified perspective. For one, Carver's characters are so empty that they reject easy identification; lacking internal dialogue and seemingly acting without understanding their own motivation, the Millers come off as ciphers. In addition, while the Millers make much of the difference between their lifestyle and that of the Stones, the narrative suggests that they are almost identical. The Millers' feeling of relative lack is based on entirely superficial premises. Perhaps most significantly, the Stones are shown to be equally trapped in a realm of commodities. Bill remembers how, when Harriet showed off her sunburst clock to Arlene, she was "cradling the brass case in her arms and talking to it through the tissue paper as if it were an infant."[62] In this simile, the child has been replaced by a commodity; here, perhaps more than anywhere, Carver depicts the idea that relationships between people have taken on the characteristics of things.

3. "What Is It?" and "Collectors" – Reified Masculinities, Diminished Selfhood

While "Neighbors" ends with a snapshot of a couple's anxiety over their own perceived inadequacy in the face of reification, Carver's two subsequent 1970s *Esquire* stories, "What Is It?" and "Collectors," deal more fully with the effect of reification on masculinity itself. Both stories treat male protagonists existing deep within this widespread cultural anxiety. The stories depict an increasingly commodified perspective, and an accompanying and increasing alienation of their male characters.

Carver's "What is it?" focuses on a defining act of reification. The story describes Leo's wife, Toni, going out to sell their convertible, in order to avoid its seizure due to Leo's bankruptcy hearings. In the first sentence, a symbolic connection is established between Toni and the convertible: "Fact is the car needs to be sold in a hurry, and Leo sends Toni out to do it."[63] As Sklenicka explains, the colloquial phrase "do it" suggests that Leo is sending Toni to sell her body along with the car.[64] Indeed, the story strongly implies that Toni sleeps with the car salesmen, and the fact that she successfully sells the car indicates that she "sells" herself as well. Carver returns to this connection a few pages later, explaining that while Toni was preparing herself to sell the car, Leo "took the jack and spare from the trunk and emptied the glove compartment of pencils, matchbooks, Blue Chip stamps. Then he washed it and vacuumed inside. The red hood and fenders shine."[65] While Toni makes herself over, Leo makes the car over; both are beautiful, ready to be sold. Furthermore, at the end of the story, Leo traces Toni's stretch marks, which are "like roads."[66] This simile is almost immediately followed by Leo remembering "waking up the morning after they bought the car, seeing it, there in the drive, in the sun, gleaming."[67] This gleaming symbol of material success contrasts the state of Leo's marriage. Even in Leo's dreams, he can only conceive of the good life in commodity terms. The car is therefore both an ironic signifier of happiness and an example of the simple sexism of the objectification of women.

The accompanying illustration in *Esquire* highlights the sexual dimension of the story.[68] The illustration depicts the interior of a car, with a bed-shaped ornament hanging from the rear-view mirror. Here, though, the illustration highlights a more traditional association – cars and sexuality – than the more specific association being made by Leo between his car and his wife. This is in keeping with advertisements in *Esquire* that featured female models, rhetorically associating car ownership with sexual desirability; for example, advertisements for the Lincoln Mercury Capri and British Leyland Motor's Austin MG (the latter published in the same issue as this story) both place single women in the passenger seat for their interior photographs.

Before Leo meets the salesman to whom he has lost his wife and his car, he learns from Toni that "He said personally he'd rather be classified a robber or a rapist than a bankrupt."[69] For the salesman (and Toni implicitly agrees), robbers and rapists may be criminals, but *at least* they have money. Just as Leo seems incapable of disentangling Toni from her car, so too is Toni seemingly unable to find value in Leo beyond his bank account. As Nesset argues, when Toni screams "Bankrupt!" she rather bluntly indicates that "Leo's value as a person is reduced to his equivalency in monetary worth. He is, in the literal sense, of no account whatsoever."[70] Both are trapped in the realm of consumer realism, unable to find value outside of money.

Leo can think of his relationship with Toni only in relation to the things they own (or do not own). His memories of a better time in their lives are firmly focused on their possessions: "Food, that was one of the big items. They gorged on food. He figures thousands on luxury items alone … They buy what they want. If they can't pay, they charge.

They sign up."[71] Leo and Toni's "good old days" involve living the kind of lifestyle promoted in *Esquire*: they spend money on the type of luxury items advertised and "sign up" for book and record clubs of the type marketed in the magazine. Their lives as consummate consumers are highlighted by their fixation on food, which they "gorged" themselves on. Leo cannot help but compare this life of bounty to the type of life he now leads, bankrupt, no better than a rapist as far as the salesman is concerned.

When Leo finally meets the salesman, Nesset notes that Carver develops the contrast between the two through a description of their clothing.[72] Leo, dishevelled, is unable to fully dress himself: "Leo tries to pull the two pieces of his shirt together, tries to bunch it all into his trousers." The salesman, conversely, "wears a white linen suit."[73] This focus on clothing, and on clothing's importance as a signifier of masculinity, is highlighted by the story's original position in *Esquire* magazine, which, as previously noted, rhetorically associates fashion with social status and the admiration of women. The story seemingly reinforces *Esquire*'s view of masculinity. At the end of "What is it?" the reader is presented with a comparison between two men, and the masculinity of the salesman – more in line with *Esquire*'s consumer masculinity – is clearly depicted as superior: he has the nicer clothes, the convertible, and he has presumably cuckolded Leo.

The consequence of Leo's loss is devastating to him. He threatens Toni with violence and realizes that "he is willing to be dead."[74] Leo finds his selfhood diminished; for example, during the night, when Toni is still absent, he receives a phone call with only a dial tone at the other end. "I'm right here!" Leo screams, but there is no answer, no recognition of his voice or identity. When Toni returns, he is unable to speak, instead cocking his fist at her and squeezing her wrists.[75] Confronted with the salesman, Leo can only begin to say "I want to tell you" without ever completing the sentence.[76] He is unable to make himself understood, and is recognized only as a bankrupt and a cuckold. Though in the final paragraph he slips into bed with Toni, she does not even acknowledge his presence.[77] This loss of dignity is brought on, however, by his treatment of his wife as an object, and is exacerbated by his, and Toni's, inability to find value in anything but the commodity form. Even having faced such ruin, Leo is unable to correct his perception, and continues to understand his relationship to people in the same terms as his relationship to things, dreaming in the end of the red convertible gleaming in the sun.

According to Goldman, one consequence of reification is that "Social relations are no longer seen as the means to the production and consumption of goods. Instead, the acquisition of goods is presented as the means of forming social relationships. The goods acquire a life history, while humans lose theirs."[78] Certainly, for Leo and Toni, the acquisition of goods is a means of forming social relations: Leo's relationship with Toni started when he bought children's encyclopedias from her,[79] and seemingly ends when she sells the convertible to a salesman, their relationship (and Toni) traded openly, as a commodity. Furthermore, the humans in the story seem to be in the process of losing their history to the car. Leo's memories, which dot the narrative, give way to a final memory of the car instead, and prior mentions of the car paralleled Toni's and his relationship. Carver's narrative depicts the car gaining in prominence as Leo's and Toni's selfhood diminishes. The couple's relationship is essentially subtracted from their selfhood and repositioned into consumer items.

This process continues in "Collectors." The unnamed narrator of "Collectors" presents one more step on the path to alienation and anxiety in the realm of consumer realism. Readers may perhaps best understand the story in light of Godden's claim that in capitalist realism, "selfhood is persuaded to reside in the isolated and full gratification of needs through commodities."[80] The narrator's dearth of commodities reflects his lack of selfhood. The narrator's lack is emphasized by the magazine tagline: "End with nothing, not even your dust."[81]

The story of "Collectors" is, like most of Carver's fiction, quite straightforward: the unnamed narrator, whose first words are "I was out of work," is lying on a sofa waiting for word from "up north," presumably about a job.[82] It is unclear if it is his apartment, or if he is squatting. A man named Aubrey Bell comes to his house and informs him that a Mrs Slater has won a free vacuum demonstration. Despite the narrator's protestations that "Mrs. Slater doesn't live here,"[83] Bell enters and demonstrates the vacuum's cleaning power. Eventually Bell picks up a letter, possibly the eagerly awaited news from "up north," claims that it is for a Mr Slater, and leaves with it. There is very little action, and unlike "Neighbors" and "What is it?" there is seemingly no change in the characters or their relationship with one another.

However, what "Collectors" does describe is a character for whom the absence of things, of material possessions, corresponds directly to an absence of selfhood. As Lauren Berlant argues of the similarly unnamed narrator of Carver's story "Fat" (published, like the stories discussed here, in Carver's first collection, *Will You Please Be Quiet, Please?*), "Many processes collaborate to make structural conditions of existence seem like properties of ... the person";[84] for the narrator of "Collectors," the primary process at work is that of reification.[85] It is fitting, then, that this is the first Carver story in *Esquire* told from a first-person perspective. This perspective, which should highlight the narrator's subjectivity, instead highlights its lack. From this first-person perspective, the reader "sees through the eyes" of a totally reified consciousness. Tellingly, the prose is even sparser than in other Carver stories. Like the apartment, almost totally empty of consumer items, the narration is lacking in adornment – it even lacks quotation marks, lessening the distinctions between the narrator's perspective, his words, and the words of Bell, and reflecting his weakened subjectivity. When the narrator does speak, his comments are rife with negative constructions, e.g., "Mrs. Slater doesn't live here"; "No car ... I don't have a car"; "It's not my mattress"; "This carpet's not worth fooling with"; and so on. Perhaps most tellingly, he twice tells the salesmen that he is "not in the market."[86] Though he means that he cannot purchase the vacuum cleaner, the phrase situates him in relation to the market, which is "the central institution in this new monopoly of the code."[87] The narrator's dialogue therefore reflects both his distance from this institution and its centrality to his consciousness.

As mentioned, the narrator is also unnamed, and so his identity is indeterminate: Bell asks if he is Mr Slater, but the narrator never responds. He repeats that "Mrs. Slater doesn't live here,"[88] but this could either mean that he is not Mr Slater, or that he is, and Mrs Slater has moved away. As Bethea argues, this indeterminacy "underscores the story's central theme involving the absence or loss of identity";[89] the fact that his identify is left indeterminate is more telling than acceptance or denial, which at least would be affirmative, instead leaving him alienated from his own selfhood.

In contrast to the unnamed narrator, the salesman goes by a proper name, and central to his characterization is his penchant for name-dropping authors. He names W.H. Auden, and mentions the good life of others: "Rilke lived in one castle after another, all of his adult life. Benefactors ... He seldom rode in motorcars; he preferred trains. Then look at Voltaire at Cirey with Madame Châtelet."[90] Bell's commentary implicitly compares the narrator's life of scarcity with Rilke's and Voltaire's life of abundance; similarly, the famous names of these authors contrast with the narrator's namelessness. Held up as exemplars of success and leisure (and therefore masculinity, according to the logic of *Esquire*), the names of these authors highlight the narrator's comparatively constrained masculinity.

Since the narrator offers so little by way of exposition or description, the reader needs to analyse his characterization based on his things. While the Stones' full apartment in "Neighbors" signifies a "full" life, at least to the Millers, this narrator's empty house correspondingly signifies a life that is lacking. Carver returns again and again to the scarcity of commodities in the narrator's house: "There was a bed, *a* window," only a few concrete objects worth mentioning. When he wants to watch Bell at work, the narrator says "I went to the kitchen and got *the* chair."[91] When Bell opens the door to the closet, there is "only a box of Mouse-Be-Gone."[92] This lack of commodities parallels the narrator's lack of selfhood, reflecting a viewpoint that recognizes no other way of identifying individuality except through the commodity form. Bell ironically comments on this fact while discussing the virtues of his vacuum, stating "Every day, every night of our lives, we're leaving little bits of ourselves, flakes of this and that, behind. Where do they go, these bits and pieces of ourselves?"[93] Here, Bell's comment refers to common detritus, but can fruitfully be read as a statement about the narrator and the narrator's selfhood.

In light of the discussion of "What is it?," it is significant that the narrator admits that he does not have a car.[94] Bethea correctly notes that this lack of a car "emphasizes his stasis,"[95] but it is worth considering this detail in relation to the importance of the car in the previous story. For Leo, the car was the only way he understood his life: it symbolized not only his relationship with Toni, but his status in the world. Losing the car amounted to emasculation and a loss of identity. In "Collectors," the narrator has no car – he either never could afford one, or, considering his employment status, and the fact that he is avoiding creditors,[96] presumably he has sold his car or had it taken from him. Whatever the reason, the narrator's lack of a car further symbolizes his loss of identity and his emasculation.

The notion that the narrator is emasculated is perhaps subtle if one does not read the story from a consumer-realist perspective. No mention is made of his sex life, and this omission would not be in itself notable if not for the lack of consumer items, which signify not only selfhood but masculinity. Given the association between cars and women established in automobile advertisements, and adapted in

"What is it?," the narrator's lack of a car is especially telling. A scene wherein Bell cleans the narrator's bed draws attention to the narrator's emasculation. After entering the bedroom, Bell explains that "You have to turn it [the vacuum] up to full strength for a job like this one." He then "extended the hose to the head of the bed and began to move the scoop down the mattress."[97] Here, Bell's vacuum takes on a phallic quality: its "full strength" suggests a corresponding lack in the narrator. In "Collectors," the narrator's lack of agency is symptomatic of his symbolic emasculation. He does nothing to stop Bell's demonstration, even when he wants him to leave: "I kept watching him," the narrator states, "That's all I did."[98] He cannot even get past Bell's vacuum cleaner to pick up the recently arrived letter, or speak a word of protest when Bell leaves with it.

Bell's final act – leaving with the letter delivered during his demonstration – has menacing overtones. Nameless and jobless, the narrator loses to Bell perhaps the only item capable of restoring both identity and employment. Like the narrator of "Fat," this story's narrator cannot even understand what the story means.[99] The shut door, the image that ends the story, takes on additional meaning, functioning as the final punctuation in the narrator's story of diminishing selfhood. In "What is it?," after mentioning Leo's financial status, Toni tells her husband "You're nothing."[100] This may not have been strictly true of Leo, but it certainly is true of the unnamed narrator.

"Collectors" goes further than either "Neighbors" or "What is it?" in representing the detrimental effects of reification. "Collectors" narrates a realm of pure consumer realism, a world where it can be taken for granted that a lack of material goods *logically* symbolizes a lack of selfhood. The narrator and his house have no characteristics of their own; they can only be characterized negatively, by the absence of commodities. The feature immediately following "Collectors" in *Esquire* highlights this absence. Entitled "The Perfect Male Shopping Spree," the article opens with the following lines:

> The problem: How to get everything you need for a fall/winter wardrobe on one grand shopping sortie, buying the best there is anywhere and actually having a good time while you're doing it.
>   The solution: London, of course.[101]

The life of wealth and luxury required for such an extravagant "shopping spree" stands in stark contrast to the narrator's jobless status and empty apartment. The article is representative of the "good life" held up as eminently desirable for men. Masculinity, for Carver's characters and for the readers of *Esquire* magazine, becomes inseparable from their display of goods. Masculinity is both a commodity and an aspect of the display of certain commodities – commodities that the narrator of "Collectors" is lacking. When read in the context of its original publication, then, one cannot help but notice that those commodities absent from "Collectors" have seemingly migrated, moving outward to densely populate the pages of *Esquire* magazine. It is a blunt illustration of the world from which the narrator is absent, declaring himself "not in the market."

4. Conclusion

Carver's short fiction of the 1970s regularly depicts lower-middle-class, blue-collar, or even unemployed workers, men who have seen their relationship with labour and capitalism change under neoliberalism, and whose relationship with patriarchy has transformed due to the many challenges of feminism, civil rights, and gay activism. The lifestyle offered by *Esquire*, which ostensibly facilitates men's successful renegotiation of their masculinity, remains largely out of the reach of Carver's characters, for whom the right commodities are financially inaccessible. Instead, their relationship with these commodities becomes characterized by voyeurism. The promise that these ads promote will forever remain tantalizing, but also tantalizingly unfulfilled.

Carver's stories both arise from, and note the problems of, a neoliberal culture that substitutes life with lifestyle and presents both gender and selfhood as commodities. This neoliberal conception of masculinity finds a paradigmatic example in *Esquire*, which establishes a *de facto* standard for male success and agency. *Esquire*'s target readership may exist in a social class well above Carver's working-class men, but its articulation of consumer masculinity nevertheless trickles down to them, shaping their culture and their masculine selfhood. In this way, Carver's stories, like the magazine in which they were originally published, are both equally examples of neoliberalism.

However, just as Carver's stories reproduce a neoliberal perspective, so too do they provide a space from which a critique of neoliberalism might be launched. Though Carver's characters cannot escape the "realism" of consumer realism, they can enact small, escapist fantasies in an attempt to renegotiate their relationship to patriarchal authority.

Carver's consumer realism may reveal a constrained masculinity for some, but this constraint can challenge, as much as be challenged, by dominant masculine forms. For example, in "Neighbors," there is a brief passage that highlights the desire for an escape from masculinity. While Bill visits the Stones' apartment, he takes the opportunity to dress up in women's clothing (1971, 11). Carver describes his cross-dressing in the same matter-of-fact manner as his consumption of goods: "He stepped into the panties and fastened the brassiere, then looked through the closet for an outfit. He put on a black and white checkered skirt and tried to zip it up. He put on a burgundy blouse that buttoned up the front. He considered shoes, but understood they would not fit."[102] In the realm of consumer realism, gender *can be* another consumer choice – it is an aspect of the individual's display of goods. Trying on another gender *could be* similar (if not identical) to consuming any other aspect of a different lifestyle, provided one has access. Still, this particular choice of consumption demonstrates a type of gender fluidity available due to the reification of gender; in this way, the increasingly constrained masculinity of Carver's male characters in his *Esquire* stories also hints at the potential for an increased freedom from gender constraints, if only his characters could identify this potential and access it.

Of course, the world might be similarly reified for Mailer and the types of characters he describes, but those reified commodities remain accessible, consumable. Carver's consumer realism may reveal a constrained masculinity for some, but this constraint can challenge, as much as be challenged by, dominant masculine forms. As Judith Butler writes, "agency begins where sovereignty wanes."[103] This statement is true for the characters found in the work of Truman Capote. Like Carver, Capote is a writer intimately associated with *Esquire* magazine; however, Capote's fiction of the 1970s provides a stark contrast to Carver's, depicting not "Low-Rent Tragedies," but the consumerist orgies of the jet-set elite. For Capote, reification leads to generative possibilities, and new forms of masculinity.

Though the 1970s saw a decline in the power of the working classes, and thus posed a challenge to blue-collar masculinity, it was also the era of disco, David Bowie, and other queer subcultures influencing the mainstream. Alternative masculinities, those not beholden to a straight masculine ideal, were beginning to enjoy social influence and new possibilities – new articulations of masculinity – were increasingly realized, even if they too were to reside in the realm of consumer realism.

4

True Men and Queer Spaces in Truman Capote's *Answered Prayers*[1]

The entire cover of the December 1979 issue of *Esquire* is given over to advertising the appearance within of Truman Capote's "non-fiction short story" entitled "Dazzle." The design is eye-catching: purple, gaudy, and intended to resemble sequins, the cover may not reflect the subject matter of Capote's tale, but at least reflects *Esquire*'s own interest in promoting the story. "Dazzle" itself is quite shocking: a supposedly true tale, it involves a young Capote visiting the local witch in the hopes that her magic will help him switch genders, exclaiming, "I don't want to be a boy. I want to be a girl."[2] The revelation that one of America's most famous authors and personalities desired, at least at some point, to assume another gender, could have caused quite a stir, especially given the venue of his admission. However, *Esquire* was seemingly more interested in controversies from Capote's recent past. In the issue's instalment of "Backstage with *Esquire*," the regular feature on the magazine's contributors, Capote commented on the uproar caused in high society by the publication of "La Côte Basque, 1965," in the magazine's November 1975 issue: "The reaction was unbelievable ... I might just as well have killed the Lindbergh baby."[3] Certainly the author discusses the style of "Dazzle" and its factuality, but the real thrust of the brief interview is to return Capote's attention, once more, to the furor around his gossipy, unfinished work, *Answered Prayers*.

Until recently, scholarly discussions of Capote's work and theoretical studies of queerness in America have largely ignored *Answered Prayers*.[4] Perhaps the academic silence surrounding the work is because it remains incomplete, though rumours abound that a full draft does, indeed, exist. The November 2012 publication of the chapter

"Yachts and Things," previously believed to be lost or non-existent, will no doubt give hope to those who wish to someday read the completed *roman à clef.* To the extent that the book has been discussed at all, the focus has been on the controversy surrounding its publication and its status as an unfinished text. This oversight is regrettable, given that *Answered Prayers* is the final work of an influential and notorious American author. Moreover, as Scott St Pierre argues, the book contains an "authentically queer agenda" and "a genuine, if unrecognised, instance of queer resistance,"[5] making it Capote's most direct dealing with the place of sexuality – specifically, queer sexuality – in American society.

According to Capote, *Answered Prayers* was to be an American *Remembrance of Things Past.* It was also a book that Capote continually put off publishing: he signed the initial contract in 1966, to be delivered on 1 January 1968, and as each deadline passed, the book's contract was renegotiated, a process that was repeated at least four times. In 1975 and 1976, more than seven years after the initial deadline, Capote began publishing excerpts in *Esquire.*[6] From these fragments, readers can divine a basic plot: the story follows the narrator, P.B. Jones – an author, masseur, and eventual gigolo – as he climbs the ladder of high society as a "friend of the rich," partaking in much gossip and imbricating himself in the sexual lives of the famous and wealthy. During his travels with the jet set he encounters Kate McCloud, and strikes up an association which (presumably) leads to his downfall. Jones retells all of this from his room at the YMCA, where, sometime later, he becomes a full-fledged gigolo. Capote made no secret that he was Jones and that the high society gossip relayed by Jones was the genuine article. The publication of the second excerpt, "La Côte Basque, 1965," caused the aforementioned stir, and so *Answered Prayers* became, as the May 1976 cover of *Esquire* proclaimed, "The most talked-about book of the year," not due to its artistic merits, but to its salacious gossip.[7]

Perhaps because it is unfinished, the published text gives no explanation of Jones's initials. According to Capote's notes, P.B. stands for "Paul Bunyan."[8] Significantly, Raewyn Connell specifically identifies Bunyan when noting that exemplars of masculinity are often frontiersman.[9] Capote's allusion may seem odd, connecting as it does a twentieth-century hustler to a legendary lumberjack. However, Jones *is* a frontiersman of sorts, though the borders he crosses are located not at the edges of civilization but at the margins of the gender order. It is therefore worth considering how Jones, like an exemplar of masculinity, provides "solutions to gender problems."[10] The particular gender problems to which Jones potentially provides solutions are quite different than those faced by standard exemplars of masculinity, who have as their main purpose the stabilization and reinforcement of hegemonic masculinity. Rather, Jones demonstrates how queer masculinities can avoid or perhaps even counter marginalization, by traversing queer spaces, social spaces in which different gender regimes allow for different gender relations, and open up the utopian possibility of a space outside of masculine domination.[11]

Thomas Johansson and Andreas Ottemo, adapting Paul Ricoeur's notions of ideology and utopia to Connell's theory of masculinity, argue that an attention to utopianism is required if we want to move beyond analysing the gender order as it is and instead reshape and reconstitute hegemonic masculinity into something else, something better.[12] Moreover, to speak of utopianism in relation to queerness is to invoke the work of José Esteban Muñoz, whose *Cruising Utopia* is the most sustained analysis of queer utopianism available. In that work, Muñoz calls for "a refunctioned notion of utopia in the service of subaltern politics" by arguing that "Certain performances of queer citizenship contain ... a sign of an actually existing queer reality, a kernel of political possibility within a stultifying heterosexual present,"[13] a present characterized by the dominance of hegemonic masculinity. Both patriarchal and capitalist power structures characterize the culture in which queer utopian spaces are contested, and so queer spaces must negotiate both masculine and economic domination in sophisticated ways. Answering Muñoz's call, my reading of *Answered Prayers* draws attention to this very negotiation, detailing how the *roman à clef* critiques the existing capitalist gender order through its delineation of social-sexual spaces and queer utopianism.

To make this argument, I first look at the shifting definition of masculinity in the 1970s; specifically, I examine the increased visibility of homosexual subcultures in the mainstream and how *Esquire* responds to these shifting gender norms. The magazine's response to these changes results in a cultural text that simultaneously promotes and critiques heteronormativity. Having established this historical and cultural context, I develop an analysis of *Answered Prayers* in conversation with twenty-first-century Capote scholars, such as Jeff Solomon and Thomas Fahy, who have sought to unveil and analyse the political dimensions of Capote's persona and his writing, especially in relation to cultural norms of sexuality, conformity, and consumption. In particular, I build on the work of these scholars to detail the role of queer spaces in *Answered Prayers*, to demonstrate how Capote critiques the relationship between economic and masculine domination, while simultaneously offering "dazzling" – and not-so-dazzling – utopian alternatives.

1. Gay Visibility and *Esquire's* Queer '70s

As discussed in the introduction to this study, when *Esquire* was first published in 1933, it sought to interpellate a white, heterosexual, consuming male audience. One of its strategies for achieving this aim was the repudiation of homosexuality. Speaking of its fashion pages, the editors assured its readers that the magazine would never become "a primer for fops."[14] Speaking in less coded language, the magazine's editor, Arnold Gingrich, later wrote that he specifically sought out contributions from Ernest Hemingway to "deodorize the lavender whiff coming from the mere presence of fashion pages."[15] Whatever *Esquire's* version of masculinity was going to look like, the editors anticipated that it could be mistaken for homosexuality, hence the pre-emptive repudiation of queerness. Both of these early editorial statements suggest that homophobia played a central role in the formulation of *Esquire's* hegemonic masculinity project.[16]

By the 1970s, the place of homophobia in the magazine, and in its masculinity project, had begun to change. The 1970s were, in some ways, a time in which the hegemonic form of masculinity was less chauvinistic than in years previous, especially in some of what Connell calls "gender regimes." The urbane, middle-brow gender regime of the *Esquire* reader existed in a wider culture of increasingly fluid gender lines and androgyny. Indeed, in the 1970s, hegemonic forms of masculinity were adapting and reacting to a gay subculture. In this post-Stonewall era, "gay issues" were tackled in mainstream media, which found a new interest in "alternative" sexual lifestyles.[17] Popular culture began to reflect, and perhaps propagate, a less rigid form of masculinity, as can be seen in the rise of disco. Surveying the decade for *Esquire*, Tom Wolfe writes that "the male-homosexual netherworld created disco. The discotheque is the 1970s' quotidian and commercial rationalization of what used to be known as a homosexual rout."[18] Wolfe further identifies Studio 54, the trend-setting nightclub, as seven-hundred and fifty men "dancing with one another to seamless music and exploding lights in a homoerotic frenzy."[19] Homophobic condescension aside, Wolfe articulates a movement of gay culture from the margins to the centre of the mainstream.

It was not only disco, but also rock and roll that pushed the boundaries of normative masculinity. As Randy Jones and Mark Bego note, the glitter and glam rock of the 1970s predominantly featured figures of ambiguous sexuality and gender (e.g., Alice Cooper and David Bowie) who unsettled binary gender structures.[20] While male pop stars were increasingly androgynous, if not outwardly transgender, 1970s fashions – fashion being a central and long-standing aspect of *Esquire* – also reflected a new take on masculinity. As Anne-Lise François explains, men's clothes in the 1970s "undermine the image of manly independence from the vicissitudes of time, body, and context, which understated masculine garb has from the Enlightenment onward sought to project."[21] For François, in other words, men's fashion traditionally remained surprisingly and statically "understated," and this understatement is, in part, explained by the way masculinity has attempted to define itself as ahistorical and natural: men's clothing less obviously changes with the times because it is the times which change, not men. However, in the 1970s, masculine garb becomes increasingly flashy (think John Travolta in *Saturday Night Fever*), including large sideburns, bell-bottom pants, and so on. While not as obviously subversive of gender norms as the flamboyant image of glam rockers, popular masculine dress nonetheless can also be read as undermining the supposed "natural" relationship between the male sex and older forms of hegemonic masculinity.

Esquire was (and remains) a magazine invested in hegemonic masculinity. As Johansson and Ottemo argue, hegemonic masculinity is "constructed through distortions – not least by media images presenting acceptable and normative definitions of gender" and also through an integrative function "creating an impression that the existing order is not only the best order, but that it has to be defended and kept."[22] These ideological functions – of distortion and integration – are frequently on display in the magazine. In the 1970s, for example, the magazine published Gay Talese's two-part article on "The Erotic History of Hugh Hefner," lionizing the *Playboy* founder and his lifestyle. Perhaps even more representative of the magazine's continued investment in hegemonic masculinities was its "Joy of Sports" special issue, the second instalment of which ran in October 1975. Connell argues that sport is the exemplary "test of masculinity," and that in men's formative school years success at sport is central to men's performance of masculinity.[23] This issue's focus on sports tellingly reveals the patterns of hegemonic masculinity, especially in the feature "Actual Size!," a series of photos of athlete's body parts that are supposedly, as the title claims, true to scale. The feature's description in the table of contents invites readers to "Try your hand (neck, thigh, arm, biceps) against these pictures!," insisting that men test themselves against these masculine ideals. Even the successful businessman, for example, must compare his masculinity against others during his reading time. Those who feel an aversion towards doing so, or who have no interest in sport, may want to turn to Alexander Theroux's supposedly humorous article "The Sissy," a lengthy screed against school-aged boys who are unathletic and therefore (it posits) effeminate. Hegemonic masculinity, in this instance, is stringently enforced.

At the same time, queer content became more visible in the magazine. If Theroux needed an example of the "sissy," he needed look no further than the pages of *Esquire*. Capote was one of several figures frequently featured in *Esquire* who, following Marlon Ross, might be labelled a "sissy": "the personification of a gender identity distinct from but inextricably linked with that of the male homosexual. As impersonation, the sissy is always figured as excessive, exaggerated, inauthentically gendered as a male person out of his gender place."[24] Indeed, Ross's examples of the sissy figure are Capote and James Baldwin (discussed in chapter 2).[25] In his theorization of the sissy figure, Ross suggests that if we forestall the rush to equate effeminacy with homosexuality, then we can better theorize the workings of homophobia. Marcie Frank's discussion of Gore Vidal,[26] another "sissy" *Esquire* writer, more fully articulates Ross's suggestion:

> To the extent that the closet names a sexual secret, Vidal cannot be said to be either properly in or properly out of it. The position that he would occupy is beside the closet. His sexual openness ... offers an alternative view of sexual definition and sexual liberation, allowing us to see the closet as a powerful historical structure that sublimates sexuality into cultural capital of various forms (most notably camp, but also other forms of wit) that only retrospectively come to be recognized as gay.[27]

Frank's analysis of Vidal calls to mind Oscar Wilde, a figure to whom Vidal was frequently compared. As James Eli Adams has argued, Wilde's nineteenth-century dandyism suggested that "masculine identity might not be a stable ground ... but instead might be a mode of performance, a set of social scripts to be perpetually enacted and revised."[28] Because Ross's sissy (like Wilde's dandy) suggests homosexuality without explicitly being labelled as such, he creates space for a thinking-through of the relationship between masculinity and sexuality that would otherwise be immediately shut off by homophobia, which in turn allows hegemonic masculinity to be refigured, if only subtly. Vidal, like Baldwin and Capote, embodied a type of nonnormative masculinity that became, as the '60s gave way to the '70s, a more frequent aspect of *Esquire*, symptomatic of the previously mentioned changes in the wider gender order.

Capote's gender became the focus of readers' attention with the publication of his first novel, *Other Voices, Other Rooms*, but not because of the book's plot; rather, the book's dustjacket featured what became an infamous photograph of Capote reclining on a couch and gazing into the camera. Hilton Als describes the photo as "an assertion, a point, asserting this: I am a woman."[29] Solomon, in a persuasive study of Capote's early photographic portraits, makes what is perhaps a more sophisticated claim, and one more in line with Ross, when he suggests that the portrait "allowed him both to be recognized as gay and to be seen and discussed as nonspecifically queer – as effeminate, childish, and strange – deviations less threatening than the bald assertion of sexual difference, although associated with homosexuality through the nexus of nonnormative masculinity." Solomon sees Capote as deliberately constructing an image of ambivalent sexuality with which to "strategically harness the simultaneous currents of fascination and repulsion with nonnormative masculinity in postwar America."[30] Like Victorian dandies before him, Capote created a persona that suggested "ostentation, or theatricality, or a calculated social role" that "observers typically attack ... as a form of effeminacy."[31]

Discussions of Capote in *Esquire* were typical of the pattern identified by Solomon. For example, it only takes Barbara Long until her second sentence to mention Capote's "thin lisping voice" in her 1966 article on *In Cold Blood*.[32] Gerald Clarke's 1972 story on Capote brings up the same discourse by having Capote object to it: "The wispy, childlike voice – 'It is not a lisp,' he says firmly – and the peculiar, yes, delicate, mannerisms that seemed so shocking in 1948 are now amusing eccentricities, always good for sales."[33] Lisping, delicate, and eccentric, Capote's strangeness and effeminacy took precedence over overt discussions of his sexuality.

Whereas Capote's persona, and his photographic representation, may have been ambivalently received, *Esquire* occasionally published more overtly queer content. Such is the case with Oliver Evans's "A Pleasant Evening with Yukio Mishima," published in the May 1972 issue. True to its title, the article describes an evening Evans spent with American playwright Tennessee Williams and Japanese author Yukio Mishima, both of whom are implicitly identified as gay (among other things, Evans refers to both authors as having "an indifference to orthodox sexual morality").[34] In a straightforward manner, Evans describes how Williams and Mishima met at a party for swingers at Williams's "West Side pad" in New York, around 1956–7; additionally, Mishima compares himself to Gore Vidal, and discusses Capote ("I don't like his mannerisms, the image he creates for himself. The effeminacy is disgusting.")[35] Despite Mishima's stated distaste for Capote's persona, his penchant for having himself photographed in service of constructing his own queer persona invites comparison to Capote. Several photographs accompany the article: black and white, and taken by Kishin Shinoyama, the photos depict the physically sculpted Mishima posing either nude or semi-nude. In one picture,[36] Mishima reclines on a Honda motorcycle, wearing only leather boots and gloves, black underwear, goggles, and a helmet for riding. Another supposedly depicts death by drowning,[37] and involves a naked, supine Mishima lying alluringly on a rock out in the water, in a pose (because of its context) reminiscent of the pin-up girls (the Petty Girls, the Varga Girls) of the magazine's early years.

Homosexuality was even a subject of reportage. The most direct discussion of homosexuality is Tom Burke's "The New Homosexuality." Published in December 1969, Burke's essay proposes the existence of a "new," macho style of homosexual masculinity, one that had yet to achieve mainstream recognition. Burke describes "the new homosexual of the Seventies," as "an unfettered, guiltless male child of the new morality in a Zapata moustache and an outlaw hat, who couldn't care less for Establishment approval, would as soon sleep with boys as girls, and thinks that 'Over the Rainbow' is a place to fly on 200 micrograms of lysergic acid diethylamide."[38] Burke further claims that "from a polite distance, he is indistinguishable from the heterosexual hippie,"[39] in part because, like the heterosexual hippie, the new homosexual is antagonistic to the Establishment. In fact, Burke sees new homosexuals as more radically individual than their heterosexual counterparts, since hippies "maintain one important allegiance with The System: heterosexuality."[40]

Burke even understands the Stonewall Riots in the context of what he calls the new homosexuality:

> When the bars of the old homosexuality were raided, patrons tended to leave the scene as rapidly as possible. The Stonewall's ejected customers, however, young and belligerent, gather on the sidewalk, complaining loudly ... 'Pig cops!' a boy shouts, and the cry is taken up. An empty beer can strikes a patrol car, then another, then rains of cans, bottles, and coins. The amazed police quickly lock themselves inside the club, as the mob charges, battering the doors with an uprooted parking meter.[41]

Burke, based on interviews with a cohort of "new homosexuals," credits the change in homosexual identity, and the type of aggressive behaviour described in the Stonewall Riots, to the notion that homophobia no longer shapes homosexual male identity. The message is clear: the thoroughly masculine and anti-Establishment "new homosexual" is a figure more-or-less amenable to the type of consumer masculinity offered by *Esquire*.

Additional queer content was not as visible. Readers could find advertisements targeting gay men, but these were often tucked away in the back of each magazine, easily overlooked. For example, from 1971 to 1975, *Esquire* regularly ran advertisements for Ah Men, a men's clothing store out of West Hollywood that cultivated a gay clientele,[42] while throughout 1970–1 there appeared ads for Roy Dean's *A Time in Eden*,[43] described as "A photo essay on MAN ... one of the most beautiful books ever published."[44] The standard advertisement is made up of four photographs of a powerfully built male nude, presumably Dean's Adam. No mention is made of Eve.[45]

In enumerating these several examples of queer or nonnormative content in *Esquire* leading up to and including the 1970s, I do not mean to imply that *Esquire* had reconceptualized its primary audience as homosexual. Nor do I mean to suggest that all of the examples are the same: the advertisements for *A Time in Eden* are targeted at gay readers of *Esquire*; "The New Homosexuality" is written to heterosexuals; and the "sissy" public figures in the magazine occupy a more ambivalent relationship with *Esquire*'s readership. The point is that in the 1970s *Esquire*, as one place where masculine hegemony is established, demonstrated how homosexual masculinity was being articulated for (and by) a heterosexual audience. *Esquire* is one place where homosexual male visibility (and invisibility) was negotiated. Staging gay male visibility and opening up queer spaces within its pages, *Esquire* demonstrates how homophobia and "the closet" were addressed, managed, or skirted in the constant making and remaking of its consumerist masculinity project.

Moreover, the increasingly visible queer content in the magazine can be described as a type of quotidian queer utopianism, a glimpse of "utopian bonds, affiliations, designs, and gestures that exist within the present moment,"[46] gesturing towards a less stultifying, less heteronormative future. For example, the readers of the Ah Men advertisements could send away for the store's catalogue. David Johnson has explained how the catalogue helped shape gay consumer identity: he quotes one anonymous man's claim that the "Ah-MEN catalog was a link to my awakening sexuality" and another who describes the catalogues as "a catalyst for awakening the hormones deep inside."[47] More immediate to the *Esquire* reader is the blatant homoeroticism of the Mishima photographs, which, I would argue, threatens to force men to renegotiate their gaze, since queer representations contain "the capacity to disturb stable definitions."[48] As Lynne Segal further explains,

> Because the affirmation of homosexuality is the affirmation of sexual desire, it inevitably symbolizes opposition to repressive sexual norms. Because the affirmation of homosexuality is outside the institution of the monogamous heterosexual family, it inevitably symbolizes the possibility of real alternatives to that institution, the possibilities of new types of community and morality which challenge patriarchal family ideology.[49]

The homoerotic images of Mishima are potentially subversive. In a way, the image of Mishima is a queer space within the magazine, one which exposes queerness as a potentiality implicit in *all* of the magazine's images, but which typically was exploited only by queer readers (such as queer uses of "muscle magazines"). In other words, the "heterosexual" space of *Esquire* is such only because it does not announce the potential for a queer enjoyment of its aestheticizing of men, but the Mishima photographs foreground such a reading. For example, in this particular case, the relationship between the reader and the images of men changes from one of comparison and competition (as with the athlete's bodies in "Actual Size!") to one of pleasure and eroticism (as with the images of Mishima). Other relationships between the reader and the text threaten to be similarly troubled, resulting in a queer "hermeneutics of suspicion," which as Lee Edelman argues, involves the suspicion of "the potential permeability of every sexual signifier."[50] In these various stagings of heterosexual masculinity, the magazine challenges – if only for a brief period – the centrality of homophobia to hegemonic masculinity and opens up the potential space for alternatives.

2. Capote's Critique of Heteronormativity

It is in this cultural and material context, analysed above, that Capote published *Answered Prayers*. Its presence in *Esquire* draws attention to how the novel negotiates homophobia through its articulation of social spaces positioned at a remove – sometimes at the margins – of the mainstream social world. To accomplish this reading, I demonstrate how *Answered Prayers* furthers Capote's critique of masculine hegemony, as scholars have so far theorized that critique. As Solomon suggests, "The destruction of the social order extends throughout Capote's work, from the disabling of the patriarch in *Other Voices* to the desecration of the upper class in *Answered Prayers*."[51] Before turning to the text of *Answered Prayers*, then, I want to briefly review the twenty-first-century scholarship that has sought to foreground the political implications of Capote's writing, to demonstrate how Capote's final work extends his critique of hegemonic masculinity. In particular, I want to focus on Capote's use of queer spaces, to demonstrate how *Answered Prayers* pushes this concept into the realm of the utopian.

Judith Halberstam refers to queer spaces as "the place-making practices within postmodernism in which queer people engage and … the new understandings of space enabled by the production of queer counterpublics."[52] Halberstam develops the term "counterpublic" from Michael Warner, who argues that counterpublics "can work to elaborate new worlds of culture and social relations in which gender and sexuality can be lived … It can therefore make possible new forms of gendered or sexual citizenship – meaning active participation in collective world making through publics of sex and gender."[53] As Warner's quotation indicates, counterpublics are especially pertinent to queer gender identities; Halberstam adds the importance of gendered spaces to the creation of counterpublics. Much of the scholarship surrounding the politics of gender identity has, indeed, focused on locality and gendered spaces. This has been especially true of gay and lesbian scholarship, whether those spaces are physical, social, or symbolic. For example, both George Chauncey and Samuel Delany, though focusing on different time periods, have discussed the importance of physical spaces to the construction, maintenance, and pleasure of gay life in New York (where much of *Answered Prayers* takes place). In *Gay New York*, Chauncey discusses gay social centres such as rooming houses, cafeterias, bath houses and the YMCA, and gay neighbourhoods such as Greenwich Village and the Bowery, in the period from 1890 to 1940. In *Times Square Red, Times Square Blue*, Delany discusses, generally, the neighbourhood around Times Square, and specifically the gay institutions found there: "clubs, bars of several persuasions, baths, tea-room sex, gay porn movie houses (both types), brunches, entertainment, cruising areas, truck stop sex, circuit parties, and many more."[54] Delany argues that these institutions – both physical and social spaces – are central to his concept of sexuality. In addition to these physical spaces and social spaces, the symbolic space of "the closet" looms large in discussions of homosexuality's "place" in society, while queer men and women are often defined as either being "in" or "out" of the closet, and the spatial metaphor of "coming out" is central. Eve Kosofsky Sedgwick plainly submits that "The closet is the defining structure for gay oppression in this century."[55]

Chauncey and Delany are discussing, at least in part, the role of queer spaces for establishing, mobilizing, and supporting different gender regimes – and this makes queer spaces, I would argue, potentially utopian. Delany's gay institutions are not only places of pleasure, but different gender regimes found within the dominant gender order. Delany therefore describes how queer spaces can exist within a heterocentric society. The significance of this discussion of gendered (queer) spaces is twofold: first, it indicates how Capote's *Answered Prayers* could itself act as a queer space within the heteronormative field of *Esquire*; next, it explains how Capote can depict queer masculinity existing within the larger gender order but without the fear of marginalization and domination, since his queer characters, ensconced in high society, exist in a kind of queer space, though the queerness of that space is limited. The term "queer space" is pertinent because it describes how different social spaces can create different gender regimes, regimes that can exist within the dominant gender order and alongside other gender regimes, and how the creation of such spaces can be potentially disruptive and transformative of the concept of hegemonic masculinity. This is why I argue that, although such space, within the diegesis of the text, is certainly not political, extra-diegetically the space is potentially utopian, in the sense of utopia as "a critique of a present order, and of the overarching dictate of how things are and will always be in an unyielding status quo."[56] If, as I argue last chapter, Carver's characters are trapped because they see the world with "commodifying eyes," then the importance of queer spaces is that their existence can potentially allow for a new way of "seeing" or negotiating one's own relationship within the dominant gender order. Capote's place-making practices therefore mobilize different gender regimes, within which different, and perhaps even subversive or utopian, versions of masculinity can exist.

Capote's critique of heteronormativity and use of queer spaces are present even in his early fiction. A queer *bildungsroman*,[57] *Other Voices, Other Rooms* follows Joel Harrison Knox, an effeminate 13-year-old who moves from New Orleans, Louisiana to Skully's Landing, a plantation in Mississippi. There, he comes to know, and become one of, the Landing's strange inhabitants, including his transsexual cousin Randolph. Fahy reads in the novel an argument that male aggression supports patriarchy by "mak[ing] sexuality an issue of social control, a way of preserving white, middle-class hierarchies."[58] Brian Mitchell-Peters argues that the novel's main characters largely avoid this male aggression, which usually takes the form of homosexual panic, when they reside in Skully's Landing. The Landing is therefore a queer space, what he calls a "fantasy location" that moves the text from "dismal realities" to "the world of queer acknowledgement and arguable homosexual awakenings."[59] Mitchell-Peters's analysis suggests that Capote's work be read with an eye to how he creates spaces – sometimes social, sometimes physical – wherein different sexualities and genders can be articulated against a heteronormative, homophobic, hegemonic culture.

Capote's critique continues in his next two book-length works of fiction: *The Grass Harp* (1951) and *Breakfast at Tiffany's* (1958). The former revolves around a group that abandons society and takes up residence in a tree house, where they avoid social conformity; the latter is the story of Capote's most famous invention, Holly Golightly, a former rural bumpkin turned café socialite in Manhattan's Upper East Side. Fahy argues that *The Grass Harp* is about resisting the conformity and materialism of 1950s America;[60] moreover, "Capote uses the nostalgia of the novel to create a yearning in his readers for a space that can make inclusiveness a lasting possibility instead of something ephemeral."[61] Regarding *Breakfast at Tiffany's*, Tison Pugh has argued that, despite foregrounding Golightly's liberated heterosexuality, the novella contains queer themes and homosexual characters, including the narrator.[62] Both Fred's homosexuality and Golightly's progressive sexual attitudes contrast with the conservative sexual mores and strict gender roles of the 1950s. However, as Fahy points out, conformity ultimately wins out in the end, since Fred and Golightly can only "pursue their own desires so long as they look and behave according to certain social stands ... [revealing] a rigid class hierarchy in America that limits personal and social freedom to those who do not conform."[63] Both novels, then, present a desire for resistance, a utopian urge to exist outside of a society that conforms to the dictates of hegemonic masculinity, enforced, most often, through male aggression and homophobia.

Answered Prayers, Capote's final (though incomplete) long work of fiction, further develops these themes of social space and queer resistance. The novel tackles masculinity, sexuality, and social hierarchies from a distinctly queer subject position and, in keeping with the era (and the magazine) in which it was published, it does so with an openness that bespeaks a refusal of homophobia. Moreover, *Answered Prayers* furthers Capote's critique of heteronormativity by foregrounding the role played by capitalism in enforcing competition and conformity. In this way, Capote's work resonates with some strands of contemporaneous feminist thought and women's writing. As Maria Farland has argued, "The rhetorical conjunction of sex oppression and oppressive social systems served as the nodal point for 1970s sexual liberation theory and fiction." Farland's argument focuses on what she calls "the property/sex oppression nexus" in Women's Liberation fiction, but *Answered Prayers* also fixates on this "nodal point" when thinking through sexuality, masculinity, and homophobia. Following the historic pattern Farland identifies, Capote's novel concentrates less on "the notion that freedom would involve a choice between one system of property and another" and turns instead to "spaces of removal from those systems."[64] A social space outside of capitalism – or at least differently positioned in relation to dominant capitalist society – might be the only space in which true gender and sexual freedom could be practiced. In keeping with the analyses of Capote's work highlighted above – in particular, the creation of queer spaces in *Other Voices, Other Rooms* and *The Grass Harp* (i.e., Skully's Landing and the treehouse) and the criticism of conformity and materialism in *Breakfast at Tiffany's* – I argue that *Answered Prayers* critiques the interrelationship of masculine and economic domination through the creation of two social spaces differently related to both: the "space" of high society, and the fantasy locale of Father Flanagan's Nigger Queen Kosher Café. In so doing, the work gestures towards "a queer utopia beyond shame"[65] and beyond masculine domination, at the extreme end of the capitalist social structure.

Most of the action of *Answered Prayers* takes place in high society. Capote depicts the jet-set crowd with whom he had been acquainted for several years as corrupt and decadent. The critique of high society can be located throughout the text, but is best symbolized by the island of Spetsopoula, which appears in "Yachts and Things." In November 2012, *Vanity Fair* published a fragment of this incomplete chapter of Capote's unfinished novel. The newly discovered fragment provides a compressed picture of some of the concerns of the existent novel: like the rest of *Answered Prayers*, it focuses on the fabulously wealthy. Taking place on and off the shores of Spetsopoula, the real-life private island of oil magnate Stavros Niarchos, "Yachts and Things" depicts a world of decadence. The narrator, Jones, describes Spetsopoula in telling terms: "the island, naturally dry and unfertile, imports its own water by tanker; it has been turned into a place as flowered and green as a Rousseau forest ... It was a bit artificial, even sinister, but nevertheless a work of art, nature tamed and reconstructed by sensibilities of a unique sort."[66] The art and artificiality of the island are paradigmatic of the adornment and materialism of the jet-set crowd. Similarly, Capote's text is littered with designer items and the names of expensive restaurants and hotels. The reference to "Verdura cuff links, classic Paul Flato cigarette cases, the obligatory Cartier watch" in "Mojave"[67] is relatively restrained when compared to the absolute saturation of such markers of a decadent lifestyle in *Answered Prayers*, in which on one page alone a reader will find references to Pernod, Deux Magots, the Ritz, Boeuf-sur-le-Toit, Brasserie Lipp, and Gauloises bleu.[68] These symbols of excess clearly delineate the social space of the text.

Within this social space, the wealthy jet set are free to indulge in the type of nonnormative sexual behaviour that would otherwise see them marginalized. Not only is the narrator a gigolo, but also every character seems to be embroiled in nonnormative sex, and many, if not most, of the characters display nonnormative gender identities or features. A list of nonnormative sex acts in *Answered Prayers* would include (but not be limited to) masturbation, pedophilia, incest, rape, bestiality, and urolangia, not to mention the repeated focus on infidelity. Similarly, a list of nonnormative gender features, identities, and behaviours would include homosexuality, androgyny, transvestism, cross-dressing, and prostitution.[69] Capote is hardly a moralist – he does not target his critique of high society at their nonnormativity, but their hypocrisy, since they can afford to engage in nonnormative behaviour while actively marginalizing those outside of their class position.[70]

Of course, the social space of high society has stark and imposing borders, and it is here that the violence of patriarchy is most highly visible. While high society allows queerness of sexuality and gender to enter, it remains a closed, racist space. Only whiteness is permitted,[71] and a great degree of racism is bandied about so often and so casually that it performs a kind of policing function, in that the saturation of racist language implies a normalization of whiteness and a hostility to other races. A few examples of virulent racism include the racist description of Jones's dog (64), Harry McCloud's mother's outburst (76), and Harry Cohn's message to Sammy Davis, Jr (118). These most egregious examples are not often of events that occurred within the queer space of high society; rather, they are only spoken of, but their open rehearsal points to the homogenous racial makeup of the space. Reflecting the racial politics of mid-century America's socioeconomic structure, high society's whiteness keeps itself strictly segregated from the nation's racialized lower classes (mirroring the continued marginalization of African Americans and other people of colour in *Esquire* magazine). High society may be a type of queer social space, but access to this space is severely limited by economic and social status, and its existence depends on the inequality propagated by capitalism. Those in the highest economic strata of society are relatively free of patriarchal domination; if one is not at the mercy of the system of economic dominance, then one is less at the mercy of patriarchy. Thus, the queer potential of the space to disrupt these borders and boundaries is delimited, a point I return to below.

Readers can see the racial-economic divide even more clearly in those spaces where racial minorities are visible: the streets. The chapter "Kate McCloud" begins with a description of Eighth Avenue, featuring a social makeup diametrically opposed to that of high society: "Prostitutes, blacks, Puerto Ricans, a few whites, and indeed all strata of street-people society – the luxurious Latin pimps (one wearing a white mink hat and a diamond bracelet), the heroin-nodders nodding in doorways, the male hustlers, among the boldest of them gypsy boys and Puerto Ricans and runaway hillbilly rednecks no more than fourteen and fifteen years old" (83–4). Jones, speaking in his own voice and not recounting high-society gossip, uses racialized descriptions, but the racist hostility is lessened. This "street-people society" is exactly what high society polices its borders against, and not surprisingly, then, they are described as a kind of detritus.

Significantly, Jones does speak up for the society of the street. When a preacher berates the denizens of Eighth Avenue, Jones finds himself coming to their defence: "'I'm no better than they are. And you are no better than I am. We're all the same person.' And suddenly I realized the voice was mine, and I thought boyoboy, Jesus, kid, you're losing your marbles, your brains are running out of your ears" (85). Jones's justification for speaking up, declaring that "We're all the same person," might sound false, but when he goes on to reveal that these words slipped out, that this was an unconscious utterance, it discloses his identification with the poor and the marginalized, and speaks to the longing for a utopian space outside of the constraints of the dominant gender order, a longing embodied in Denham Fouts's fantasy of Father Flanagan's Nigger Queen Café (28). This longing highlights the insufficiency of high society as a queer space, its inability to fully extricate itself from the patriarchal gender order, and perhaps even its insufficiency as a space for the production of a queer counterpublic. The economic homogeneity of high society makes it especially problematic as a queer space, especially considering that one of Delany's major interests is how queer spaces allow for challenges to class policing, in so far as they become a site of class mingling, rather than separation. Access to high society is simply too limited, and this points to the fact that while it provides a space which unsettles heteronormativity, it remains firmly ensconced within the dominant gender order, and is therefore limited in its capacity to challenge patriarchal institutions. The desire to escape this gender order motivates the creation of queer spaces within the text. Since access to the queer space of high society is highly limited, queer characters need to come up with a strategy for penetrating its borders, and the principal way this is achieved is through the process of reification.

3. Fugitives from the Gender Order: Best-Kept Boys and Queer Utopias

Denham Fouts, P.B. Jones, Aces Nelson – none of them are born wealthy, none are "natural" members of the jet set, and yet each has reached the apex of high society. To do so, each has, to a certain degree, made himself into an object of sexual pleasure. This is true when Fouts is described as the "Best-Kept Boy in the World," and when Nelson is labelled as "a friend of the rich," both of which describe Jones's role in the jet set before becoming a gigolo. The roles of the three men, when members of the jet set, are best explained by Jay Hazelwood, who, speaking of Nelson, declares that "He's sweating for his supper ... Keeping the Geritols happy in their oceangoing salons. That's how he makes his walking-around money. The rest of it comes from pumping broads of various ages and hungers – rich quim with husbands that don't give a damn who does them as long as they don't have to" (62). Tellingly, she further uses racist language to describe this sort of labour, claiming that "Being a friend of the rich, making a living out of it, one day of that is harder than a month's worth of twenty niggers working on a chain gang" (62). Here, Hazelwood clearly indicates how one from the lower classes can enter high society while also starkly declaring the limits of such mobility. A man can enter high society if he turns himself into an object, and if his labours are not menial but pleasurable; however, this possibility is specifically limited to white men. (Importantly, what these figures lack in actual capital, they tend to make up in cultural capital: Jones is a short story writer, Fouts and Nelson are exceedingly well-travelled and capable, as the above description implies, of hobnobbing with the elite.)

Recently, queer scholars Kevin Floyd[72] and Muñoz have turned to the work of Herbert Marcuse to describe alternatives to the patriarchal gender order. Both Floyd's focus on reification and Muñoz's discussion of queer utopianism are informed by Marcuse's cultural analysis, and both topics are central to the type of queer critique of hegemonic masculinity at work in *Answered Prayers*. Marcuse's work largely focuses on reconceptualizing psychoanalysis, and thus much of his scholarship resides outside of the framework for this study; however, in "The Affirmative Character of Culture," Marcuse does comment on reification. Importantly, Marcuse finds the possibility of liberation in the concept of reification, but only at the stage of the absolute reification of the body, by which he means the marketing of the body as a source of pleasure, stating that such a form of reification is only held in contempt by members of the larger gender order (though he does not use this term – Marcuse talks more generally of the "performance principle," the rationalization of culture) because it represents an alternative to the procreative, familial forms of sexuality upon which capitalist culture is based.[73] Marcuse's argument is that bourgeois society regulates sexuality, attempting to shape society's sexuality into the best formulation for advanced capitalism. Bourgeois society and capitalism are therefore intimately connected to patriarchy, and founded on what Marcuse calls "genital supremacy." Resisting this bourgeois imperative, the proletariat can resist the dominant gender and economic orders.

As Floyd explains, Marcuse developed this line of thought further as his career progressed. Floyd points to a passage in Marcuse's most well-known work, *Eros and Civilization*, where Marcuse declares:

> No longer used as a full-time instrument of labor, the body would be resexualized ... The body in its entirety would become an object of cathexis, a thing to be enjoyed – an instrument of pleasure. This change in the value and scope of libidinal relations would lead to a disintegration of the institutions in which the private interpersonal relations have been organized, particularly the monogamic and patriarchal family.[74]

Marcuse's description of "The body in its entirety" as "an instrument of pleasure" describes, to a certain extent, the ways Jones, Fouts, and Nelson can be viewed as resistant figures, returning us to the discussion of the photographs of Yukio Mishima. Their "resexualized" bodies, like the pictures of Mishima, symbolize "the possibilities of new types of community and morality which challenge patriarchal family ideology."[75]

Marcuse's criticism is relevant to the extent that it draws a clear connection between economic domination and masculine domination, a connection borne out by Capote. Capote's high society is a social space outside of economic domination, and so is a space relatively free of masculine domination. Fouts, Nelson, and Jones can be seen "triumphing" over reification, or at least its most detrimental effects, precisely because they have suffered "the most extreme reification," by turning themselves into "beautiful things," objects of exchange.

The menagerie of marginalized individuals found in the description of Eighth Avenue (83–4) demonstrates how the mobility of these reified individuals is still limited to race and cultural (if not economic) class. Barred entrance to high society, members of "street-people society" remain taboo objects, and are thus marginalized to the violent streets and largely denied the "new happiness" foretold by Marcuse; instead, the streets and theatres are depicted as a kind of hell, where "leather-boys" urinate on transvestite prostitutes and septuagenarian "wrecked whores" offer oral sex for a dollar (84, 85). In comparison, Jones, Nelson, and Fouts live in a world of material excess and physical pleasure, though while access to this kind of happiness might be new for these individuals, it is hardly the "new happiness" Marcuse seems to prescribe.

Importantly, then, this rent-boy reification is not part of a revolutionary change. This is not reification as praxis, but as individual social mobility. Either Marcuse vastly underestimates the power vested in the overall economic and gender order or his theory of beautiful things is predicated on revolutionary, communal action; otherwise, the result is, as with Jones, individual and largely incapable of producing a counter-patriarchal discourse. *Answered Prayers* may therefore be read as a critique of the gender order, or perhaps more fittingly the libidinal economy. The equation that roughly parallels the economic system to patriarchy, and which orders gender accordingly, reveals a grossly unequal and illegitimate system. What is desired, Capote reveals, is a queer enclave, a utopian space, within the borders of which the specter of hegemonic masculinity and masculine domination cannot be found.

This desiring takes its most concrete form in the novel in Father Flanagan's Nigger Queen Kosher Café. As described by Denham Fouts, in the "Best-Kept Boy in the World" (20), the Café represents just this sort of queerness, as a grotesque Promised Land that haunts *Answered Prayers* and its characters:

Tell me, boy, have you ever heard of Father Flanagan's Nigger Queen Kosher Café? Sound familiar? You betcher balls. Even if you never heard of it and maybe think it's some after-hours Harlem dump, even so, you know it by *some* name, and of course you know what it is and where it is ... There it is: right where they throw you off at the end of the line. Just beyond the garbage dump. Watch your step: don't step on the severed head. Now knock. Knock knock. Father Flanagan's voice: 'Who sent ya?' Christ, for Christ's sake, ya dumb mick. Inside ... it's ... very ... relaxing. Because there's not a winner in the crowd. All derelicts, especially those potbellied babies with fat numbered accounts at Crédit Suisse. So you can really unpin your hair, Cinderella. And admit that what we have here is the drop-off. What a relief! Just to throw in the cards, order a Coke, and take a spin around the floor with an old friend like say that *peachy* twelve-year-old Hollywood kid who pulled a Boy Scout knife and robbed me of my very beautiful oval-shaped Cartier watch. The Nigger Queen Kosher Café! The cool green, restful as the grave, rock bottom! That's why I drug: mere dry meditation isn't enough to get me there, keep me there, keep me there, hidden and happy with Father Flanagan and his Outcast of Thousands, him and all the other yids, nigs, spiks, fags, dykes, dope fiends, and commies. Happy to be down there where you belong: Yassah, massuh! (28)

In the novel's fragments, its narrator, P.B. Jones, never reaches the Café, though he wishes he could "dash downstairs and find a bus, the Magic Mushroom Express, a chartered torpedo that would rocket me to the end of the line, zoom me all the way to that halcyon discotheque" (79). For Jones, the Café signifies the type of queerness identified by Muñoz, queerness as "a structuring and educated mode of desiring that allows us to see and feel beyond the quagmire of the present."[76] Alas, like the reader of *Answered Prayers*, Jones can never reach this promised end-point, but desires to do so.

Desire is central to queer spaces. Queer spaces are, according to Jean-Ulrick Désert, "desires that become solidified: a seduction of the reading of space where queerness, at a few brief points and for some fleeting moments, dominates the (heterocentric) norm, the dominant social narrative of the landscape."[77] Such queer spaces are, according to Samuel Delany, one of the few social spaces that foster interclass relationships,[78] in direct opposition to the largely intraclass space of high society (which is, as explained, delineated by class). Interclass relationships at the Café include Fouts's dance with the "Hollywood kid," and the proximity of the "potbellied babies with fat numbered accounts at Crédit Suisse" and the "commies." Delany's argument is that the "stabilizing discourse" which supports the infrastructure – what I would call hegemonic discourse – "sees interclass contact as the source of pretty much every thing dangerous, unsafe, or undesirable in the life of the country right now."[79] Patriarchy is largely defined by its hierarchization of the social: take, for instance, the way in which Connell's taxonomy of masculinity organizes the gender order into masculinites that are hegemonic, complicit, or subordinated, and how this internal differentiation is always predicated on the domination of women by men. The type of queer space symbolized by the Café brings this high level of order into a high level of disorder.

While the outcasts of the Café have reached "rock bottom," the Café-goers have nevertheless embraced their marginalization. On the one hand, with neoliberal masculinity, the only kind of gender capital that can be "cashed in" is *actual* capital. On the other hand, the outcasts of the Café are "all derelicts" who are "happy to be down there where [they] belong." Their dereliction, their marginality, is embraced: "yids, nigs, spiks, fags, dykes, dope fiends, and commies" have given up on their patriarchal dividend, and have found "relief" in finding an exit from the realm of hegemonic masculinity. The Café outcasts therefore take part in "the rejection of normal love that keeps a repressive social order in place."[80] In addition, the Café-goers differ from the street-people of Eighth Avenue to the extent that they might produce a queer counterpublic. Michael Warner argues that counterpublics, "can work to elaborate new worlds of culture and social relations in which gender and sexuality can be lived ... It can therefore make possible new forms of gendered or sexual citizenship – meaning active participation in collective world making through publics of sex and gender."[81] It is the queer space of the Café that allows for the possibility of a counterpublic.[82] Father Flanagan's Nigger Queen Kosher Café is therefore a type of queer utopian enclave, a space that exists within, but separate from, the dominant gender order. Contrary to the "prison house" of the heterosexist present, the Café represents a striving, "in the face of the here and now's totalizing rendering of reality, to think and feel a *then and there*."[83] While it is not overtly stated, it seems to be a place exclusive to marginalized *masculinities* in particular – Fouts's word choice, "You betcher balls," is directed to Jones, but might imply that the Café outcasts are traditionally male; additionally, the only identifiably female group identified with the Café, "dykes" – that is, lesbians – might well be understood as representatives of female masculinity. Those who have been marginalized within the gender order find an equally marginalized space – beyond the garbage dumps, past the severed heads – wherein they can be "hidden and happy." Even former enemies, such as Fouts and the Hollywood kid who once mugged him, can form new relationships, in this instance joining together in dance. The kid from Hollywood robbed Fouts of his Cartier watch, the type of lavish adornment typical of the high society Jones spends most of his time with. In the queer enclave of the

Café, there is no need for such outward signs of wealth, nor is there competition over goods. The implication is that without market competition, there is no sexual competition; a less aggressive, less toxic, and altogether different form of masculinity can exist.

4. Conclusion

Capote's *Answered Prayers* demonstrates the degree to which the economic and gender order are entwined, illustrating how a late capitalist gender order can structure sexuality, prohibiting some forms of sexuality and gender while allowing others free reign. One the one hand, qualified sexual (and gender) freedom is available to those whose wealth places them at a remove from the centre of economic domination. Capote's queer masculinity – usually subordinated and victimized within the dominant gender order – can avoid any feeling of emasculation or homophobia precisely because they can afford to. On the other hand, Father Flanagan's Nigger Queen Café represents a utopian desire to exist outside of the dominant gender order, a space where, following Muñoz, subaltern politics might be exercised and queer citizenship performed. I focus on the term "desire," however, because of the Café's always-deferred status; it is a place that Jones can never reach and, to the extent that no one has found a completed version of the manuscript, it remains a place that the reader can never access. The Café represents a kind of queerness we cannot touch, but that "we can feel … as the warm illumination of a horizon imbued with potentiality."[84] This desire for a queer space makes explicit the limits in the gender order that are implemented by the prohibitive nature of hegemonic masculinity.

While I have argued that *Answered Prayers* demonstrates the close relationship between the gender order and the economic order, and therefore the tight link between masculinity and wealth, it also demonstrates the 1970s as an era when queer masculinity gained increased cultural visibility and influence. This post-Stonewall era would mark a high point for queer masculinity's access to the patriarchal dividend. The 1980s would see the ascension of Ronald Reagan and a new cultural conservatism that would attempt to "remasculinize" America. The result would be a renewed marginalization of queer masculinity and a mobilization of conservative exemplars of masculinity. As we shall see in chapters 6 and 7, this attempt to re-establish a unified representative (white, heterosexual) masculinity paradoxically calls attention to the impossibility of doing so, and highlights instead hegemonic masculinity's fragmentation. However, *Answered Prayers* reminds us to search out those kernels of political possibility, out beyond the garbage dumps, right at the end of the line.

PART THREE

Cold Warriors of the 1980s

5

Sexual Fallout in Tim O'Brien's
The Nuclear Age

"Am I crazy?" Tim O'Brien's *The Nuclear Age* immediately confronts readers with this question, which constitutes the first three words of the novel. It does not take long for O'Brien to establish that, regarding the narrator, William Cowling, the answer is obviously "yes." However, the real question that dominates O'Brien's 1985 Cold War satire is not *if* William is crazy, but what has caused his madness. Though William's troubled mental state is ostensibly a result of living under the constant threat of nuclear annihilation, in actuality his problematic relationship to masculinity is the source of his insanity. *The Nuclear Age* returns us to the discourse of masculinity in "crisis" that provided the context for Norman Mailer's *An American Dream*, but also delineates and criticizes the way cultural institutions mobilize culturally conservative, ideologically charged symbols in an attempt to maintain patriarchy. William questions his sanity because he finds himself alienated from patriarchy: though a white, heterosexual male, he finds himself continually failing to demonstrate the characteristics of hegemonic masculinity and therefore fails to benefit from his privileged position within an unequal gendered hierarchy. He represents what Connell calls a "complicit" form of masculinity: that is, William either does not, or fails to, practice hegemonic masculinity, yet he nonetheless expects his "patriarchal dividend." Though he practices a number of masculinity projects – including as a fighter, a husband, and a father – he continually fails to achieve hegemony. The novel presents this problem as a contributing factor to his insanity, since William has been culturally indoctrinated to believe that masculine domination has been naturalized, and that as a man he has certain rights and privileges that guarantee his dominant place in society, especially over women.

Instead, he finds his authority constantly threatened, resulting in his own feelings of obsession and paranoia. In this way, William's relation to hegemonic masculinity is one of "cruel optimism," which, as Lauren Berlant explains, "exists when something you desire is actually an obstacle to your flourishing ... it might be a fantasy of the good life, or a political project."[1] William's failures are felt most keenly because he attempts to access patriarchal authority in the very ways that the Reagan era endorsed and authorized; in particular, he does so by attempting to practice "cowboy" masculinity and "civil defense."

O'Brien was a frequent contributor to *Esquire*, especially in the 1980s, when he published five short stories which would eventually make up the majority of his most well-known work, *The Things They Carried*.[2] During the same decade, *Esquire* also published two excerpts from *The Nuclear Age*. Using the methodology established in previous chapters, I use *Esquire* to provide a historical context for an analysis of Reagan-era (white, middle-class) masculinity, then, reading radially, I move the analysis outwards, to the cultural signifiers found in the magazine, and to the complete, published novel itself.

In the 1980s, *Esquire*'s hegemonic masculinity project reflected the cultural politics of Reaganism and what Scott Duguid calls that era's "addiction to masculinity."[3] This is not to say that *Esquire* always endorsed Reagan's "Cold Warrior" masculinity[4]; rather, the magazine strategically endorsed or rejected these conservative notions of gender in an attempt to negotiate a hegemonic masculinity project for its ideal readers. Significantly, though, *Esquire* demonstrates how cultural symbols were activated in the American gender order in the 1980s. Read in conversation with the magazine, *The Nuclear Age* dramatizes how two such conservative symbols were marshalled to reinforce patriarchy: the exemplary masculinity of the cowboy and the gendered space of the bomb shelter. These symbols recur throughout the novel, but dominate certain sections. The three sections of the novel (Fission, Fusion, Critical Mass) broadly delineate different eras of William's life. Each section is divided into several chapters, many of which are entitled "Quantum Jumps." These chapters depict William in the present of the novel, when, in 1995, he begins digging a hole in his backyard, presumably to construct a bomb shelter, a project that will accelerate the deterioration of his nuclear family. The other, variously titled chapters form an autobiography of William's life, from childhood to parenthood. While the bomb shelter is present throughout the novel, the dominant image of the autobiographical chapters is the cowboy, while "Quantum Jumps" chapters foreground the shelter. More importantly, the novel not only depicts the use of these symbols, but also criticizes them, demonstrating how the larger cultural discourses of the Cold War participate in an endless sheltering of heteronormative gender roles, roles perceived as always on the edge of destruction.

The Nuclear Age does not depict the failure of patriarchy; rather, what the novel depicts is a historic moment during which the strategy used to renegotiate hegemonic masculinity is anachronistic and insufficient for the new social and economic reality, and specifically for a white-collar gender regime. This failure to renegotiate gender relations in the 1980s does not result in an immediate threat to those in a position of actual hegemonic power: their position is far too entrenched. It does, however, result in a failure whereby non-hegemonic men – whether they represent subordinate, marginalized, or complicit masculinities – find the basis of their relationship to patriarchal power disrupted at a discursive, cultural level. This disruption complicates the access to what Connell calls a patriarchal dividend. It is therefore not patriarchy itself – that is, the institutions which materialize patriarchy – that is immediately weakened, but the cultural discourse that naturalizes patriarchy. However, if the cultural discourse weakens, then the social structure loses some of its ability to reproduce itself, and so weakens in that regard. The result, in the case of O'Brien's novel, is a complicit masculinity that is unable to practice a single, unified configuration of gender, and instead is completely fragmented. In the case of O'Brien's narrator, William, the result of this fragmented masculinity is paranoia, delusions, and obsession, which leads to a total undermining of his patriarchal authority. Since O'Brien sets up William as a representative man of his age, and since, in Connell's formulation, "complicit" masculinities make up the largest number of masculinities, the novel depicts William's fragmented masculinity as symptomatic of the era.

While the cracks that appear in the façade of hegemonic masculinity do not completely undermine its structure, they do represent opportunities – or the beginnings of opportunities – for gender subversion and the materialization of a counter-patriarchal discourse. While these possibilities are not fully explored in the novel – and cannot be, since it is told by a masculine voice speaking from within the failing discourse of hegemonic masculinity – they are presented in a nascent form in the female characters in the novel, most promisingly in the figure of William's daughter, Melinda. The last part of this chapter therefore focuses on the female characters in *The Nuclear Age*, characters who subvert Connell's notion of "emphasized femininity."[5] In doing so, they provide alternatives to the ideology of hegemonic masculinity responsible for William's madness.

1. Cold War Discourse and Gender Trouble in *The Nuclear Age*

To analyse *The Nuclear Age*, I first need to contextualize the novel in the cultural (especially gendered) politics of Reaganism. This process requires a double focus, since the era mobilized a gendered, Cold War discourse, focalized in the 1950s and early 1960s, to undertake what Susan Jeffords has called the "remasculinization" of America.[6] This hegemonic masculinity project was a response to America's experience in Vietnam, and also a reaction to the relatively queer-friendly decade of the 1970s (discussed in the previous chapter). During this time, Reagan-era America returned to ideas of "Cold Warriors" and "civil defense" to reinforce strict gender roles and heterosexual patriarchy.

Esquire itself drew attention to the "macho" masculine posturing of the era's Cold Warriors. In an article entitled "Getting Ready for War" – published in April 1979, setting the stage for the Reagan 1980s – Richard Reeves openly contemplates the possibility that the Cold War is about to erupt into all-out war. Reeves sees the national press as partly responsible for laying the groundwork for war, claiming "Give yourself a couple of weeks of reading and you're ready – anxious, for a John Wayne movie."[7] The most edifying solution to Cold War anxiety is, Reeves suggests, a bit of hard-line masculinity typified by Wayne. This explains the "astonishing sales" of a new line of World War II-themed titles published by Time-Life and Bantam[8] – there is a thirst for manly action. Reeves is, in fact, incredulous about a new generation of men who view Wayne-style masculinity as laudable: "younger men don't seem quite as hung up about excessive masculinity as do their elders who survived feminism. A lot of kids don't seem to think that movies like *Grease* or songs like 'Macho Man' are put-ons or put-downs – to say nothing of the violent enthusiasm for things like *The Warriors*."[9] The late-70s' nostalgia for a supposedly lost hypermasculinity has potentially dire political significance:

> When men were men, they fought for what they wanted. When America
> was America, it wasn't pushed around in Afghanistan. There seems to be

real frustration in the country, dangerous frustration. How will we react if we really face the prospect of a lowered standard of living because of a bunch of goddamned commies and Arabs? Are we going to take that or are we going to act like men? Fight! That's where the new macho talk may be leading us.[10]

At the dawning of a new decade, Reeves sees how hegemonic masculinity is beginning to be renegotiated – over and against the supposed "softening" of the queer 1970s, the 1980s would be an era of stolid heterosexuality, muscular action, and potent agency. In many ways, Reeves's article calls to mind Schlesinger's 1957 "The Crisis of American Masculinity." Schlesinger argued that men should self-actualize through tasteful consumption and that "Masculine supremacy ... was the neurosis of an immature society."[11] Reeves sees American men falling back into this neurosis.

The Cold War discourse invoked by Reaganism might be thoroughly masculinist and heteronormative, but it is, as Reeves suggests, neurotic, paranoid, and fraught with contradiction. Throughout the novel, William conflates gendered threats with nuclear threats in a manner paradigmatic of the discourse surrounding civil defence. Elaine Tyler May's *Homeward Bound* remains the most comprehensive discussion of the ways Cold War culture attempted to retrench strict gender roles through an overvaluation of the nuclear family, as well as explicit antagonism towards alternative sexualities and sex outside of the family. For example, May discusses the fact that homosexuals were targeted during the "Red Scare," their attackers using the faulty logic that so-called "sexual degeneracy" was equivalent to moral weakness, and thus the "sexual degenerate" was vulnerable to communist influences.[12] Alternative forms of sexuality were not only outside of the mainstream, but seen as potential dangers, if for no other reason than they could be blackmailed by the Soviets.[13] Their potential threat to heterosexual masculinity was re-encoded as a threat to national security.

Cold War culture also depicted female sexuality as threatening if not contained in monogamous, heterosexual, domestic relationships. As May points out, during the Cold War, sexually available single women were given the explosive label "bombshell" (106), reminding us that the hydrogen bomb dropped on the Bikini Islands had a picture of Rita Hayworth attached to it. Furthermore, the creator of the "bikini" swimsuit, which would become a standard uniform for "bombshells," named his design after the infamous islands to suggest the swimwear's "explosive potential."[14] Jacqueline Foertsch further elaborates on this issue, explaining that the so-called "bombshell" represents both the explosive power of the bomb and the "possibly fatal threat to men's cultural centrality which she simultaneously 'radiated.'"[15] What May and Foertsch here demonstrate is that Cold War discourse conflated female sexuality with nuclear warfare. Female sexuality is therefore both an object of desire and of fear: if it can be harnessed (especially in the domestic sphere), then it can be a powerful tool for the defence of hegemonic masculinity (the Bikini Island tests were, after all, an act of offence figured as a defence of national security), but if female sexuality cannot be controlled, then it threatens to annihilate the American way of life.

The potential explosiveness of female sexuality, combined with the "Red Scare" distrust of queer sexuality, demonstrates how Cold War culture figured alternative forms of sexuality – alternative, specifically, to monogamous, married, heterosexual relationships – as threats to patriarchy. Patriarchal authority, embodied in the U.S. government, sought to use fears of nuclear war to label any potential counter-hegemonic gender practices as dangers to the nation, thus shoring up patriarchy and ensuring its continued connection with military supremacy and national defence. Cold War discourse, then, saw the gendered landscape of America as primed to explode – volatile single women and insidious queers besieged good, clean heterosexual families, the backbone of patriarchy and the American way of life.[16] Or so the supporters of civil defence would have us believe.

In *The Nuclear Age*, William lives out this drama of civil defence, and its associated gender panic. Though William obsessively identifies the source of his fears as nuclear annihilation, the threat he is unconsciously responding to is one to his masculinity in particular, and to patriarchy in general. In this way, William's life exemplifies the gendered Cold War discourse, which, in mobilizing a campaign of civil defence against nuclear threats, sought to retrench the nuclear family and reinforce the dominant position of white, heterosexual, complicit men in society – a gendered discourse that O'Brien ultimately parodies.

O'Brien spends a good deal of time establishing a connection between William and the nuclear age itself, making him a model of complicit masculinity. William is a baby boomer, born in 1946, making him roughly the same age as the bomb. His last name, "Cowling,"

may sound like a play on "coward" or "cowering," but as Mark Heberle notes, "cowling" was originally a term for the hood covering
an airplane's engine and was extended in the nuclear age to refer to
the outer canopy of a rocket engine.[17] Not only is William connected
to the bomb – the symbol of the age – but he also takes great pains
to explain his own typicality, stating that he "carved out a comfortable slot for [himself] at the dead center of the Bell-Shaped Curve."
His average-ness is reinforced by his dress ("blue jeans and sneak-
ers"), his batting average (".270 – not great, but respectable") and his
grades ("mostly B's").[18] Toby Herzog argues that even the chapters
themselves further link William's life to the age itself: the titles (e.g.,
"Chain Reactions," "First Strikes," and "Escalations") refer both to
mankind's progress towards a supposedly unavoidable nuclear apocalypse and the periods of William's lifetime.[19] William's averageness,
when considered alongside the novel's era-defining title, adds an alle-
gorical weight to his identity and actions. To put the allegory bluntly,
the threats to which William responds are threats the whole age feels.

William begins the story of his life by recounting a formative event
from his childhood, one that illustrates the subconscious connection he establishes between nuclear threats and sexual ones. Fearing
nuclear annihilation, little William constructs a bomb shelter in his
basement out of a Ping Pong table.[20] Confusing graphite for lead,
William lines the top of his shelter with pencils in an attempt to stave
off nuclear radiation. William overhears his father mocking his shelter, which is embarrassing enough, but his anger really rises when his
mother joins in (21). Following this episode, William skips school to
read up on civil defence at the library, where a sexual drama enfolds.
When a librarian, described as "all hips and breasts and brains" (23),
approaches William, his reaction is specifically targeted: "As she bent
down, one of her breasts accidentally pushed in against my neck"
(22). William's sexual attraction is quickly confused with his desire for
safety. William believes that, unlike his mother, the librarian takes civil
defence seriously. His time with the librarian leads to embarrassment,
though, when he breaks down crying, and she calls his parents to pick
him up. When William's parents take him away, he states, "I wanted
to crawl into her lap and curl up for a long sleep, just the two of us,
cuddling, that gentle hand on my knee. All I did, though, was sigh and
take a last fond look at her chest, then I headed for the door" (24).
William displaces his sexual desire for the librarian with a desire for
shelter – in this case, the shelter offered by a mother to her child, her

breasts a symbol of maternal nurture. Commenting on this passage, Daniel Cordle rightly notes that William views women as both erotic and maternal.[21] More specifically, the passage indicates an Oedipal confusion, in which he longs for a nurturing family/mother, but he also yearns for the power the father represents (hence his anger over hearing his parents laugh at his shelter). William's confused sexual attraction and his embarrassment in front of the librarian leads him back into his homemade bomb shelter, which his father eventually convinces him to deconstruct so that they can play a few games of Ping Pong. As Susan Farrell notes, this part of the story ends by clearly associating William's mental state with global nuclear politics (21),[22] with William claiming that "for the decade my dreams were clean and flashless. The world was stable. The balance of power held" (32). William's mental state and world geopolitics are here shown to be intertwined, his (sexual) confusion a confusion of the era.

However, William's obsession with the bomb shelter is not solely the product of duck-and-cover lessons at school: Arthur Saltzman correctly notes that William's sexual problems predate his nuclear fears.[23] The cause of his anxiety may be a much earlier injury to his penis, which he sustained through "an embarrassing bicycle accident" which, in his own words, left him with "a mangled pecker. A huge gash, and it hurt like crazy" (18–19). The damage to William's penis is permanent, since Dr Crenshaw decides to stitch the injury without anesthetic, leaving stitches "like railroad ties." William asserts, "I've still got the scar on my pecker to prove it. Great big tread marks, as if I'd been sewn up by a blind man" (19). William's phallus, the symbolic centre of masculine authority, is irreparably marked at a young age, metaphorically denoting the problematic relationship he will have with masculinity throughout his adult life.

Perhaps William's originary trauma is the wounding of his "manhood"; perhaps it is his father's annual performance as Custer at the Battle of Little Bighorn, with its requisite death and symbolic scalping (more on this below). In any event, William's nuclear anxiety is forever linked with sexual anxiety, in much the same way that his culture confuses the two.[24] William reacts to threats against his masculinity as though they were nuclear threats against his safety, and he responds accordingly. First, he turns a Ping Pong table into a bomb shelter, since his parents do not provide the kind of comfort and safety he imagines the librarian offering, and also after his doctor symbolically castrates him by inadequately treating his "pecker." Later, William digs a massive hole in his backyard, ostensibly for shelter, after his wife's in-fidelity threatens his masculinity. What William's behaviour displays, at the larger cultural level, is the degree to which the practice of civil defence is understood as panicked, compulsive, and inherently patri-archal and heteronormative. In other words, when William's mascu-line status is in question, he can call on this larger cultural discourse to reinforce, or at least protect what remains of, his patriarchal position.

Through the figure of William Cowling, *The Nuclear Age* demon-strates the effects of these conflated threats on complicit forms of masculinity, specifically one who is not, for most of his life, connected with actual hegemonic power, but who, as a straight, white male, none-theless expects that the benefits of patriarchy should be available to him. When William feels his masculine authority challenged, he falls back on these Cold War discourses to defend his position, but finds them inadequate to the task. William's story, then, demonstrates not only how hegemonic masculinity was renegotiated during the Reagan era, but also the failings of that renegotiation, and the effect that fail-ing had on masculinity.

2. Cold Warriors and Cowboys: "Somewhere the Duke Is Smiling"

If the bombshell was the figure of both the power and threat of Ameri-can women's sexuality, then both the Cold War and the 1980s cul-tural return to the cowboy signal the attempt to posit a masculinity that can corral (if you will) the power of that sexual energy. Kathleen Starck calls this dominant formulation of gender practice during the Cold War "realist masculinity" or (following Suzanne Clark) the "Cold Warrior." Quoting Clark, Starck further argues that "Cold Warrior" masculinity relied on "the gendered mythology of an American West as the site of the hero, the warrior."[25] This follows Clark's claim that the Cold War mobilized discourses of the old West in order "to claim that there was and always had been only one real American identity."[26] During the early Cold War, then, figures such as John Wayne, most often associated with the role of the cowboy, became important exem-plars of "Cold Warrior" masculinity.

In American culture in general, the cowboy is an especially poi-gnant figure, a symbol of masculine hegemony. He was also an im-portant exemplar of masculinity during an earlier period of *Esquire*'s masculinity project. For example, beginning in 1949 and continuing into the next decade, the magazine prominently featured Western stories: the table of contents began listing Westerns (and mysteries) separate from the rest of the fiction, under their own headings. More significantly, during the same period the magazine published a regular feature entitled "There Was a Man." Each instalment featured a different figure from history, and the men chosen for this honour were regularly frontiersman or cowboys, such as Wild Bill Hickok,[27] Daniel Boone,[28] Davy Crockett,[29] and George Armstrong Custer.[30] Each article retold the manly exploits (usually bravery, vigour, and violence) that made its subject a man to be cherished and emulated. Significantly, each article also located this heroic masculinity in the distant past, implicitly arguing that the modern world has no place for such men, and making a supposedly "true" masculinity the object of nostalgia.[31] Writing about the cowboy stereotype, Kimmel summarizes his key traits as bravery, emotionlessness, and impeccable ethics, but more importantly he notes that the cowboy is characterized by his mission "to reassert natural law against those forces that would destroy it," including, in the twentieth century, communism.[32] This cowboy figure plays a prominent role in American popular culture, especially in Hollywood and in the White House: one need not have too long a memory to remember the cowboy persona of George W. Bush, but both Ronald Reagan (discussed below) and John F. Kennedy (discussed next chapter) used cowboy and western imagery during their presidencies.

It is no wonder, then, that the cowboy is a recurring exemplar of masculinity held up to ridicule in *The Nuclear Age*.[33] The novel's association with *Esquire*, however, emphasizes the cowboy as an outdated and anachronistic cultural figure. *Esquire* magazine's ideal readership comprises white-collar professionals, and so Cary Grant, for example, portrays a type of hegemonic masculinity that they might wish to emulate. The magazine therefore has a complicated relationship with more conservative, violent forms of masculinity, such as John Wayne. On the one hand, the magazine was quick to rely on traditional, conservative notions of masculinity; on the other, it might just as easily mock such a masculinity project. Bethan Benwell, analysing more recent British "lad" magazines, finds a similar ambivalence between what he calls "a traditional masculinity within which attributes such as physicality, violence, autonomy and silence are celebrated" and "a more ironic, humorous, anti-heroic and self-depreciating masculinity."[34] Benwell's conclusion is that the ideal reader "subtly oscillates" between these two roles. In much the same way, *Esquire* can sometimes

embrace cowboy, "Cold Warrior" masculinity, or reject it, depending
on the context and on what, at the time, would most benefit the magazine's hegemonic masculinity project.

Consider the April 1980 issue: depicted on the cover is John Wayne,
standing among the clouds and complete with cowboy hat and angel
wings. The caption reads, "Somewhere the Duke is Smiling – A Guide
to the New Hard-Line Culture." The accompanying article by Peter
W. Kaplan, described in the table of contents as "A tough guy guide
to the new Hard Line," offers a series of comparisons between the old
"soft-line" and the new "hard-line" culture. This "hard/soft" dualism
was a direct throwback to McCarthy-era political rhetoric: as K.A. Cuordileone has shown, Cold War culture "put a new premium on hard
masculine toughness and rendered anything less than that soft, timid,
feminine, and as such a real or potential threat to the security of the
nation."[35] According to Kaplan, the new "hard-line" was much like the
old "hardline" – hence the Duke's posthumous smile. The article provides a wide range of examples: for instance, soft-line sex is identified
as "foreplay," while hard-line sex is identified as "making babies";[36]
soft-line villains are multinationals, while hard-line villains are "Soviets, traitors, and flu carriers";[37] and the soft-line hero is identified as
Alan Alda, specifically in his TV role as wise-cracking surgeon Hawk-
eye Pierce, while the hard-line is associated with Larry Hagman in his
TV role as J.R. Ewing, cowboy-hat-wearing oil baron.[38] Each of these
examples of hard-line masculinity is culturally conservative: sex is for
procreation, not pleasure; villainy is not systemic, but individual; and
heroes are, well, cowboys, not surgeons. If Wayne's presumed blessing
was not enough to underline which type of culture was dominant in
the 1980s, then the obviously phallic terms used to differentiate the
two – hard and soft – make the supposedly superior category clear.

Esquire uses Wayne on the cover because he stands as the iconic
example of the cowboy, and thus, with a single image, calls into
being an entire American mythology.[39] Wayne's masculine persona
was so strong, and so ubiquitous, that a number of stress disorders
suffered by Vietnam veterans came to be identified as "John Wayne
Syndrome."[40] These syndromes involved "the soldier's internaliza-
tion of an ideal of superhuman military bravery, skill, and invul-
nerability to guilt and grief, which is identified at some point with
'John Wayne,'" an ideal up to which the soldier could never possibly
live.[41] "John Wayne Syndrome" perfectly demonstrates how an exemplar of masculinity functions in the real world: he provides men

with an ideal version of masculinity for them to emulate, one based, in this instance, on the "cowboy" characteristics of bravery, emotionlessness, and ethical action. In addition, readers of *Esquire* can consume Wayne's image without going to the extreme of having to practice it, as the aforementioned Vietnam veterans did. After taking in the image of Wayne, the reader who flips the cover confronts a two-page advertisement for Marlboro cigarettes, featuring a typical "Marlboro Man"–type cowboy saddled atop a horse. The Marlboro Man's rhetorical message can be phrased as "real men smoke Marlboros." Wayne acts for the magazine as a whole as the cowboy does in this particular advertisement.

Esquire's use of Wayne's image to advertise a "new" form of masculinity is ambivalent: his placement on the cover demonstrates that they know the image of Wayne sells magazines (particularly magazines advertised to men), but the "hard-line" masculinity he represents simply does not represent *Esquire*'s hegemonic masculinity project. What this ambivalence demonstrates is how exemplars of masculinity can be mobilized. Like the discussion of the "White Negro" and sixties' counterculture in the first chapter of this study, Wayne represents a kind of masculinity that *Esquire*'s ideal readership should not practice, but a kind of masculinity that they can nonetheless consume.

The importance and specific functions of this conservative figure to the "panicked" maintenance of patriarchal power (to echo Judith Butler) are best shown by an article published one month after the original publication in *Esquire* of "Civil Defense," which would later become, in a revised version, the second chapter of *The Nuclear Age*. The article, "American Beat: A Wolf in Wolf's Clothing," offers a counterexample to this conservative notion of masculinity embodied by the cowboy, only to then reinforce the need for what is presented as a more foundational and natural masculinity. In the September 1980 piece on millionaire playboy Nick Nickolas, writer Bob Greene describes a threat to masculinity that he labels the "New American Man":

> The nation's social fabric has been embellished in recent years by the arrival of something called the New American Man. In his extreme and exotic form, the New American Man drinks white wine and cries a lot and is so achingly sensitive that he often finds himself quivering. He is constantly searching for the feminine side of his own personality. He is a staunch supporter of feminist theology; in many cases, his wife has left him, but he is secretly proud that she was able to show such strength.[42]

Greene importantly labels this type of masculinity "new," setting up a comparison between it and the conservative type of masculinity exemplified by John Wayne's cowboy persona. Importantly, this "new" masculinity allies with feminism, an actual political and cultural threat to patriarchy. Greene characterizes this alliance as emasculation: the New American Man sips chardonnay while weeping, "quivering," all while trying to be more like a woman. Such masculinity is marginalized by or at least subordinated to the type of hegemonic masculinity that Wayne is seen as exemplifying. Whereas previously the magazine mocked Wayne's cowboy masculinity, here such a conservative and nostalgic version of masculinity was mobilized both to sell magazines and other consumer items and, in the process, to buttress the patriarchal structures of the Reagan era by reifying "real" masculinity as an object that men – men presumably threatened by feminism – can purchase and therefore "own" as part of themselves.

Scott Duguid has argued that this nostalgic masculinity buttressed America's political and economic situation,[43] and accuses Reagan-era culture of being "addicted" to masculinity. There is no better example of the fact that this version of cowboy masculinity was tied to political and ideological power than Ronald Reagan himself.[44] Enacting the figure of the cowboy, Reagan sought to assure Americans that political problems could be overcome through tough and assured masculine action – or, perhaps more appropriately, "true grit."[45] Wayne died the year before Reagan won the election; following in the footsteps of Wayne, Reagan became America's foremost exemplar of masculinity for the 1980s.[46] Reagan accomplished this performance by creating masculine images of himself: for example, he was sometimes represented as "chopping wood, breaking horses, toughing out an assassination attempt, bullying congress, and staging showdowns with the Soviet Union."[47] The Reagan administration therefore sought to define political leadership through masculine example.

Of course, neither Wayne nor Reagan was a "real" cowboy; they only played them, either in the movies or in the White House. This performance is not unusual – exemplary masculinities are, by their nature, fantasy figures – but the fact that actors were now the paradigmatic exemplars points to the fact that such masculinity is an artifice, a performance. It also makes it plain, to some, that the cowboy is no longer a "real" figure (if it ever was). Rather, by the 1980s, the cowboy cannot only be mobilized as an exemplary masculinity for some,[48] but can also be viewed as a kind of fourth order simulacrum, an image that, according to Jean Baudrillard, "bears no relation to any reality whatever."[49]

It is therefore helpful to examine the ways in which O'Brien continually evokes the figure of the cowboy only to subject that figure to parody or ridicule and, most often, to emasculation, in a way similar to *Esquire*'s invocation of Reagan's cowboy masculinity.[50] Unlike Mailer's "White Negro," who was a historically specific answer to the "problems" facing patriarchy, the cowboy is an anachronistic figure, out of place in the 1980s. Indeed, *The Nuclear Age* is full of cowboys, but each of their performances is not only inadequate, but points to the necessary inadequacy of the cowboy as an exemplary masculinity.

The first cowboy introduced in the novel is William's father, who, every year, re-enacts Custer's Last Stand, playing the title role. Every summer of his childhood, then, William witnesses the "death" and scalping of his father – his scalping acting as a symbolic castration. William makes this connection between scalping and castration clear in a later chapter, when at university he attends a "Custer's Last Stand" Carnival. Ned Rafferty, a "big-shit linebacker" dressed as Crazy Horse, dips William's hair in a bowl of ketchup (85). Moments later, when William is dancing with Sarah Strouch, Rafferty cuts in, getting between our protagonist and the novel's "bombshell" character. William's reaction is telling: "Scalped, I thought. First my father, now me" (91). William makes clear here what he otherwise seems to realize only unconsciously: that he understood his father's repeated scalping as a form of emasculation.

Aside from connecting the cowboy to issues of gender – and, more specifically, masculine anxieties about gender – William's father's annual performance as Custer also establishes a connection between the cowboy and American history, expansionism, cultural genocide, and patriarchal governmental power. Like Wayne and Reagan, he is also, in this instance, an actor playing a role, and his performance of this exemplary masculinity has a profound effect on young William:

> I worshipped that man.
>
> I wanted to warn him, rescue him, but I also wanted slaughter. How do you explain it? Terror mixed with fascination. I craved bloodshed, yet I craved the miracle of a happy ending ... It was the implacable scripting of history; my father didn't stand a chance. Yet he remained calm. Firing, reloading, firing – he actually smiled. He never ran, he never wept.

He was always the last to die and he always died with dignity. Every summer he got scalped. Every summer Crazy Horse galloped away with my father's yellow wig. The spotlights dimmed, a bugler played Taps, then we'd head out to the A&W for late-night root beers. (10–11)

Here, William describes just how successful his father's performance is: like a "true" cowboy, he displays manly discipline in the face of overwhelming odds, and dies with dignity. Not surprisingly, young William wants his father to survive, but he also craves his death. This familial (and communal) drama might be Oedipal, but more to the point it reveals the formative violence in the cowboy conception of masculinity, and, perhaps, the failure of older models of masculinity that still hold sway over a generation of men.

It is worth asking just *why* William's father has this privileged position in the town's annual historical pageant. He is not the mayor, nor, would it seem, does his job make him a significant figure; however, he might be recognizable, since the librarian, for example, is able to phone William's home without even asking who he is (23–4). I raise this questionnot to speculate on the diegetic reason for William's father's role, but to underline its symbolic importance: if William is an "average" and therefore representative man in the nuclear age, then the fact that William's father plays the role of Custer, and that William must witness this performance annually, demonstrates that the novel points to a historical problem with masculinity, culminating in the 1980s. The men in the 1980s are not directly connected to a cowboy lineage, but only to a simulacrum thereof; however, that empty image still rules over them. That William is representative of this cycle is clear not only from his father's role as Custer, but from the fact that even as a child his father "hails" him as "partner" (32) and "cowboy" (192), performing an act of what Althusser calls interpellation, whereby ideology "'recruits' subjects among the individuals ... or 'transforms' the individuals into subjects."[51] William even used to dress the part: a photograph of him as a child, introduced late in the novel, represents young William as "a handsome child: blond hair and a cowboy shirt and a big smile" (250). In this photo from William's childhood, the reader gets to see William's initial, highly problematic connection to the figure of the cowboy.

Rafferty, who O'Brien first introduces dressed as Crazy Horse, is himself a cowboy, as William later learns. Further along in the novel, when both are members of a guerilla organization called the

Committee, and in a moment of brotherly bonding, Rafferty tells William that he is a "Ranch kid – I ever tell you that? Grew up on a ranch. Dumb cowboy. Home on the range. All I ever wanted, some cows and dope and git along little dogie" (237). Rafferty expects William's disbelief: his past identity as a cowboy, and all the ideological underpinnings that brings with it, do not easily match with Rafferty's role as a counter-cultural, anti-patriarchal guerilla, nor, more importantly, with his role as the hen-pecked partner to Sarah Strouch. Rafferty, then, is portrayed as having taken up several masculine roles – brave, football player, and, later, guerilla – the most significant of which, for this discussion, being the cowboy; yet, these all fail to naturalize gender hierarchy, leaving him instead the lesser partner in his relationship with Sarah. Rafferty's cowboy masculinity fails to rein in – or subordinate – Sarah's femininity.

The most obvious parody of the cowboy figure comes in the form of William's schoolmate and eventual Committee member Ollie Winkler. Ollie has the typical trappings of the cowboy: wearing "a white cowboy hat and fancy high-heeled boots" (75), Ollie is the most aggressive, action-oriented member of the resistance. He is introduced to the reader when he approaches William during William's peaceful anti-bomb demonstration. Immediately, Ollie demands action: "'This bomb shit,' he said, 'a catchy tune. Who do we assassinate?'" (75). But his cowboy dress and demeanour are comically undercut by the contrast with his stature; described as "A Friar Tuck facsimile," William decides that Ollie might not be quite a midget, "but there was obvious evidence of a misplaced chromosome" (75). When Ollie puts on the hat and boots, he invokes the exemplary masculinity of the cowboy; however, he cannot overcome the masculine deficit engendered by his physical form, though he endeavours to do so with his (inevitably comical) masculine performance.

Ollie's performance of the cowboy may be comedic because of his stature, but it would be wrong to assume that Ollie's bad copy implies an authentic original. Rather, as Thomas Strychacz has argued in a discussion of the matador in the fiction of Ernest Hemingway, "the confusion of a fantasy that keeps getting recorded as real works to unsettle the priority of original over copy."[52] Strychacz's perspective is indebted to Judith Butler, who writes that gender is a "*kind of imitation for which there is no original*; in fact, it is a kind of imitation that produces the very notion of the original as an *effect* and consequence of the imitation itself."[53] The problem, according to Strychacz, "is that the process of manhood-fashioning ... alienates what appears to be 'true' manhood by showing that it too derives from copies, from repeated performances, from discursive iteration."[54] Even supposedly "real" cowboys are citing or performing previous performances, and these are performances not of a single originary cowboy figure but of other performances – John Wayne's, for instance – resulting in a form of alienated, pathological masculinity.

In the case of the cowboy in *The Nuclear Age*, it is not merely enough to say that the novel represents gender as performative, but that the gendered discourse of the Cold War impels nearly all of the male characters to perform this specific "Cold Warrior" iteration of hegemonic masculinity. This gendered Cold War discourse is what Butler calls a "regulatory norm." She writes that "regulatory norms materialize 'sex' and achieve this materialization through a forcible reiteration of those norms. That this reiteration is necessary is a sign that materialization is never quite complete, that bodies never quite comply with the norms by which their materialization is impelled."[55] Each of the male characters practices a version of "cowboy" masculinity, but Rafferty's is inadequate, Ollie's is comical, and William's father's necessarily entails emasculation and death. Trying to practice "cowboy" masculinity leads to failure, not dominance. The novel therefore reveals the workings of hegemonic masculinity while simultaneously parodying them. The figure of the cowboy – so central to the Reagan era in which the novel was written – has a very real effect on the men in the novel, and on masculine identity in America, but the poor attempts to enact the cowboy make not only the characters, but the cowboy itself, seem comical. Parodying the cowboy exposes heterosexual masculinity "as an incessant and panicked imitation of its own naturalized idealization."[56]

Though William does not practice cowboy masculinity like the others, he is nonetheless associated with the role. For instance, as previously noted, William's father regularly refers to him as "cowboy" (13, 26) or "partner" (32). As Susan Farrell notes, O'Brien added these forms of address after he revised the *Esquire* "Civil Defense" excerpt into the second chapter of the novel, stressing the town's frontier history[57] and strengthening the pattern of associations between characters and the cowboy figure. While William does not practice cowboy masculinity, he nonetheless attempts a similar role as a revolutionary guerilla. While John Wayne never played a revolutionary, he nonetheless played a number of soldiers, a role similar to a guerilla, though the soldier is a role that William specifically tried to avoid. After running from the draft and refusing the role of the soldier, William and his associates in the Committee take up with Ebenezer Keezer and Nethro, two specialists who put them through a kind of guerilla boot camp. Here, William learns that what it takes to be an armed radical is the same as what it takes to be a soldier. On the weapons range, William discovers that his friends – Sarah, Rafferty, Tina and Ollie – "knew the whys and wherefores of deadly force" (185). Conversely, William loses control of his bowels when he fires his automatic rifle. His mishap is clearly identified as a masculine failing: Ebenezer Keezer, directly eyeing William, later refers to the group as "regulation panty-poopers" (186). The supposed radicals have, perhaps unwittingly, become an institution so similar to the military that, rather than challenge society, they merely reproduce its patriarchal logic. Given the "cowboy" presidency of Reagan, and his involvement with guerillas during the Iran-Contra scandal, the novel subtly criticizes radical groups, presenting them as another iteration of Cold Warrior masculinity.[58]

At the "final exam," a quasi-military drill featuring live ammunition, William completely shuts down, attempting to bury himself in the sand rather than move forward. He hallucinates his father, who says "I love you, cowboy" (192), underlining William's failure in the primary skills that denote the cowboy: an ability to remain cool and in-control in adverse situations (think of his father's calmness during the Little Bighorn re-enactment), and mastery over his weapons, which demonstrates his privileged access to violence. William does not fit either the military or the resistance, because he does not fit patriarchy and the practice of masculinity that it demands.

William's eventual turn away from "Cold Warrior" masculinity marks a shift in the novel, from William as a guerilla to a more domestic version of masculinity. Following his failure during the "final exam," William's role becomes increasingly domestic: he becomes a sort of housewife for the movement, explaining that his job at meetings involved "serving coffee, washing the breakfast dishes" (214). As he rationalizes it, "it wasn't heroism or cowardice. Just non-involvement: potato chips and coleslaw and iced tea" (219). His marginalization from the violent members of the group leads him into fantasy, where he expresses nostalgia for the nuclear family: "I tried not to listen. I scoured the frying pan and hummed *Happy Birthday*, pretending I was back home again, my father outside raking leaves, my mother in the bedroom wrapping gifts" (215). In his fantasy, William fits into both the role of the mother and the child – he is actually washing dishes, a stereotypically feminine role in the domestic sphere, while in his mind he awaits presents from his parents. Here, William fantasizes about both femininity and immaturity, two roles against which masculinity typically measures itself. William therefore fails to fit into the masculine roles offered by a violent, "Cold Warrior" culture.

3. Retrenching the Domestic Sphere in "Grandma's Pantry"

But William, after failing to gain power within a series of patriarchal roles (be they within the sexualized realm of adolescence, or the violent realms of the military and the resistance), will not allow his domestication to turn into emasculation, and seeks yet another patriarchal institution in which he can finally discover his masculine identity. Soon after this shift is made, William begins seeking out Bobbi and a domestic life similar to the one he remembers having in his childhood – a life like the one he had in Fort Derry, fishing with his father, but omitting the night terrors. This nostalgia for the nuclear family will lead William into his next masculine role: the family patriarch. In an attempt to secure this role, William begins to dig a hole in his backyard, presumably to build a bomb shelter; in doing so, he invokes the gendered Cold War discourse of "Civil Defense." The bomb shelter is – according to this Cold War discourse – a physical space that can create and maintain a patriarchal gender regime. As opposed to the queer spaces discussed in the last chapter, which seek to avoid a patriarchal gender hierarchy, William hopes to provide an exaggerated, heteronormative space.

The bomb shelter is, like the figure of the cowboy, a symbol from the past that returned to prominence in the political culture of the Reagan era. As Margot Henrickson explains, many works responded to Reagan's resuscitation of Cold War rhetoric and renewed nuclear policies, such as his Strategic Defense Initiative (the so-called "Star Wars" program.)[59] Foertsch concurs, adding that the Reagan-Thatcher era was characterized by Cold War fears suggestive of the early 1960s (474).[60] As Allan Winkler notes, these Cold War tensions led to a resurgence in civil defence during the Reagan years, eventually resulting in the 1983 budget for civil defence doubling the previous year.[61]

Esquire registered the renewed fear of nuclear war throughout the decade by publishing numerous articles on defence strategy, civil defence, and nuclear weaponry.[62] In a November 1982 article, "In Case of Cataclysm," Adam Smith notes that, according to Gallup, "Most Americans ... now think World War III may break out in the Eighties."[63] These fears have resulted in the growth of civil defence: "Twenty years ago we had ridiculous backyard bomb shelters. We had school-children crouching under their desks. That was absurd. All American civil defense has been a kind of posturing. John F. Kennedy urged Americans to build bomb shelters. Jimmy Carter asked for $2 billion to plan the evacuation of American cities. Ronald Reagan asked for $4 billion." Rather than seeing this investment as money well spent, Smith dismisses civil defence as "right-wing and kooky."[64]

The Nuclear Age comments on the cultural discourse of Reaganism by foregrounding the over-determined, gendered place of the shelter. As Henrickson explains, the shelter was central to each proposed civil defence policy.[65] The bomb shelter was a central image both of the Cold War and of domestic safety and retrenchment. This image drives William, who attempts to recast his dissolving family into a model, nuclear family, by re-establishing the domestic realm in the form of a shelter. However, just as the novel reveals that the figure of the cowboy was too obviously an insufficient masculine figure by the 1980s, so too is the bomb shelter exposed as too anachronistic and outdated to serve as a model by which to reinforce and restructure hegemonic masculinity.

In a 1951 article referenced by May, Charles Clarke argues that one of the major challenges of a post-nuclear America would be sexual. In a piece entitled "VD Control in Atom-Bombed Areas" in the *Journal of Social Hygiene*, Clarke argues that in the panic following a nuclear attack,

> Families would become separated and lost from each other in the confusion. Supports of normal family and community life would be broken down ... Under such conditions, it is to be expected that moral standards would relax and promiscuity would increase. With this increase, the venereal disease rates and the number of illegitimate births would mount ... the chances are that the venereal disease rates would increase by 1,000% or more.[66]

Here, Clarke shifts the focus away from such common post-nuclear concerns as radiation, looting, and the scarcity of food and resources, towards the threat of venereal disease and illegitimate babies. Clarke's suggestions include policies ensuring that sexuality be strictly policed in this nightmarish, post-apocalyptic America, arguing for the "vigorous repression of prostitution and measures to discourage promiscuity," as well as championing "social and religious services." "Every effort should be made," Clarke warns, "to re-unite family groups, to safeguard morals, to support or restore morale."[67] Commenting on Clarke's essay, May notes that just as nuclear energy was to be contained, so too was "the social and sexual fallout of the atomic age itself."[68] What is most at risk in a nuclear war, the article suggests, is the continued survival of the traditional family unit.

Following this logic, the bomb shelter not only protects your family from nuclear annihilation, but also protects America from the threat of dangerous sexuality – that is, the type practiced outside of the confines of the heterosexual, socially sanctioned family unit. The bomb shelter, then, was a highly gendered place. As May notes, some of the literature referred to the shelter as "Grandma's pantry," while in civil defence publications, "safety was represented in the form of the family."[69] Constructing the bomb shelter was a masculine activity, connected to the contemporaneous cultural fixation on Do-It-Yourself work.[70] While men would take on the role of protectors and providers,[71] women had an important role to play as well. Jean Wood Fuller, the Assistant Administrator of the Federal Civil Defense Administration (FCDA), called on women to use their domestic skillset to help out with the Cold War.[72] In the domestic realm of the bomb shelter, they would be homemakers, while in the post-nuclear world they would be relied on to perform the all-important role of mother. As Georgia Senator Richard Russell put it, "If we have to start over again with another Adam and Eve, then I want them to be Americans and not Russians, and I want them on this continent and not in Europe."[73] Indeed, the fallout shelter acts to consolidate the powers of patriarchy: women's sexuality is forced back into the domestic sphere and directed entirely towards their husbands, while homosexuals and other so-called "degenerate" sexualities, understood in the Cold War as threats to national security, are directly excluded from safety. Alternative masculinities are thus marginalized while the dominance of men over women is confirmed. The building of a fallout shelter is the figural retrenchment of patriarchy, while the space itself is literally a bomb-proof domestic sphere.

It is therefore fitting that the chapter in which William discusses his nostalgic, domestic childhood is entitled "Civil Defense," the appellation given to America's bomb shelter strategy. When "Civil Defense," which would go on to become the second chapter of *The Nuclear Age*, was originally published in the August 1980 issue of *Esquire*, the magazine featured three articles on the then-presumed Republican presidential nominee, Ronald Reagan. The original publication of the story, then, had an even more explicit connection to the president than its later publication as a novel. One of these features, Joel Kotkin and Paul Grabowicz's "Dutch Reagan, All-American," begins by describing Reagan's version of his childhood home of Dixon, Illinois:

> A sunny day in a nineteenth-century town entering the twentieth century. Victorian houses, small factories, boys in straw hats, girls in party dresses, summer afternoons at the creek. Wise town doctors, hard town villains, small-town government. Hard work, school plays, chores to be done, civics as ethics, football as worshipful activity. Galena Avenue, the war memorial, the house where Lincoln slept one night. A good place to raise your children, and a place that one of those children could look back on and say, "I realize now that we were poor, but I didn't know it at the time." Did that world exist? … It's important to ask, because it's that little town, more than any other place, to which Ronald Reagan would like us to return.[74]

Compare this description of Reagan's purported idyllic small-town past to O'Brien's description of William's childhood home, as it was originally published in "Civil Defense" in the same issue:

> Fort Derry, Montana, was your typical small town, with the usual gas stations and parks and public schools, and I grew up in a family that pursued all the ordinary small-town values. My father sold real estate, my mother kept house. During the summers we would sometimes hike up into the mountains above town, the Sweetheart Mountains, and my dad would show me how to cast for trout, and my mom would fry the catch over an open fire, and things were just fine. I was a regular kid. I played war games, tried to hit baseballs, started a rock collection, rode my bike to the A&W, fed the dog, messed around. Normal, normal. I even ran a lemonade stand out along the sixth fairway at the golf course, ten cents a glass, plenty of ice: a regular entrepreneur.[75]

Both are depictions of a stereotypical "small town." Like Reagan, William is convinced that he must return to this supposedly unspoiled past. In the second example, William – telling his story in retrospect, as an adult and a father – depicts a time when he was "regular," and when the domestic sphere was an inflexibly gendered place. Dad works; mom stays home. Dad catches the food; mom cooks it. William describes himself as an All-American boy, playing baseball (America's official pastime) and war (America's unofficial pastime), and involving himself as both a producer and consumer of goods – a kind of nascent capitalist.

Capitalism, gender roles, and even masculine aggression are all tied, here, to the "good life." As Berlant notes, the "good life" is the central fantasy of cruel optimism: "Fantasy is the means by which people hoard idealizing theories and tableaux about how they and the world 'add up to something.'"[76] For William, the good life is dependent on the safety – or shelter – of normalcy. However, William's repetitive insistence of his normalcy ("Normal, normal") suggests, following Butler, that something is not normal about this "normal" life – that normalcy must be iteratively re-expressed because it is not actually a solid origin. One might ask of William's origin the same question that the *Esquire* writers put to Reagan's "small town" upbringing: "Did that world exist?" In the present of the novel, William hopes to transport his family back to this nostalgic image of the past, just as Reagan tries to remake the country in the image of Dixon, Illinois, circa 1920. William's individual story serves as an allegory for the culture of Reaganism as a whole.

A series of parallels motivates the comparison between William's childhood past and his present as a father and cuckolded husband. William's adult family mirrors the makeup of his childhood family: husband, wife, and child. His home is even near the Sweetheart Mountains, which he used to visit with his family when he was young. Moreover, the novel makes the connection even clearer: in the "Civil Defense" chapter, William's first memories are of when he was a kid of "about Melinda's age" (9). This parallel between William's childhood and his present underscores the ways William's obsessive digging of a bomb shelter has, at its source, a desire to force his family back into a conservative notion of the past, one which may never have existed to begin with, considering that William introduces his childhood by explaining that he was a "frightened child" who in his dreams "watched the world end" (9). Having supposedly failed as a man in a world of cowboys, William's desire for patriarchal control turns towards the home front, ostensibly motivated by his ongoing fears of nuclear annihilation, but actually provoked by Bobbi's infidelity, as symbolized by her missing diaphragm (286). Bobbi's infidelity comes to represent, for William, "an erosion of the traditional family structure" (197), and even makes him question whether his daughter, Melinda, is actually his own (196). "What happens when those fantasies start to fray," Berlant asks of people's attachment to the good life, "depression, dissociation, pragmatism, cynicism, optimism, activism, or an incoherent mash?"[77] At his home near the Sweetheart Mountains, William begins obsessively digging; when Melinda asks what the hole is for, William's response is that "It's a shelter" (5). William's response is complicated by the fact that the hole never becomes a shelter – that, in the end, it is nothing but a hole – but the act of digging is clearly the culmination of William's lifelong obsession with shelter.

In Cold War culture generally, and for William specifically, the bomb shelter metonymically links safety and domesticity. This is perhaps most clearly shown in a *Good Housekeeping* editorial, noted by Winkler. The November 1958 article, entitled "A Frightening Message for a Thanksgiving Issue," describes the precautions that would need to be taken to survive a nuclear attack, and is essentially an advertisement for family bomb shelters.[78] The editors conclude that "All this may happen. You have the choice of believing that it can't. But if you recognize the possibility of war between major powers, you must go further and acknowledge that atomic bombs will be dropped. On us."[79] This is a message that William seems to have taken to heart: his continued insistence that the "bombs are real" echoes *Good Housekeeping*'s contention that atomic bombs *will* be dropped. More to the point, that the call for bomb shelters was published in this particular magazine demonstrates how the shelter was a part of the domestic sphere: building and maintaining a shelter should be of pivotal concern to "good housekeepers."

However, despite *Good Housekeeping* and the label of "Grandma's pantry," the domestic space of the bomb shelter was specifically not a feminized place. Much of the Cold-War 1950s cultural discourse had taken great strides to turn the homestead into a masculine realm. One way this happened was through the Do-It-Yourself movement. As Steven Gelber explains of the 1950s movement, "household maintenance and repair permitted the suburban father to stay at home without feeling emasculated or being subsumed into an undifferentiated entity with his wife."[80] *Esquire* even took part: beginning in the June

1951 issue, the magazine began featuring a regular "Housing" section, with articles on home décor and DIY projects intended to make the home a masculine domain. The unattributed editorial in that issue introduced the new section, identifying as a problem the wife's control of the domestic sphere and inviting men to read and enjoy the "Housing" section each month, stating "Let your wife look over your shoulder, if you want (she'll do it anyway, just as the gals always sneak a look at Esquire's strictly masculine fare) but don't forget – we're talking to *you*, man to man."[81] The section remained a regular feature of the magazine until November 1953.

In the 1950s, then, men made the domestic sphere masculine through home construction and various home projects. William demonstrates, in satirical fashion, how Do-It-Yourself still keeps the domestic space sufficiently masculine, when he barricades his wife and child into a bedroom and builds a service hatch through which he can communicate and pass them food and other necessities. He says of the service hatch, "I'm proud of it. It's a brilliant piece of engineering: a rectangular hole in the door, nine by twelve inches, wide enough to permit the essential exchanges, narrow enough to deflect foolish thoughts of flight" (194–5). William's DIY project makes his household safe for patriarchy, insofar as he uses his masculine set of skills to imprison his wife and daughter and force them to maintain the charade of a happy nuclear family. The bomb shelter does this on a larger, cultural scale: Lichtman calls it "an ideologically charged national do-it-yourself project that permeated America's post-war consciousness more than its physical landscape."[82] William's actions, then, were emblematic of a larger cultural attempt to shelter heteronormativity and patriarchy.

Despite William's new sense of security, one should not view the shelter as the opposite of the bomb; rather, the bomb shelter is a symbol of the regulatory practices of Cold War culture, authorized by the threat of nuclear warfare. Civil defence is just another aspect of nuclear warfare. Jean Baudrillard makes the connection: "The risk of nuclear atomisation only serves as a pretext ... to the installation of a universal system of security, linkup, and control whose deterrent effect does not aim for atomic clash at all ... but really the much larger probability of any real event, anything which could disturb the general system and upset the balance. The balance of terror is the terror of balance."[83] Baudrillard's claim is that the nuclear threat is a mere pretext for the increasing powers of the military-industrial complex, the very seat of masculine hegemony.[84] Derrida, writing (fittingly enough) in 1984, makes a similar point:

> For the "reality" of the nuclear age and the fable of nuclear war are perhaps distinct, but they are not two separate things. It is the war (in other words the fable) that triggers this fabulous war effort ... "Reality," let's say the encompassing institution of the nuclear age, is constructed by the fable, on the basis of an event that has never happened (except in fantasy, and that is not nothing at all).[85]

Here, the connection between hegemony and gender is clear: civil defence is, according to Baudrillard and Derrida, a "pretext" for structuring society – and that includes gender relations – according to the logic of technology and militarism. The masculinist images of Cold War discourse in general, and the fallout shelter in particular, clearly link "safety" and authority with masculinity. Furthermore, the fallout shelter not only figuratively entrenches the family, but creates a domestic sphere that is also a militarized zone – the family home as bunker. The man must be in charge not only because he is the *pater familias*, but also because he is the commanding officer. Mapping their more general theories onto this specific situation, one could say that both Derrida and Baudrillard agree that there is no clear distinction between nuclear warfare and nuclear defence. Civil defence is but a part of nuclear discourse, which itself is a regulatory practice, one which – among other things – seeks to reinforce patriarchy. The fear of nuclear war is the impetus behind adhering to strict gender roles in the name of national security.

O'Brien's novel sees nuclear threat and nuclear defence as part of the same madness – the hole William builds is both safety for, and threat to, his family – and this united nuclear discourse serves to regulate and normalize clearly defined gender roles. It is a clear action of hegemonic masculinity: those in power use nuclear discourse not only to ensure patriarchy, but actually to entrench even stricter gender norms. The bomb shelter not only links safety and domesticity, but also stands in for the regulatory norms of the Cold War. Because he is white, male, and heterosexual, William believes that he is able to bring the regulatory powers of patriarchy to bear on his family by constructing the bomb shelter; however, by metonymically linking patriarchy with Cold War notions of civil defence, O'Brien points to the illegitimacy of both, and he does so by making William take this connection to an absurd extreme.

Just as the cowboy is a figure inadequate to the task of reviving patriarchy in the 1980s, so too is the bomb shelter, as a highly gendered space, too outdated to perform its role of retrenching the domestic sphere. The result is that the bomb shelter becomes too visibly a symbol of the subjective violence of patriarchy. In the process of digging the hole, William alienates his wife and daughter, who threaten to leave him. To avert this crisis, William barricades them in the house, forcing them to share one domestic space while he prepares another. Rather than becoming a potential home for William's family, though, the hole becomes a potential tomb; instead of building a shelter in the giant hole, William rigs it with dynamite and, in the final chapter, drugs his family and lowers them into it. Here, we witness the symbol of the bomb shelter transformation, so that it comes to symbolize visually the usually subjective violence of hegemonic masculinity. The gaping hole, the drugs, the dynamite – William's "shelter" becomes an image of the illegitimacy of patriarchy, the inverted shelter threatening to scatter his family across the countryside.

Luckily, Melinda recovers from her sedation before he can detonate the explosives, and William seemingly suffers a change of heart, committing himself to a new outlook on life. One form of retrenchment replaces another, and, if anything, William has simply moved from a material shelter to a mental one:

I will trust the seasons. I will keep Bobbi in my arms for as long as she will stay. I will obey my vows. I will stop smoking. I will have hobbies. I will firm up my golf game and invest wisely and adhere to the conventions of decency and good grace. I will find forgetfulness. Happily, without hesitation, I will take my place in the procession from church to grave, believing what cannot be believed, that all things are renewable, that the human spirit is undefeated and infinite, always. I will be a patient husband. I will endure. I will live my life in the conviction that when it finally happens – when we hear that midnight whine, when Kansas burns, when what is done is undone, when fail-safe fails, when deterrence no longer deters, when the jig is up at last – yes, even then I will hold to a steadfast orthodoxy, confident to the end that E will somehow not quite equal mc^2, that it's a cunning metaphor, that the terminal equation will somehow not quite balance. (312)

William's plan, as he describes it, is to destroy the bomb shelter, and instead to live a life of quiet conformity – to embrace the life that Mailer railed against, as described in the first chapter of this study. This is barely progress for William, but a move sideways. As Cordle has convincingly argued, the novel comments on a cultural discourse that equates security with conformity, and suggests that the Cold War culture of consumerism and containment was itself a kind of psycho-logical sheltering.[86] In effect, William's decision marks an embrace of a more socially acceptable form of shelter – a life of consumerism. This is exactly the life *Esquire* has to offer its readers, should they, too, require a similar type of "safety valve" while living under the threat of nuclear annihilation.[87]

4. "Ovaries Like Hand Grenades": Emphasized Femininities in *The Nuclear Age*

Given that the novel was first excerpted in *Esquire* magazine, it might not be surprising that, at first glance, there would not seem to be much room in *The Nuclear Age* for female characters. Melinda is only a child, Sarah is killed off by a mysterious disease, Tina Roe-buck seems to exist solely to have her weight mocked, and Bobbi, most obviously, never actually speaks – the reader's only access to Bobbi's character is through Melinda, as a proxy, and through her poetry. To a certain degree, this only makes sense – in my reading, *The Nuclear Age* deals largely with the conflict between a man and his place within hegemonic masculinity, and so women are necessarily marginalized. However, the novel clearly demonstrates not only the fact that these women work within patriarchy, but also that they are subject to the regulatory norms of the Cold War era as well, even as they attempt to escape them. This is most obvious in the problem-atic relationship between the female characters and domesticity, and in the way that Bobbi and Sarah complicate the concept of em-phasized femininity. While neither Bobbi nor Sarah have enough agency and freedom to be the author of a truly counter-patriarchal discourse, they do provide examples and hope for Melinda to be just such a character.

Both Bobbi and Sarah complicate what Connell calls "emphasized femininity." Emphasized femininity is the feminine equivalent of he-gemonic masculinity; however, based on the very nature of hegemonic masculinity, no woman can actually have access to hegemony – women

are always subordinated within the gender hierarchy. Rather, emphasized femininity is based on compliance with this unequal and illegitimate gender structure. Emphasized femininity is constructed around
women's subordination to men and "oriented to accommodating
the interests and desires of men";[88] emphasized femininity therefore
maintains hegemonic masculinity through acquiescence and collabo-
ration. Superficially, Bobbi and Sarah might fit this description, especially when considering the fact that Bobbi's job as a stewardess[89] and
Sarah's role as a cheerleader threaten to place them in the role of
male fantasy figures; however, Bobbi's desire to escape, and the clear
presentation of domestic violence, troubles such an idealized relationship, as does Sarah's evolution into a radical.[90]

One characteristic of emphasized femininity is the "acceptance
of marriage and childcare as a response to labor market discrimination against women."[91] Even as William attempts to force his family
members into thoroughly domestic roles, the female characters of
the novel feel the cultural pressure of which William's actions are
symbolic. This is most prevalent in the character of Tina Roebuck,
who is obsessed with losing weight. Despite what is revealed to be her
surprising competency as a radical guerilla, Tina longs to fit a more
conventional concept of femininity, papering the walls of her room
with "photographs of fashion models – trim, well-tailored girls out
of *Vogue* and *Seventeen*, shapely specimens out of *Cosmopolitan*" (115).
Mostly, Tina's obsession is played for laughs – William looks back with
nostalgia on "Tina with her Mars bars and anorexic dreams" (115) –
but it is telling that one of the members of a radical, anti-nuclear paramilitary unit is still subjected to the cultural dictate to conform to
emphasized femininity, just as its male members repeat the fascination with violence, within a model of complicit, if not hegemonic,
masculinity. Sarah finds herself drawn even more powerfully to a
strictly domestic lifestyle, admitting to William that "Part of me wants
to run away. Like to Rio, or anywhere. Have babies and clip coupons.
Be your wife, maybe – something normal – anything" (172). Later
in the novel, even more desperate for William's attention, she insists
that "My doctor says I've got this gorgeous womb – ovaries like hand
grenades – I'm built for motherhood – I can cook and rob banks and
manage money. I can sew. I know how to make pickles. Just name it"
(276). Even radicals like Tina and Sarah, it seems, cannot escape a
patriarchal discourse that advertises a life of domesticity as an ideal
choice for women.

However, Sarah's simile, "ovaries like hand grenades," and the description that follows, conflate her potential role as a housewife with her symbolic role as a bombshell. Sarah's supposedly explosive reproductive organs highlight the danger that she potentially poses to patriarchy. First, the sheer size of Sarah's ovaries – organs which produce, among other hormones, testosterone – is threatening, given that her ovaries might stand in for testicles, making her more "manly" than William, or most men for that matter. Second, the particular simile she uses makes her reproductive organs potentially destructive. Sarah seems to be stuck in a liminal space between emphasized femininity and counter-hegemonic radicality. Never finding a real place for herself, Sarah eventually dies from a form of meningitis. As a sexual outlaw, she has no place in the rigid gender order of the Cold War, and is thus silenced.

If Sarah offered no more resistance than her guerilla actions, then she would not have much to offer as a potential counter-hegemonic figure. Her death, in the text, would seem to be an example of a failure to imagine a place for her in a patriarchal society, or perhaps a fitting punishment for her failure to conform. Sarah does, however, describe a fantasy, a possible alternative to the patriarchal aggression and violence of the nuclear age. One evening in Key West, Sarah describes her dream to William, a dream of being, fittingly, a cheerleader for the Dallas Cowboys. It is Super Bowl Sunday, and the teams do not show up:

> [B]ut here's the stunner. Nobody cares. Nobody notices. Because yours truly is out there blowing their dirty little minds with cartwheels. Cartwheels you wouldn't believe. Nobody's even thinking football – cartwheels, that's all they want. Crowd goes bananas. Super Bowl fever, they're all screaming for more cartwheels ... They love me. They really do, just love-love-love. Who cares about football? War's over. Just love. It's all completely reversed. At half time the two teams trot out for a cute little twenty-minute scrimmage and then – bang – back to the action – me and my cartwheels. (243)

Sarah's dream describes an America where Cold Warrior masculinity is no longer central, where "love-love-love" replaces the militarism and violence of the cowboy. Such an analysis is not unproblematic: Sarah's vision of the future is largely narcissistic ("They love me") and still features a highly sexualized female figure as a focal point for spectacle. However, the revolutionary aspect of Sarah's dream comes from the complete reversal she envisions: the war is over, and the football game – a ritualized form of male aggression that is war's correlative – is marginalized. In its place is love, which finds its correlative in Sarah's "billion beautiful cartwheels" (243). It is worth noting, too, that one of the benched football teams is the Dallas Cowboys, and so here Sarah imagines a world where she has symbolically overcome the exemplary masculinity that has cast such a shadow over the text, and over American masculinity itself. With the motions of her body, those "beautiful cartwheels," Sarah hopes to write the cowboy out of history.

While Sarah hopes to challenge patriarchy with her cheerleading, Bobbi's contribution comes through her poetry, which can fruitfully be read in opposition to William's masculine writing. Based on an analysis of the works of Norman Mailer, Peter Schwenger has argued that William writes in the "language of men": "conversational, even colloquial; slangy; occasionally foul-mouthed; and above all anti-literary."[92] *The Nuclear Age* focuses on, among other things, its protagonist's problematic relationship with masculinity. As Schwenger notes, William's style is defensive – his "manly" writing is yet another example of William mobilizing discourse in an attempt to access patriarchal privilege.[93] Stated another way, William uses his writing on the one hand as a way to elide the effeminacy of some of his actions, and on the other he uses it to essentially omit femininity from the text.

But if O'Brien writes in the "language of men," in Schwenger's terms, then what we might call the "language of women" manages to work its way into the narrative only by sneaking into the cracks that form in the masculine façade. The most obvious examples are Bobbi's poems; take, for instance, her short poem entitled "Relativity," apparently composed while William digs his hole and Bobbi contemplates leaving him:

> *Relations are strained*
> *in the nuclear family.*
> *It is upon us, the hour*
> *of evacuation,*
> *the splitting of blood*
> *infinitives.*
> *The clock says fission*
> *fusion*
> *critical mass.* (122, italics in original)

William calls a similar poem "Horseshit of the worst kind" (65), denying that there is any worth to Bobbi's only form of communication,
and demonstrating the aforementioned dislike of the literary. Even
Foertsch, a critic of the novel, seems to share William's opinion, calling them "childish and fragmentary," before dismissively explaining
that Bobbi "Donna Reed-ly pin[s] them to pajama tops and cereal
boxes as if they were any Saturday's 'honey-do' list."[94] Better than any
male character, Bobbi perceives the comparisons between the or-
dering of the domestic sphere and the regulatory norms of nuclear
rhetoric. As Cordle argues, at the end of the novel the change in William's perspective is characterized by a change from his old point of
view, which denied metaphor – "No metaphors, the bombs are real"
(4) – to one that embraces "the metaphoric power of the science
behind the bomb."[95] Bobbi's poems represent a third option, unacknowledged by William at the end of the novel: her poems contain
"powerful metaphors for domestic crisis, but they also indicate how
the language of power and control, and the way of thinking that ac-
companies it, permeates society from the macrocosm of international
politics to the microcosm of the family unit."[96] As a poet-critic, Bobbi
is able to correctly identify the root of her husband's problems: he
simply is not able, or willing, to comprehend.

   Though Bobbi's occupation as a stewardess threatens to make her
another male fantasy figure, her position also indicates mobility and
freedom. It is Bobbi's very mobility that causes William problems. After Bobbi meets William on a flight from New York to Miami, she
writes him a poem entitled "Martian Travel." Later, William goes to
great lengths to track Bobbi down. The pursuit leads William on a
merry chase: staking out the gate area of Bobbi's airline; flight from
Denver to Salt Lake; New York City; Bonn, Germany; an American
Air Force base in Wiesbaden; University of Minnesota; and finally
back to New York where she works for the UN. Along the way William
learns of Bobbi's various lovers: a navigator named Andy Johnson, a
Professor named Scholheimer, an unnamed Air Force adjutant, another Professor named Johnson. He learns that men love her and
women hate her, that she leaves a trail of broken hearts behind her,
and that he is not the only recipient of "Martian Travel." When the
adjutant claims that Bobbi "had this way with words," Sarah derisively
responds, "Like a Xerox machine" (279), while earlier another stewardess claims that Bobbi would "pass them out like peanuts" (227).
So Bobbi, like Sarah, exists in a kind of liminal space in the novel. In

many ways, she seems to embody the male fantasy of the sexy stewardess, and others treat her poems as consumer items. At the same time,
her poems touch on deeper truths than any other form of discourse
in the novel, and her mobility is a resistant tactic to domestication and
emphasized femininity.

The long pursuit required to track down Bobbi, and the stories William hears about her romantic history, certainly foreshadows her eventual infidelity to William; however, more importantly, what the chase
symbolizes is Bobbi's resistance to domestication. That she continually does settle down with someone, if only for a little while, only emphasizes how central the domestic life is to hegemonic masculinity's
conception of women, and the cultural pressure to conform. Bobbi's
voice is absent from the text, and her presence often mediated, because she is a figure who cannot adequately be pinned down and fully
represented in William's "language of men." She exists in a liminal
space, one that denies full representation. William cannot fully represent or understand her because she has access to a discourse outside
of patriarchy – or she at least skirts its perimeter. Trapping Bobbi in
a domestic sphere and therefore removing the mobility that defines
her character is the only way William can begin to understand and
represent her, but those moments are transitory and fleeting. Bobbi
can be represented, inasmuch as she conforms to some definitions
of emphasized femininity and domesticity, but she cannot be represented to the extent that she continues to elide these definitions. It is
not surprising that William eventually decides to destroy her.

It is Bobbi's child, Melinda, who represents perhaps the best prospect for a counter-hegemonic future, though it needs to be emphasized that this is only a *possibility* opened up by the text, and in no
way a certainty. It is Melinda who is able to reverse her father's downward spiral towards murder-suicide, and who breaks the spell that the
hole has on him. She is also the character who continually answers his
opening question, telling him he is crazy. Her character draws further
significance from a comparison between her childhood and her father's. When William retells the story of his childhood bomb shelter,
he begins by explaining that it occurred when he was a kid, "about Melinda's age" (9). While little William is obsessed with building bomb
shelters, Melinda is critical to dismantling them. While in both cases
it is the father who destroys the shelter, it is crucially important that
not only was Melinda not involved in the construction of the hole,
but that the impetus to destroy it comes from her, not from William.

Heberle makes clear this significance, arguing that while William's ping pong shelter was disassembled by a loving father, his final shelter is dismantled through the love of his daughter (151). Heberle focuses on William's action, but Melinda's role needs to be emphasized: in effect, Melinda refuses to be a victim of history, like her father, and it is the child who saves the father, not the other way around. If the lineage of fathers and sons forms a sort of patriarchal history, then here Melinda severs this chain. If William's relationship with his father prefigures his gender problems, then perhaps Melinda, by both saving her father and rejecting his authority, opens the path for a better future. Bobbi and Sarah provide examples of the possibilities for women, but are too situated in history to truly break free and create a space outside of patriarchy. The possibility is there, however slight it may be, that Melinda, and her generation, could change all of that.

5. Conclusion

Lying in bed as a young man, William dreams of "a concrete igloo" and "a tree house made of steel" (38). These unlikely images of shelter illustrate William's anxiety, his need for safety – the safety provided by farcical images of exaggerated security. When William's anxieties are recognized as gender anxieties, these absurd images come to emphasize not only his anxiety about his access to patriarchal authority – William's culturally enforced desire to retrench and maintain patriarchy – but also the insufficiency of the images currently being marshalled to do so. *The Nuclear Age* critiques such Reagan-era images as the cowboy and the bomb shelter, images pulled from a conservative notion of America's past and mobilized to reinforce patriarchy. Sometimes, these images work: remember, for example, how *Esquire* used John Wayne to sell its readers on the idea that the "New Hard-Line" of masculinity would involve ruthless business practices and sex for solely reproductive purposes, or when the Cold War rhetoric of civil defence convinced homeowners to entrench the domestic sphere in their own backyard. William, feeling his masculinity threatened, attempts to mobilize these images to access his patriarchal dividend, but finds that they lack the cultural power to do so for him.

The Nuclear Age sees the 1980s as a decade when hegemonic masculinity fails to successfully renegotiate its boundaries. The cowboy is held up to ridicule; the bomb shelter becomes a tomb. Even the domestic sphere itself is challenged as an adequate way to reinforce an unequal gender hierarchy. In attempting to benefit from all of these different images and discourses, William's complicit masculinity becomes fragmented, and madness follows. However, his final decision, contra Mailer, is to embrace conformity and, in particular, consumerism. This embrace of consumerism points towards a gender practice that can suture together these fragmented pieces of masculinity: what John Beynon calls "bricolage masculinity." Bricolage masculinity is a type of "hybridized masculinity that is experienced and displayed differently at different times in different situations ... the result of 'channel-hopping' across versions of 'the masculine'" and "in which fashion and 'image management' are clearly primary elements."[97] This bricolage masculinity is sufficient, if only to the extent that it allows men to go from one version of masculinity to another, with great alacrity, to cobble together a masculinity which responds to the momentary problems of patriarchy. When William cannot be a cowboy, he will be a father and husband, and when that fails, he will be a consumer. When that fails, another form of masculinity will take its place.

As Beynon's references to "channel-hopping," fashion, and "image management" suggest, bricolage masculinity is a practice of masculinity intensely related to consumption. Rosalind Gill, taking up Beynon's term, argues that masculinity and consumption became increasingly interrelated as the twentieth century advanced, and that representations of masculinity were increasingly fragmented. Furthermore, by the 1980s, a wider range hegemonic masculinity practices was available for men.[98] Gill discusses bricolage masculinity as a type of consumer masculinity that responds to this situation. While he situates her discussion in an analysis of "lad" magazines in the UK in the 1980s and 1990s, it nonetheless suggests that men's interest magazines are an ideal field in which bricolage masculinity can be practiced. As Stefan Cieply argues, *Esquire* promotes the idea of understanding identity as lifestyle.[99] Readers of the magazine can consume dissent, as in the 1960s case of Mailer and *An American Dream*, or they can consume images of cowboy masculinity. Conversely, they can reject these images in favour of other masculine practices, practicing a type of strategic mobilization of certain kinds of masculinity. In this way, magazines such as *Esquire* allow men – especially those men practicing a form of complicit masculinity – to access the patriarchal dividend and feel comfortable in their masculinity without forcing them to choose a particular hegemonic masculinity practice that may not fit the consumerist gender regimes in which they primarily operate.

For William, raised in a supposedly idyllic, conservative notion of the past, one to which he longs to return, such a bricolage masculinity might not be tenable, and until he accepts it as a possibility, his fragmented sense of masculinity leaves him obsessive and possibly insane. Perhaps it will be men of a later generation who can embrace such a multifaceted masculinity, finding strength in bricolage; this may be the case, but no such men exist in *The Nuclear Age*. As we shall see in DeLillo's *Libra*, masculinity continues to fragment, and those men engaged in hegemonic masculinity projects even more acutely feel the paranoia and sense of emasculation characterized by William's complicit masculinity. Furthermore, this paranoia and emasculation is generalized to masculinity at large. Like Capote's *Answered Prayers*, *The Nuclear Age* motions towards the existence of a realm outside of patriarchal discourse, but it does so through its female characters. If masculinity is fragmented, then Bobbi's poetry and Sarah's cheerleading gesture towards those cracks, however small, and hint that these cracks open up a space outside of patriarchy, however insignificant it might be.

6

Don DeLillo in the American Kitchen

As I was working on *Libra*, it occurred to me that a lot of tendencies in my first eight novels seemed to be collecting around the dark center of the assassination. So it's possible I wouldn't have become the kind of writer I am if it weren't for the assassination. Certainly when it happened I had no feeling that it was part of the small universe of my work, because my work, as I say, was completely undeveloped at that point.

– Don DeLillo[1]

As argued in the previous chapter, O'Brien's *The Nuclear Age*, published in 1985, depicts a time when masculinity fragments, when the idea of a unified, representative masculinity becomes untenable. Don DeLillo's *Libra*, published three years later and, like *The Nuclear Age*, excerpted in *Esquire*, picks up on many of the same issues. Whereas O'Brien's novel focuses on the fragmenting effects of "Cold Warrior" masculinity on complicit forms of masculinity, *Libra*, with its vast narrative scope and shifting narrative focus, turns its attention to "Cold Warriors" and other men practicing hegemonic forms of masculinity. *Libra*, moreover, moves beyond identifying the symptoms of a fragmented masculinity, instead positing the Kennedy assassination as a watershed moment during which a fantasy of a coherent, unified, and hegemonic American masculinity was destroyed.

In an interview with Anthony DeCurtis, quoted in this chapter's epigraph, DeLillo refers to the assassination of President John Fitzgerald Kennedy as the "dark center" around which his earlier novels had been collecting. He elaborates in another interview, observing that he explicitly mentions Lee Harvey Oswald in *Players* and *Running Dogs*, and that *Americana,* his first novel, ends with his protagonist driving through Dealey Plaza, the site of the assassination.[2] Even DeLillo's later novel, *Underworld,* features a screening of the Zapruder film.[3] This "dark center," then, is a significant, central historical moment for the author, an event that DeLillo is compelled to represent again and again.

Of course, Kennedy's assassination is not just a watershed moment for DeLillo, but for the whole of America: the assassination of JFK is "the seven seconds that broke the back of the American century."[4] Several critics echo this sentiment: Jeremy Green describes the assassination as "the catastrophic occasion which appeared to shatter a consensual narrative of nation."[5] Peter Boxall declares it "a moment in [American] history at which narrative *fails* to cohere."[6] And Mark Osteen sees it as "America's Mysterium Magnum; like any religious mystery, it is both radiantly overdetermined and heavily shrouded."[7] For each of these critics, the assassination is a crisis for America: it disrupts narrative (for Green and Boxall) and initiates a new era of mystery (for Osteen). Other critics cast an even wider net, finding in the assassination implications for the world and culture at large. Thomas Carmichael sees the assassination as "the first postmodern historical event. In popular terms, it is best known both as the original site of a contemporary nostalgia and as the moment at which all that follows in the postmodern period was violently interjected into contemporary experience."[8] For Fredric Jameson, it was "the coming of age of the whole media culture," and should be understood as "a unique collective (and media, communicational) experience, which trained people to read such events in a new way."[9] Both Carmichael and Jameson see the assassination as a sea change, one that drastically alters the culture not just of America, but of the Western world.

While the importance of the event – both as an historic event in American politics and culture, and as an aesthetic event highlighting the difficulty of representation and the distance between history and narrative – is well established in the literature, Jameson, for instance, argues that its significance cannot be explained by Kennedy's political status alone.[10] While Jameson is correct, to the extent that it is not Kennedy's position as president *alone* that makes this event so meaningful, I would like to interrogate the role of the man central to this event. Kennedy's masculine persona was already firmly ensconced in American culture at the time of his death, and has since only grown in significance. The repercussions of Kennedy's assassination were therefore keenly felt in the American gender order.

Looking at a wide range of media, Randi Gunzenhäuser finds a distinctly gendered dimension in reactions to Kennedy's assassination, arguing that "presentations of the president's death are in part characterized by the effort of recovering a strengthening frame for the heterosexual white male body and identity via the myth of male sacrifice and the stabilizing of gender relations."[11] Challenging this view, Craig Warren, responding directly to Gunzenhäuser, insists that Kennedy's broken body can act "as a symbol of liberation from normative white masculinity."[12] While both scholars come to opposite conclusions about the cultural uses of Kennedy's death, both nevertheless suggest that the assassination should be understood as a moment in which American gender ideology is reconfigured. That is to say that, especially in the American cultural consciousness, Kennedy's assassination is a privileged site in which hegemonic masculinity is reshaped, contested, and potentially fragmented.

At the centre of this profound postmodern moment is a preeminent exemplary masculinity. Even before his death, Kennedy functioned within hegemonic masculinity in a fashion similar to previously discussed exemplars of masculinity (e.g., John Wayne, Mailer's "White Negro"). He was an important figure for *Esquire*: for example, it was there that Mailer published his famous essay on Kennedy, "Superman Comes to the Supermart." Arthur Schlesinger, Jr, whose "The Crisis of American Masculinity" was published in the magazine and discussed in the introduction, was an advisor to Kennedy, and went on to write *A Thousand Days: John F. Kennedy in the White House*, which won both the Pulitzer Prize for Biography or Autobiography and the National Book Award in History and Biography. In addition, Tom Wicker published in *Esquire* two important articles on Kennedy following his assassination: "Kennedy Without the Tears" and "Kennedy Without End, Amen."[13] Add to these specific instances multiple covers, articles, and references, and it is clear that *Esquire* was, and has since been, invested in Kennedy's presidency, finding him an important exemplar for their own hegemonic masculinity project.

However, Kennedy is doubly significant to the nation as a whole because of his political stature. As Dana Nelson argues, as president, Kennedy represented "the concrete correlative for national manhood."[14] Moreover, Kennedy, with the help of many who wrote about him, cast himself as a representative man, a "man whose developmental trajectory stands not for the achievement of the individual ego but for the integration of the state."[15] Kennedy therefore embodied several important discourses about American masculinity, and his representation could be used as an exemplar of masculinity in specific gender regimes (such as *Esquire*'s ideal male readership), or to make claims about the larger gender order. His death did not limit these uses, but multiplied them, and so Gunzenhäuser and Warren can make opposing claims about the significance of Kennedy's assassination for American masculinity, and both can be correct, depending on what discourse each is mobilizing. One man – exemplary, representative, or otherwise – cannot hope to adequately represent all men, or even all men's ambitions or desires.

Building on this scholarly disagreement, I argue that in *Libra*, De-Lillo scripts the Kennedy assassination as the centre of a crisis for twentieth-century American masculinity. The novel depicts a group of "Cold Warriors" – men practicing a paradigmatic form of Cold War hegemonic masculinity – who feel their masculinity threatened by domestication and a supposedly "queer threat." In the face of this threat, Kennedy is offered as the (always deferred) masculine solution. However, Kennedy is a solution that does not quite work, in part because, as a particularly ubiquitous form of exemplary masculinity, he not only figures as a solution to the "problem" of patriarchy, but also represents what James Messerschmidt calls a "masculinity challenge."[16] Finally, DeLillo implies that the postmodern, ironic author is an exemplary masculinity that *does* work. *Esquire* supports this point of view, offering in DeLillo's definition of masculine authorship an exemplar of masculinity suitable to its ideal male readership.

With *Libra*, DeLillo provides an entire masculine metanarrative, one that diagnoses the problems of twentieth-century American manhood and prescribes a type of remedy in the figure of the author himself, recalling the three "techniques of liberation" (satire, art, and politics) offered by Schlesinger in his essay on "The Crisis of American Masculinity."[17] The pattern repeats itself: twentieth-century consumerism and materialism is believed to threaten masculinity, and so masculinity is renegotiated through the tools of consumerism and materialism themselves. Materialism, the domestic sphere, exemplary masculinities, the place of the American author – these seem like disparate topics, but there is one place that they are regularly united: *Esquire* magazine.

1. "Men in Small Rooms": American Masculinity, American Kitchens

Libra returns us to the popular discourse of "masculinity in crisis" of chapter 1 and the "Cold Warrior" masculinity of the preceding chapter. Despite years of ideological labour, the type *Esquire* magazine engaged in, certain forms of masculinity remain averse to, and threatened by, domesticity and materialism. Certainly by the 1980s, there remained a sense of "agency panic"[18] for those who continued to equate consumerism (in all of its forms) with femininity, and conformity with castration.[19] These men feel as though they are meant to produce things, to fix things, to work with their hands: anything else represents a lack of masculine agency. DeLillo perhaps best describes this masculine anxiety in his earlier 1980s work, *White Noise*, in which the narrator, Jack Gladney, explains his discomfort around his father-in-law:

> There were times when he seemed to attack me with terms like ratchet drill and whipsaw. He saw my shakiness in such matters as a sign of some deeper incompetence or stupidity. These were the things that built the world. Not to know or care about them was a betrayal of fundamental principles, a betrayal of gender, of species. What could be more useless than a man who couldn't fix a dripping faucet – fundamentally useless, dead to history, to the messages in his genes? I wasn't sure I disagreed.[20]

Here Gladney, an influential professor of "Hitler studies," describes his relationship with his father-in-law in terms that espouse his own gender insecurities. Vernon Dickey (whose last name emphasizes his masculinity – and perhaps his attitude as well) *attacks* Gladney with his knowledge of tools, themselves symbols of his physicality. Gladney does not have these supposedly useful physical skills; instead, he is a white-collar worker, and his labour is of the intellectual sort. Because of this, Gladney feels that his masculinity is inferior to Vernon's. The result of this anxiety is, as is often the case in DeLillo's fiction, violent action: Vernon, the more stereotypically masculine character, gives Gladney a gun,[21] an obvious phallic object, which Gladney later uses to shoot Mink.[22] DeLillo's male protagonists often resort to violent action as the remedy for a loss of agency,[23] and the symbol of this lost agency is usually the encroachment on the male subject of materialist, domestic space.

DeLillo's concern with materialism's (and often specifically domesticity's) effects on characters is not new to *Libra*. Indeed, this is a recurring concern for DeLillo, one that is also a major focus of works he
previously published in *Esquire*. For example, "In the Men's Room of
the Sixteenth Century" (December 1971) focuses on a cross-dressing
detective known as "Lady Madonna" and is thematically concerned
with the sacred and the profane; however, the profane is identified as
much by nonnormative sexuality as it is by consumerism (e.g., "the homoerotic wax museum," "the paraplegic sex exhibit," and the "pubic-
wig boutique").[24] The one act that draws violent response from the
story's protagonist is a business suggestion, made by one Grambling
Douglaston Clapper: "We've recently become interested in possession
by demons and plan to start a nationwide chain of clinics, to be run on
a franchise basis, devoted to exorcism and general postoperative therapy. We need somebody to run things from the spiritual standpoint.
We're basically business-oriented, you see."[25] The commercialization
of spiritualism seems to be the ultimate example of the dehumanizing
effects of materialism. The story implies that what is lacking in this
nightmare landscape is a proper form of masculinity, one that would
police strict gender roles and keep materialism in check.

"Human Moments in World War III" (July 1983) ignores questions
of the sacred, but provides perhaps the ultimate example of "men in
small rooms."[26] The narrative focuses on two astronauts who become
alienated from themselves and from humanity, feeling increasingly
impotent while orbiting the earth in a space capsule. Their capsule is
both weaponry and a domestic space, in which the astronauts listen
to "old radio shows" and feel "a sensation of prosperous well-being,
the consumer's solid comfort."[27] However, the story that most keenly
focuses on the negative effects of a consumerist-materialist lifestyle on
individual agency under late capitalism is "Players" (April 1977) published as a novel later that year. (The version in *Esquire* involves several
excerpts from part one of the novel, and concludes with "The Motel,"
the final scene from the complete novel.) DeLillo characterizes Lyle,
the story's male protagonist, through the objects around him. One
of Lyle's recurring characteristics is his television-watching habits: he
flips through the channels incessantly, finding comfort not through
the narrative or the images that the TV offers, but from the ritual
of technology itself.[28] Another of his rituals highlights the degree to
which Lyle depends on material things: "Lyle checked his pockets
for change, keys, wallet, cigarettes, pen, memo pad. He did this six

or seven times a day, absently, his hand skimming over trousers and jacket while he was walking, after lunch, leaving cabs. It was a routine that reassured him of the presence of objects and their locations."[29] Lyle's life is so caught up in the material world that he seemingly cannot extricate himself from the objects that surround him. His self-hood seemingly collapses into materialism.

A masculinity project that is uncomfortable with consumerism is therefore out of place in an advanced, consumerist society, and so cannot be properly hegemonic. At the centre of *Libra* is Win Everett, a semiretired CIA operative who practises a type of masculinity adversarial to consumerism. Everett's plot to shoot at Kennedy (and miss) stems from doubting, and wanting to prove, his own masculine agency. It is no surprise that the highly patriarchal gender regime of the CIA,[30] from which Everett is semiretired, fittingly punished Win for his past transgressions by finding him a position on the faculty at Texas Woman's University (19). Everett primarily hopes to re-establish his masculinity through the authoring of secrets,[31] contrasted with the domestic lifestyle he is forced to live in their absence.

The section of *Libra* that introduces Win was published, in excerpted form, in the September 1988 issue of *Esquire* under the title "The Lone Gunman Theory." Tellingly, Everett's domestic environment prefaces his first appearance:

> American kitchens. This one has a breakfast nook, where a man named Walter Everett Jr. was sitting, thinking – Win, as he was called – lost to the morning noises collecting around him, a stir of the all-familiar, the heartbeat mosaic of every happy home, toast springing up, radio voices with their intimate and busy timbre, an optimistic buzz living in the ear. The *Record-Chronicle* was at his elbow, still fresh in its newsboy fold. Images wavered in the sunlit trim of appliances, something always moving, a brightness flying, so much to know in the world. He stirred the coffee, thought, stirred, sat in the wide light, spoon dangling now, a gentle and tentative man, it would be fair to say, based solely on appearance. (15–16)

"American kitchens" take precedence over Everett in the paragraph's structure, subtly emphasizing the influence of Everett's surroundings over the plot he is soon to author. Everett's home life hedges him in and defines him: his introduction to the reader is crowded with domestic sounds and images from which he separates himself, "lost" in thought. But the reader might not see Everett as separate, as distinct, since this introduction is overwrought with breakfast smells and sounds, and kitchen appliances, as though Everett lives in a home décor catalogue.

The problem of distinguishing Everett from his material context reflects the problem of distinguishing the story from its material context in *Esquire*. As published in the magazine, domestic images surround and hedge in the excerpt itself. As Ruth Helyer has argued, DeLillo's fiction "suggests that masculinity ... is an insecure construction based on dominant societal norms and presented via mediated images."[32] It is therefore worthwhile to analyse DeLillo's fiction as it was contextualized within a field of such mediated images. Full page advertisements focused on food and dining, such as Rémy Martin cognac and *Food & Wine* magazine,[33] interrupt the text of "The Lone Gunman Theory," as well as advertisements which implicitly identify the reader's masculinity as being in need of supplementing by way of consumption: for example, a JCPenney advertisement for men's wear states that "You've got to get up pretty early to beat a Stafford Man," while an ad for Foltene Shampoo states that "One Out Of 20 Needn't Worry About Thinning Hair. This Is For The Other 19."[34] At the end of the novel excerpt, another full-page advertisement shows a couple kissing; the top of the ad features a quotation that reads "We've told each other 'I love you' a thousand times. But it took a diamond like this to leave her speechless."[35] These advertisements rhetorically suggest that the reader is insufficiently masculine to succeed in the contest between men (a contest often fought over women). The Foltene advertisement, for example, is directed towards the supposed 95 per cent of men who need help with their thinning hair, not the 5 per cent who do not; moreover, it implies that thinning hair needs help, since thinning hair is a sign of aging that undermines the practice of hegemonic masculinity. These advertisements hail the reader: if successfully interpellated, he must identify his own masculinity as deficient, either based on his appearance (clothing, hair) or in his relationship with women, and consequently turn to the consumer solutions offered within the magazine. The Service Merchandise ad vows that diamonds can provide a form of mastery over women which standard communication cannot; furthermore, standard communication implies mutual dependence, whereas capitalist interpellation – based on mechanisms of ownership – implies mastery and control. These consumer items promise to supplement masculinity, but only by defining the reader's masculinity as always already deficient.

These processes of hailing and interpellation, and the rhetoric of masculinity as either surplus or lacking, are intrinsic parts of how men negotiate hegemonic masculinity in the marketplace. *Esquire* directs its masculinity project at an ideal readership that is conversant in consumerist processes and understands them as lifestyle choices. However, men like Everett do not see masculinity as something negotiated in the marketplace, and therefore find materialism emasculating. Everett later describes his domestic routine as a kind of Sisyphean ritual: "He checked the front door. The days came and went. Bedtime again. Always bedtime now. He went around turning off lights, checked the back door, checked to see that the oven was off. This meant all was well" (148). DeLillo firmly situates his character in the domestic sphere: Everett measures out his daily life in bedtime routines, and he finds his masculinity depleted by the signs of materialism and domesticity all around him. In this way, at least, he is like Lyle in "Players," feeling his selfhood diminishing into materialism and domestic ritual.

Despite the continued normalization of the progress of consumer culture into everyday life, we have seen throughout this study that certain men – certain masculinities – continue to feel threatened by consumerism and domesticity. A significant part of the continuous renegotiation of hegemonic masculinity relates to finding new ways to assuage this anxiety. In this way, Everett's anxieties are fairly common, and his response to these anxieties is another iteration of agency panic. As Timothy Melley has argued, *Libra*'s male characters, fearing the emasculation of domesticity, come to equate self-sufficiency and self-determination with the keeping of secrets.[36] Indeed, while Everett is introduced in the kitchen, seemingly "a gentle and tentative man," he is in fact "thinking about secrets. Why do we need them and what do they mean?" (16). For Everett, "there's something vitalizing in a secret" (26), implying that secrets carry with them a kind of potency absent from his domestic life of coffee and breakfast nooks, which are depicted as feminine spaces. In Everett's case, the association between the feminine and the domestic is firmly established in the figure of his wife, Mary Francis, who "worried about the worn-out rug, thought about breakfast, thought about lunch, tried not to be too foolishly proud of the renovated kitchen, large, handsome, efficient, with its frostless freezer and color-matched appliances, on the quiet street of oak and pecan trees, forty miles north of Dallas" (31). Everett thinks about secrets, authors conspiracies, and plots his revenge against the agency that he feels abandoned him; Mary Francis thinks about her *things*. Mary Francis's pride in her renovated kitchen clearly genders the domestic sphere as feminine, within which Win, surrounded by the kitchen but lost in thought, is clearly uneasy. It would be easy to see this chauvinist conception of gender as a symptom of the novel's gender politics – that is, to compare Everett's "important" thoughts to his wife's superficial concerns – but DeLillo, I would argue, is too so-phisticated a commentator on gender, and especially masculinity, for one to make such a facile assumption. Rather, it is worth considering that Everett's obsession with secrets, with control and agency, and his discomfort in the domestic sphere, reveal a masculine anxiety which is held up to scrutiny in the novel, and which is manifested in the trope of small rooms. Furthermore, Everett's anxious masculinity points to the superiority of *Esquire*'s hegemonic masculinity project, since it spe-cifically exerts dominance through the marketplace.

Several critics have commented on the centrality of small rooms to the novel. Marilyn Wesley, for instance, refers to the small room as the "predominant setting, connoting confinement, debasement, isolation, powerlessness, and unreality, contradicts (even as it recalls) the deviant power, illicit passion, and esoteric knowledge of the epic-inspired 'undergrounds' of traditional literature and revolutionary politics."[37] Similarly, Lino Belleggia, in an article focused on the small rooms in the novel, argues that this recurring motif is DeLillo's met-aphor "for the claustrophobic condition of postmodern subjects in postmodern society."[38] Belleggia points to a statement made by De-Lillo regarding the significance of small rooms:

> I see contemporary violence as a kind of sardonic response to the prom-ise of consumer fulfilment in America. Again we come back to these men in small rooms who can't get out and who have to organize their desperation and their loneliness, who have to give it a destiny and who often end up doing this through violent means.[39]

Most of the small rooms in *Libra* are domestic spaces – bedrooms, kitchens, and so forth. These small rooms are sometimes notable for their surfeit of consumer items (such as Everett's kitchen) or for a dearth of them (as in Oswald's many living spaces); in either case, the small rooms are the material manifestation of the male characters' threatened masculinity.

Jack Ruby, Oswald's eventual assassin, haunts small rooms. Despite his being a strip club owner and an eventual assassin, much of Ruby's narrative is confined to, and concentrated on, his home. Much is made of Ruby's domestic situation: he lives with a roommate, George Senator, because "Living alone was a pressure situation" (346). Ruby remembers the time when "he took a room in a cheap walk-up hotel and isolated himself for eight weeks with the shades drawn, eating only enough to stay alive. He was a nothing person" (345). Ruby's fear of isolation takes on the familiar form of the small room. His home is bigger, messier, more expansive; like many of the novel's characters, he spends much of his time at home in the kitchen. Ruby is perhaps even more ambiguous about his sexuality than Oswald, asking one of his strippers, "Do I look swishy to you, Janet? What about my voice? People tell me there's a lisp. Is this the way a queer sounds to a neutral person? Do you think I'm latent or what? Could I go either way? Don't pee on my legs, Janet. I want the total truth" (352). Following the pattern set in the novel, the small domestic spaces that Ruby inhabits are emblematic of his anxiety about his own masculine heteronormativity – an anxiety that he explicitly addresses in the above quotation – and this masculine anxiety is a contributing factor to his later violent outburst, in which he murders Oswald.

Everett and Ruby may feel hedged in and emasculated by their domestic surroundings, but fittingly it is Lee Harvey Oswald, the novel's principal character and would-be assassin, who is most obviously shaped in the kitchen. He teaches himself to play and subsequently practices chess at the kitchen table (6, 36), does homework there (38), sleeps on a cot in the kitchen when in Fort Worth (133), and writes one of his subversive histories there (141). Following the established pattern, Oswald's domestic surroundings seem to be the material manifestation of his problematic relationship to his masculinity. Philip Nel outlines several of the "masculine failings" that underpin Lee's violent actions, including not only his attempt on Kennedy's life, but also his assaults on Marina (232, 240–2) and his attempt on the life of Edwin Walker (269–92), the latter excerpted in *Esquire* as "Oswald in the Lonestar State." Nel argues that "DeLillo does not portray Oswald as a gay man but one who is persecuted for being read as gay, for not conforming strictly to 'norms' of heterosexual masculinity."[40] Again and again, throughout the narrative, Oswald's heterosexuality is called into question, and his masculinity is thus threatened with subordination. This repetition establishes a pattern, and this pattern

highlights the connection between a supposed dearth of masculinity
and the kind of violent search for agency in which Oswald engages.
As Wesley notes, *Libra* is "an examination of violence as agency in
contemporary society";[41] more importantly, though, this connection
between violence and agency is only present in the male characters,
who seek agency through violence because they feel that their own
masculinity is threatened or deficient.

DeLillo's novel features a cast of male characters who are troubled
with their masculinity, feeling a lack of agency and control as something that results from a highly consumerist world. As Wesley argues,
the heroes of DeLillo's novels "experience lack of communal meaning and social order as a problem of power and try to re-establish the
terms of masculine selfhood that is supposed to support it."[42] In opposition to these alienated and fragmented masculinities is the idea of
a truly hegemonic form of masculinity that can re-establish patriarchy
and masculine control. This is Kennedy himself, who, as president,
acts as an exemplar of masculinity and a representative man. And,
indeed, he does act as a unifying form of masculinity inasmuch as the
male characters in the novel seemingly unify in a loose conspiracy
against him.

2. "Suck in That Gut, America!": JFK's Exemplary Masculinities

On 22 November 1963, Tom Wicker, the then relatively unknown
White House correspondent for *The New York Times,* was riding in the
presidential motorcade when Kennedy was shot. Wicker's subsequent
reporting of the event launched him into the national limelight:

> The searing images of that day – the rifleman's shots cracking across
> Dealey Plaza, the wounded president lurching forward in the open
> limousine, the blur of speed to Parkland Memorial Hospital and the
> nation's anguish as the doctors gave way to the priests and a new era –
> were dictated by Mr. Wicker from a phone booth in stark, detailed prose
> drawn from notes scribbled on a White House itinerary sheet. It filled
> two front-page columns and the entire second page, and vaulted the
> writer to journalistic prominence overnight.[43]

Subsequently, Wicker published two articles on Kennedy in *Esquire.*
The first, published only months after the assassination – and in the
same issue as one instalment of Mailer's *An American Dream* – was

entitled "Kennedy Without the Tears." The second, published years later, was entitled "Kennedy Without End, Amen" and offers some insights into understanding the retrospective importance of Kennedy.

In this later piece, Wicker explains what Kennedy had come to represent in the years immediately following his death: apparently, young people asked questions about Kennedy "in tones that suggest he is to them a mythic figure – not because of Vietnam but in spite of it, not that they believe in Camelot as a fact or an achievement, but because they have an idea that there was a time, associated with him, of action and hope, youth and confidence, long before today's drift and deadlock and rancor."[44] Kennedy, then, came to represent a kind of "golden age" for America, one associated with the young president's characteristics, characteristics which, during his time in office, were associated with his masculinity. Wicker goes on to suggest, "Merely that he was cut down as he was on a sunlit day, in the bloody mess of his mortality, might have been enough to establish him forever as the symbol of all our incompleted [sic] selves, spoiled dreams, blasted hopes."[45] Because these words were published in *Esquire*, and because of the masculine image that Kennedy fostered and enjoyed during his lifetime (and afterwards), I would suggest that one way the image of Kennedy functions is as an exemplar of a hegemonic form of masculinity, one suited to face the supposed problems of the time, specifically problems to be faced by "men."

By the beginning of 1960, Arthur Schlesinger, Jr argued that "exhaustion" caused the "torpor" of the fifties, resulting in "sterility in our conduct of foreign affairs" and "the politics of fatigue."[46] The president most associated with the 1950s was Dwight D. Eisenhower, the paternalistic elder statesmen. Only youthful vigour would remedy the "exhaustion," "sterility," and "fatigue" of the Eisenhower years: as Schlesinger claimed, "the Sixties will confront an economy of abundance. There are still pools of poverty which have to be mopped up, but the central problem will be increasingly that of fighting for individual dignity, identity and fulfillment in an affluent mass society."[47] What was needed was not just a leader, but a vigorous leader – an exemplar of masculinity.

Even before his presidential inauguration, Kennedy had been inaugurated as an exemplary masculinity, as demonstrated in the pages of *Esquire*. When asked who should be president in the January 1960 issue of the magazine, Norman Mailer replied "If I have a choice at all it is probably Kennedy. I doubt if he possesses any more political

courage than the other candidates, but I suspect he is a little more tal-
ented *as a man.*"[48] Hardly a resounding endorsement of Kennedy as a
politician, but Mailer's qualification of his choice is telling, especially
considering Jackson Katz's argument that an American president's
success as president is directly linked to his masculine performance.[49]
Mailer's comment reflects this popular perception: he chooses Kennedy above all others because he assumes that his masculinity will
equate to success in the Oval Office.

Mailer would go on to discuss Kennedy at length, especially in the
pages of *Esquire*. It was in that magazine that he published his famous
essay "Superman Comes to the Supermart," where he dubs Kennedy
"The Hipster as Presidential Candidate" and discusses him in terms
that underline his position as an exemplar of masculinity:

> No one had much doubt that Kennedy would be nominated, but if
> elected he would be not only the youngest President ever to be chosen
> by voters, he would be the most conventionally attractive young man ever
> to sit in the White House ... Of necessity the myth would emerge once
> more, because America's politics would now be also America's favorite
> movie, America's first soap opera, America's best-seller ... "Well, there's
> your first hipster," says a writer one knows at the convention, "Sergius
> O'Shaugnessy born rich," and the temptation is to nod, for it could be
> true, a war hero, and the heroism is bona fide, even exceptional, a man
> who has lived with death, who, crippled in the back, took on an opera-
> tion which would kill him or restore him to power, who chose to marry
> a lady whose face might be too imaginative for the taste of a democracy
> which likes its first ladies to be executives of home-management, a man
> who courts political suicide by choosing to go all out for a nomination
> four, eight, or twelve years before his political elders think he is ready, a
> man who announces a week prior to the convention that the young are
> better fitted to direct history than the old.[50]

Significantly, Mailer lavishes praise on Kennedy for his masculine
exploits (his war record, his beautiful wife, his political boldness)
rather than focusing on any of his political positions. More to the
point, Mailer sees in Kennedy as the embodiment of an exemplary
masculinity he himself fashioned years earlier – the Hipster, or "the
White Negro." Kennedy is not only politically powerful, but fits that
role which Mailer identifies as the future of white, hegemonic masculinity. For Mailer, the Hipster is the identity necessary for breaking the

stultifying bonds of social conformity, which he connects with the figure of the "square," a figure associated with 1950s conformity. As the
1960s began, the Hipster was set to ascend to the presidency, making
Kennedy doubly significant as an exemplar of masculinity.

As the comparison to Mailer's "White Negro" character suggests,
Kennedy was an exemplar of a "new" – or at least newly dominant –
formulation of hegemonic masculinity, one that resonated with *Esquire*. Indeed, Stephen Marche argues that Kennedy was "the ideal
subject for *Esquire* magazine," further noting that "No one has been
written about in *Esquire* more regularly or more thoroughly," and "No
one has appeared on more *Esquire* covers."[51] K.A. Cuordileone, discussing Kennedy's masculinity and Mailer's essay, sees in the president
a competing figure to the dreaded Organization Man of 1950s conformity. Kennedy's masculinity was characterized by "virility as well as …
much-touted style."[52] Kennedy's presidency reconciled "intellect, education, cultural refinement, and liberalism itself with masculine virility" (169–70), and was therefore "bound up with the cultural trends
that male dissenters like Mailer and Hefner shaped."[53] The reference
to *Playboy* founder Hugh Hefner is significant: Cuordileone argues
that Kennedy's masculinity was exemplary of the "Liberal as *Playboy*," a
gender project characterized by "power, style, youth, glamour, adventure, and virility,"[54] one that was exalted in *Playboy* magazine.

However, I would argue that it would be more accurate to see in
Kennedy an exemplar of masculinity more in keeping with *Esquire*'s
hegemonic masculinity project. Stefan Cieply, referencing Barbara
Ehrenreich's influential *The Hearts of Men*, explains the difference between *Esquire* masculinity and *Playboy*'s gender project: "Hedonism,
Ehrenreich argues, represented a cathartic liberation from the stifling
responsibilities of work, family and respectability. To this end, *Playboy* promised a way to elude the 'bondage of breadwinning.'"[55] However, while Kennedy fits many of the characteristics of the playboy, he
hardly represents a flight from family and responsibility. As Cieply
argues, *Esquire* provides a counter-example to the type of *Playboy* masculinity under discussion. *Esquire*'s ideal readers are consumers, like
the Playboy, but in consuming they do not abandon commitment and
family.[56]

The importance of highlighting this distinction is to note that the
men who feel threatened by Kennedy – Everett, Banister, and Oswald –
are the ones who perceive the domestic sphere as emasculating. They
therefore practice a type of masculinity that cannot adequately maintain

patriarchy in a consumerist society – their claims to hegemony (and thus their sense of emasculation) are challenged. Kennedy, on the other hand, represents a kind of masculinity that embraces consumerism *and* responsibility, domesticity *and* virile toughness. Kennedy represented the hegemonic masculinity for *Esquire* that, as Cieply argues, was "invested in fashioning an identity of sophisticated toughness that neutralised the problematic anti-consumerist rhetoric of much mid-century social criticism, all the while advocating the critics' calls for a dynamic, virile and authentic masculine individualism."[57] In Kennedy, *Esquire*'s readers find an exemplar of sophistication, toughness, and masculine individualism that was at home in the mediated world of consumption.

This is not to say that Kennedy's masculinity was directly opposed to "Cold Warrior" masculinity; on the contrary, Kennedy's masculine persona was similarly based on the belief that power was central to politics[58] and relied on the figure of the cowboy. Importantly, Kennedy, through the media, fashioned a type of "Cold Warrior" masculinity that sutures the (gendered) features of the cowboy to an urbane, intellectual form of masculinity, one at home with consumption and a life of luxury. Though his life seemed to exemplify sophistication, Kennedy flavoured his rhetoric with appeals to the American frontier, in a style Reagan would later elaborate. In his acceptance speech at the 1960 Democratic National Convention, Kennedy famously stated that "we stand today on the edge of a New Frontier – the frontier of the 1960's – a frontier of unknown opportunities and perils – a frontier of unfulfilled hopes and threats." Robert Dean finds in Kennedy's cabinet the "composite picture of the ideal 'New Frontiersman.'" Kennedy's staff and cabinet were not only competent men, but "exemplars of masculine virtue."[59] Kennedy augmented his masculinity not only through the company of these "New Frontiersmen," but also by projecting "an image of youth, 'vigor,' moral courage, and 'toughness.'"[60] Kennedy's masculine persona was constructed and disseminated in the same manner as a Hollywood star's, even if the venue was not the red carpet but the White House.

It is therefore worth comparing Kennedy to another exemplar of masculinity, one that plays an important role in DeLillo's novel: John Wayne. Comparing Kennedy to Wayne demonstrates how DeLillo comments on the mobilization of exemplary masculinities, and how Kennedy is both similar to and significantly different from a "standard" exemplary masculinity. Indeed, throughout the novel, Oswald's augments his masculine fantasies with other exemplary masculinities.

Oswald makes reference to several exemplary masculinities, each of which represents a life he hopes to emulate, but that he can never achieve. Two of them are familiar faces in this study. For instance, when in Russia, Oswald explains that he wants to model his career off of Ernest Hemingway (161). More significantly, in Atsugi, Oswald (Ozzie) meets with John Wayne:[61]

> He wants to get close to John Wayne, say something authentic. He watches John Wayne talk and laugh. It's remarkable and startling to see the screen laugh repeated in life. It makes him feel good. The man is doubly real. He does not cheat or disappoint. When John Wayne laughs, Ozzie smiles, he lights up, he practically disappears in his own glow. Someone takes a photograph of John Wayne and the officers, and Ozzie wonders if he will show up in the background, in the passageway, grinning. (94–5)

Oswald's idolization of Wayne, and Wayne's role as a fantasy figure is highlighted by the narrative voice, focalized in Oswald, that cannot ever refer to John Wayne as merely "Wayne," the person's last name, and instead can only refer to "John Wayne," the full name of the celebrity persona that cannot be shortened. Oswald's attraction to Wayne is that the latter is real – "doubly real" – and so Oswald wants to say to Wayne something "authentic." For Oswald, Wayne's "realness" contrasts the supposedly virtual, inauthentic world of the American kitchens in which so many of DeLillo's characters find themselves. This is, of course, paradoxical, since what Oswald is reacting to in Wayne is not the "real" person but his celebrity. Wayne himself is a consumer item, an image.

What Wayne provides for Oswald is a model for a masculine fantasy of violent agency. As Philip Nel notes, Lee learned to equate violence and masculinity from a host of "hypermasculine" figures, including Wayne, and Lee performs the role of the assassin in much the same way that Wayne played the role of the cowboy.[62] Films and novels provide exemplary masculinities from which Oswald can extract a model of behaviour: after taking up the role of a spy, he even begins reading a James Bond novel (182). Similarly, shortly before the assassination he watches two films: *Suddenly*, in which Frank Sinatra plays a combat veteran intending to assassinate the president, and *We Were Strangers*, in which John Garfield plays a revolutionary. Nel astutely notes that by closely positioning the assassination to the scene of Oswald watching the two films, DeLillo encourages the reader to equate the violence of heroic Hollywood masculinity with Lee's shooting of the president.[63] Oswald surrounds himself with fantasy figures who promise agency through violence, and therefore he finds himself driven to achieve the same agency through both violence and the quest to become, like Wayne, an icon.

Wayne is "doubly real" to Oswald, but the doubling of his realness comes from the fact that Wayne matches the image of John Wayne. This is a capacity that Wayne shares with Kennedy, of whom it is said that "He looked like himself, like photographs, a helmsman squinting in the sea-glare, white teeth shining" (395). As Carmichael argues of Wayne (though it could be equally true of Kennedy), "the complete coincidence of John Wayne with his own specular image which makes Wayne so appealing for Oswald is precisely that which is denied Oswald everywhere."[64] Oswald hopes, in some small way, to also become "doubly real," inasmuch as he hopes to exist in a photograph with Wayne; in this way, he would exist as both man and image, just as John Wayne does, though to a much lesser extent. This double existence is, perhaps, exactly what Oswald achieves in his final moments:

> There was something in Oswald's face, a glance at the camera before he was shot, that put him here in the audience, among the rest of us, sleepless in our homes – a glance, a way of telling us that he knows who we are and how we feel, that he has brought our perceptions and interpretations into his sense of the crime. Something in the look, some sly intelligence, exceedingly brief but far-reaching, a connection all but bleached away by glare, tells us that he is outside the moment, watching with the rest of us. (452)

Here, Oswald has, perhaps, achieved his goal, by becoming one with his image, in the instant before the shot that kills him. Oswald has, in a sense, done what "Cold Warrior" masculinity demanded: he has tried to augment his masculinity through recourse to violence, and modelled his behaviour after the exemplary masculinities that surround him in the cultural field. The fact that this leads to infamy, not agency, only underscores the fact that hegemonic masculinity is defined by exclusion, not inclusion, and that exemplary masculinities are fantasies which, as symbols, authorize hegemonic masculinity, but whose actual behaviour cannot guarantee hegemonic status. Oswald's death gives the lie to the implicit promise of exemplary masculinities, that supposedly masculine traits actually equate to hegemonic power.

It is clear, then, that the novel reflects just how exemplary masculinities work, and that Kennedy is like Wayne in that they both seem to enjoy this status. More to the point, *Libra* develops an aspect of exemplary masculinities which Connell's analysis has not touched on: that is, as much as exemplary masculinities reinforce hegemonic masculinity, they can also alienate men by baldly demonstrating a degree of exalted masculinity to which they do not favourably compare. To return to the Foltene Shampoo advertisement from *Esquire*: the one in 20 men who does not have thinning hair represents a figure to emulate, but his rare, desirably masculine characteristics are also a reminder of how most men do not have what he has. The advertisement works by demonstrating what most men lack to create the desire to fill this lack. Similarly, John Wayne may provide a model for masculine behaviour, but, as discussed in the last chapter, attempting to emulate Wayne might result in "John Wayne syndrome." Kennedy's exemplary status provides a model for American men – especially the consumerist, white-collar men to whom *Esquire* is targeted – but it can also alienate men by demonstrating their insufficient masculine characteristics.

Kennedy's role as president exacerbates his exemplary masculinity and the role it plays in the gender order, as Marina's dreaming demonstrates:

> She wondered how many women had visions and dreams of the President. What must it be like to know you are the object of a thousand longings? It's as though he floats over the landscape at night, entering dreams and fantasies, entering the act of love between husbands and wives. He floats through television screens into bedrooms at night. He floats from the radio into Marina's bed. There were times when she waited for him, actually listened late at night for a few words of a speech or a news conference recorded earlier in the day, waited for the voice of the President, the radio on a table near the bed. (326)

Marina's fantasy highlights Kennedy's own fantasy status, allowing him total access to America, or at least to the American imagination. For Marina, the President is the object of a thousand longings; these longings give him power, especially over women.

This passage, which highlights JFK's role as a fantasy figure and his dominance over women, also explains that while he obviously reinforces patriarchy, his status actually alienates the majority of men. Here, Kennedy enters the domestic realm and comes "between husbands and wives." Kennedy potentially cuckolds men, and therefore his exemplary status can actually threaten men with emasculation, as demonstrated in the novel by Guy Banister's discussion of the president:

> "It's not just Kennedy himself," Banister was saying on the other side of the door. "It's what people see in him. It's the glowing picture we keep getting. He actually glows in most of his photographs. We're supposed to believe he's the hero of the age. Did you ever see a man in such a hurry to be great? He thinks he can make us a different kind of society. He's trying to engineer a shift. We're not smart enough for him. We're not mature, energetic, Harvard, world traveler, rich, handsome, lucky, witty. Perfect white teeth. It fucking grates on me just to look at him." (68)

Banister's description of his hatred for Kennedy is telling. He begins by discussing Kennedy's persona, the fantasy figure of the president that fulfills the role of an exemplary masculinity. Banister is aware, at least in the beginning, that he is not describing the president himself, but his image, or perhaps more precisely Banister is describing how Kennedy's persona is consumed as an image. Unlike Oswald, then, Banister recognizes this exemplar of masculinity as an unattainable fantasy, and responds to this unattainability with anger. If there is any doubt that Banister's involvement in the plot against Kennedy is motivated by his feeling of wounded (or insufficient) masculinity rather than, for example, simple pride or even revenge, these doubts should be erased by his discussion with his co-conspirators, when he asks "How much of my manhood is watery puke? That's what I want to know" (64).

Furthermore, Banister connects Kennedy's (fantastic) masculine image with the president's (real) plans for the country. He ends his description by enumerating the characteristics of Kennedy's masculine persona, virtually echoing – or in this case, prefiguring – the details of Dean's previously noted sketch of the "New Frontiersman": "youth, 'vigor,' moral courage, and 'toughness.'"[65] In doing so, he echoes Wesley's description of the "representative man." Describing the aspects of the epic she sees at play in *Libra*, Wesley argues that, "the contemporary epic records the continued longing for the whole and representative man, the man whose developmental trajectory stands not for the achievement of the individual ego but for the integration of the state."[66] Wesley goes on to discuss Oswald as DeLillo's attempt at crafting a "representative man," but the quotation points towards the equally important example of Kennedy. Kennedy may not have been a monarch, but aside from being America's head of state, he also belonged to a political dynasty, and his presidency was popularly referred to as "Camelot." In *Libra*, DeLillo emphasizes this connection to the monarchy, noting that Kennedy kept a scrap of paper on him, with the words "*They whirl asunder and dismember me*," from Shakespeare's *The Life and Death of King John*, scribbled on it (396).[67] Much of Kennedy's symbolic importance stemmed from the fact that he seemed to represent an American aristocracy, an ideal version of American masculinity for the 1960s.

Connecting Kennedy's political and cultural designs for "a different kind of society" with a description of his image, Banister seems to conflate the body of the president with the state of the nation, in a manner reminiscent of medieval associations between king and country. Furthermore, he seems concerned that the nation simply cannot live up to Kennedy's image, that "we" (perhaps the "we" of "We the people") are not smart enough, rich enough, handsome enough.[68] What Banister is detailing here is the tension that arises when a so-called "representative man," an epic hero, and an exemplary masculinity are merged in one persona, and, more to the point, when this happens in a democratic society.

It may seem contradictory to describe JFK as both *representative* and *exemplary*. Kennedy is the people's actual "representative" in the democratic sense, yet Donald Pease argues that when the characters of democratic representatives are idealized, they stop being reflective of who the people really are and instead become what the American people would like themselves to be.[69] It is worth remembering that Kennedy is not only a "representative" of the people, but "representative" to the extent that he (or at least his image) embodies certain characteristics, or even ideals, of a generation (or of whatever group he is believed to represent). Both "representative man" and exemplars of masculinity are fantasy figures. The representative man is a fantasy, since, as Nelson states, "No single citizen can stand for the 'whole' unless 'we' are all radically and repressively the same, unless some (even many) of 'us' drop out (or into the margins) of the picture."[70] Through his election to the office of the president, Kennedy becomes "representative," an embodiment of the will of the people.

Mailer presents a similar perspective in his famous essay on Kennedy: "a hero embodies his time and is not so very much better than his time, but he is larger than life and so is capable of giving direction to the time, able to encourage a nation to discover the deepest colors of its character."[71] Recalling Wesley's statement that, in the tradition of the epic, the representative man's "developmental trajectory" represents "the integration of the state,"[72] it follows that the body of Kennedy is a powerful locus for the forces of masculine domination. Through his masculine embodiment, masculinity becomes the hinge between democratic representation *and* hegemonic domination.

However, Kennedy is not an unproblematic exemplar of masculinity. As Banister's ruminations on Kennedy make clear, Kennedy's masculine status may reinforce patriarchy, but this image is not just an "unattainable fantasy" but a *simulacrum* of masculinity, after DeLillo's usual modus operandi. As Jesse Kavadlo notes, critics have often associated Jean Baudrillard's simulacrum with DeLillo's novels, especially *White Noise* and its "Most Photographed Barn."[73] According to Baudrillard, in "the era of simulacra and simulation" we can no longer "separate the false from the true, the real from its artificial resurrection, as everything is already dead and resurrected in advance."[74] Kennedy, like Wayne, is *like* his image; the image of Kennedy takes precedence over the man – thoroughly disseminated, as his image is, through cultural institutions – until finally he becomes an exemplar of a hyperreal, postmodern masculinity, baring no relation to real men whatsoever.

Consequently, Kennedy's masculinity can only offer a kind of negative integration for other masculinities, and his exemplary and representative status is understood as more of a threat than a salve to the characters of the novel – a reminder, first, of their own imperfect manhood, but also of the imperfectability or insufficiency of all masculinity. Alternatively, a less evident form of unifying masculinity is found in the role of the author, a figure, exemplified by DeLillo himself, who can make sense and take control of the world around him.

3. Getting a Grip on the Runaway World: The Author as Exemplary Masculinity

If there is still room for the self-made man in America, the autonomous or even rootless individual man who can exist removed from the system and still maintain his agency, then according to Don DeLillo, that figure is the novelist:

> The writer is the person who stands outside society, independent of affiliation and independent of influence. The writer is the man or woman who automatically takes a stance against his or her government. There are so many temptations for American writers to become part of the system and part of the structure that now, more than ever, we have to resist. American writers ought to stand and live in the margins, and be more dangerous. Writers in repressive societies are considered dangerous. That's why so many of them are in jail.[75]

Here, DeLillo speaks of authorship in a way that sets the writer up against the previously discussed figure of the Organization Man, succinctly reproducing this crisis narrative. For DeLillo, the writer "stands outside of society," somehow able to extricate himself from the systems within which DeLillo's own characters find themselves fully imbricated. From this privileged position, the writer fights the system, or, in this case, the Establishment. DeLillo even describes the writer's particular form of agency according to the logic of the masculine anxiety we have been discussing: he sees the writer's actions as "dangerous," implying the writer's capacity to do violence, if only a symbolic form of violence, to the systems he opposes. It is the figure of the author, then, who is held up as an exemplary masculinity: he cannot mend the fractured masculinity of the so-called "American century," but he can begin to make sense of it, creating for it – in this instance – a unifying narrative about that very fracturing.

Libra itself continually reflects on the role of the author, which recommends bringing an analysis of DeLillo's concept of authorship into the discussion. At least two characters attempt to find their agency through authorship: Everett and Oswald. Everett, of course, is the author of the conspiracy, the plot against Kennedy. Everett constructs the plot out of "Pocket litter" (50), sitting at a desk in his basement. This process is described as though he were a novelist constructing a narrative: "Mackey would find a model for the character Everett was in the process of creating. They wanted a name, a face, a bodily frame they might use to extend their fiction into the world" (50).[76] The plot is a "fiction," and Oswald is the main character. This fiction that Everett is creating, a pro-Castro attempt on Kennedy's life, will prove his control of the world, his masculine agency. Everett not only wants his

old enemy Castro to be blamed for the attempt, thus potentially resulting in a war against Cuba and possibly Castro's death, but he also
hopes to implicate the CIA in the plot, avenging himself against his
former employers:

> He would not consider the plan a success if the uncovering of its succes-
> sive layers did not reveal the CIA's schemes, his own schemes in some
> cases, to assassinate Fidel Castro. This was the little surprise he was keep-
> ing for the end. It was his personal contribution to an informed public.
> Let them see what goes on in the committee rooms and corner offices.
> The pocket litter, the gunman's effects, the sidetrackings and back alleys
> must allow investigators to learn that Kennedy wanted Castro dead, that
> plots were devised, approved at high levels, put into motion, and that
> Fidel or his senior aides decided to retaliate. This was the major subtext
> and moral lesson of Win Everett's plan. (52–3)

Everett describes his hopes for his plan in terms associated with fictional narratives, noting the plan's "subtext" and "moral lesson," but
the major motivator seems to be self-aggrandizement (the fact that his
own schemes would be revealed, and the sheer breadth of his plot)
and revenge against the agency which relegated him to Texas Woman's University and "emasculated" him into semi-retirement.

However, while Everett is an author figure, he proves to be a failed
author. In short, his narrative gets away from him: he is unable to
maintain authority over the text. He reveals his worries in a passage
that further connects his plot with the writing of fiction, claiming that
"Plots carry their own logic. There is a tendency of plots to move toward death. He believed that the idea of death is woven into the nature of every plot. A narrative plot no less than a conspiracy of armed
men ... He worried about the deathward logic of his plot" (223). Indeed, Everett loses control, having authored not a failed assassination attempt, but an unintentional and successful assassination. As
Timothy Parrish argues, "Everett finds that the world responds [to his
fiction] with counterfictions. He becomes the author of plots never
intended."[77] As the plot gets away from him, Everett's presence in *Libra* lessens: we learn that he cooperates with the Agency's internal in-
vestigations (446), and in 1965 is found dead in a motel room where
he is staying under an assumed name (381–2).

Oswald, like Everett, seeks to gain prominence in his life through
authorship. He is a frequent diarist, constantly working on his

"Historic Diary." This is a document which "He wrote ... in two sittings, breaking for coffee at 4:00 A.M. He wanted to explain himself to posterity. People would read these words someday and understand the fears and aspirations of a man who only wanted to see for myself what socialism was like" (212). As with Everett, here there is an element of self-aggrandizement, a desire to write himself into history. However, Oswald is dyslexic, a handicap he cannot seem to overcome: "He made wild tries at phonetic spelling. But the language tricked him with its inconsistencies. He watched sentences deteriorate, powerless to make them right. The nature of things was to be elusive. Things slipped through his perceptions. He could not get a grip on the runaway world" (213). This last sentence, especially, highlights what is at stake for Oswald with his writing: writing is an act of making sense of the world. Indeed, before Oswald turns to violence, he sees writing as a method by which he may enter history; in fact, Parrish argues that "What makes Oswald coherent as a character is his desire to transform his self into language."[78]

The result of Oswald's dyslexia is fragmented and occasionally impenetrable prose: "*She is flabbergassed, but aggrees to help. Asks me about myself and my reasons for doing this. I explaine I am a communist, ect. She is politly sym. but uneasy now. She tries to be a friend to me. She feels sorry for me I am someth. new*" (150–1). Oswald's poor writing makes him a target for ridicule, especially when measured against his goals as a writer. Indeed, Oswald wants to model himself after Ernest Hemingway, explaining to Kirilenko that "I want to write short stories on contemporary American life" (161).[79] Hemingway is, of course, perhaps the American writer most associated with masculinity.[80] Oswald therefore models himself after *Esquire*'s original exemplar of masculinity; however, Oswald lacks the capability to describe and diagnose "contemporary American life" – a capability DeLillo himself demonstrates in writing *Libra* – and by comparing his own failed writing to Hemingway's Oswald only highlights his own masculine failings.

In addition to Everett and Oswald is Nicholas Branch, whose most prominent characteristic is his failure to write the Secret History of the assassination. Branch's project is therefore similar to DeLillo's; however, Branch's failure underscores DeLillo's apparent success. As Parrish explains, there is a significant difference between Branch and DeLillo: "DeLillo's fiction gains a purchase on the assassination precisely because it surrenders claims to historical veracity."[81] Both men are writers, but it is the novelist, not the historian, who can get a grip on the runaway world.

Oswald's goal of being like Hemingway reinforces the notion that it is only the author who can "get a grip" on the world around him. Branch implicates another modernist writer in his description of the Warren Report as "the megaton novel James Joyce would have written if he'd moved to Iowa City and lived to be a hundred" (182). As Parrish notes, "DeLillo's allusion to Joyce reveals the extent to which he remains attached to the traditional modernist ideal of the writer who can master the universe he writes."[82] Like Hemingway and Joyce, DeLillo can construct out of fragments a representation of the world around him: he cannot create a totality, the kind of fictive totality represented by Kennedy's masculinity, but he can make sense of the pieces.

Here, it is worth remembering Sandra Gilbert and Susan Gubar's classic discussion of Western society's traditional association of the penis with the pen. After citing Gerard Manley Hopkins's statement that "The male quality is the creative gift," Gilbert and Gubar explain that "Male sexuality, in other words, is not just analogically but actually the essence of literary power. The poet's pen is in some sense (even more than figuratively) a penis" within the patriarchal tradition.[83] According to this frank equation, by demonstrating a failure of authorship, Oswald, Everett, and Branch are in fact demonstrating their own impotence. Consequently, though Everett notes that "It is essential to master the data" (447), the data masters him, and as a result, he becomes fixated on his passive state, three times identifying his office as "the room of growing old" (14, 59, 450). Similarly, as Everett considers the plot getting away from him, he fantasizes about cooperating with the Agency (364–5). He slips at the top of a stairway, and his wife, Mary Frances, immediately "take[s] him by the elbow and lead[s] him inside," after which he confides in her: "I couldn't even begin to carry on if you somehow weren't well. I count on you for everything that matters" (366). The "Cold Warrior," questioning his competency as an author, finds himself, more than ever, subordinated to his wife who, as discussed, is thoroughly associated with domesticity.

Gilbert and Gubar further explain that patriarchy and authorship have a history of being confused one for the other. Western literary tradition has long held the notion that the writer is the "father" of his text; referencing Edward Said, they note that "the metaphor is built into the very word, *author*, with which writer, deity, and *pater familias* are identified."[84] DeLillo himself describes American literature as a patriarchal institution, a history of great men:

> Think of the postwar generation of writers. I'm talking specifically about male writers. Styron, Mailer, Vidal, Baldwin, and so on. Then think of the subsequent generation. Pynchon. McElroy. McGuane. Stone. Myself. A couple of others. If you were to give each group a choice of writing a novel about John F. Kennedy or Lee Harvey Oswald, what would be the result? It seems to me that the first group would choose Kennedy, and the second group, my group, would almost invariably choose Oswald.[85]

This quotation is significant, not, in this case, because of how DeLillo characterizes these two groups of writers, but because he perceives of American literature as being a paternal line of generations, implying fathers and sons and a completely homosocial national literature. Indeed, DeLillo's statement matches Gilbert and Gubar's argument even more closely, insofar as it sides the second generation with the figure who murders the figure representing the first generation: i.e., this is precisely the Oedipal relation that Gilbert and Gubar, relying on Harold Bloom, analyse and critique for its denial to women of authorship. DeLillo therefore demonstrates Bloom's "anxiety of influence" as read through Gilbert and Gubar's feminist lens, repudiating female authorship completely.[86]

Esquire itself is guilty of reinforcing the notion of authorship as essentially masculine. In July 1988, fiction editor Rust Hills introduces the "summer-reading" issue of the magazine by tying its current fiction to that published in the 1930s: "In those early days, our own Founding Fathers published the most-celebrated American writers of the time – Hemingway, Fitzgerald, Wolfe, Steinbeck – all the ones you recognize by their last names alone, as you do here with DeLillo and Mailer and Oates."[87] The inclusion of Joyce Carol Oates in this lineage of American writers keeps it from being a completely masculine collection of names, but she is listed last, while on the cover her name comes after not only Mailer and DeLillo, but the lesser known Bruce Jay Friedman and Jay McInerney. Hills's description of *Esquire*'s literary history parallels DeLillo's description of a homosocial, paternalistic American literature.

The aforementioned "summer-reading" issue features one of the two excerpts of *Libra* published in *Esquire*. Entitled "Oswald in the Lone Star State," the excerpt comprises much of the chapter "In

Dallas" from the finished novel. Incidentally, the cover features a close-up of Norman Mailer; his contribution to the issue is the first piece of his fiction that *Esquire* has published since its serialization of *An American Dream*. The magazine dedicates itself to the "Lives of the Authors," emphasizing the individuality and authority of each. The first page of "Oswald in the Lone Star State" is printed opposite a full-page portrait of DeLillo, aestheticizing DeLillo in much the same way as models found in the advertisements throughout the magazine. The author's name is also the predominant feature of the first page, significantly dwarfing the title of the piece. A highlighted box of dialogue advertises DeLillo, not his novel: "Back from the Future: DeLillo's made a habit of anticipating next year's disaster, of getting into the future to send back dispatches of bone-chilling humor from an America made exotic by technology. 'I've been prescient in poker games. A novelist just *sees* things before other people.'"[88] These highlighted side-boxes recur throughout the excerpt, two of them containing extreme close-ups of DeLillo, all of them containing his commentary. These boxes are darker and placed near the centre of the page; the effect is that the text of "Oswald in the Lone Star State" is subordinated to DeLillo's authorial intrusions.

Kavadlo, in a study of the role of authorship in the work of DeLillo (and specifically in *Underworld*), offers a way of conceptualizing how *Esquire* emphasizes an "elevated" idea of the author in *Libra*, arguing that real function of *Libra*'s Author's Note is "to remind the reader that the book was authored ... DeLillo's stance on silence, even when broken, seems to re-establish Romanticism and modernism's elevation of the author, albeit reflexively and perhaps ironically."[89] While DeLillo's aesthetics distance the author from the work, his photos and interviews in *Esquire*, which emphasize his reclusiveness and his separateness, actually elevate the author.

Of course, DeLillo is the author of *Libra* and the excerpt itself, but he is not the author of *Esquire* – the placement of his image and his extra-textual words on the page, and the design of the excerpt, were no doubt left up to the magazine, not the novelist. What is important, though, is how the magazine circulates the image of the author in much the same way that it circulates its advertising. What is for sale, in this instance, is the image of a certain kind of masculine agency that DeLillo seems to personify. Whereas JFK's exemplary masculinity seems possibly threatening, the author himself steps in as a suitable figure of "dynamic, virile and authentic masculine individualism." A subsequent dialogue box in "Oswald in the Lonestar State" implies just how DeLillo can be sold as an antidote to the emasculating effects of domesticity: it states that DeLillo "disdained the 'around-the-house-and-in-the-yard' fiction of domesticity popular then [in 1982]. 'It's ironic I wrote *White Noise* as a domestic novel' – the only one that features a toxic cloud, Hitler studies, and a pill to erase the fear of death."[90] Domesticity itself might be bad for masculinity, but DeLillo's satire of domesticity somehow provides a safety valve, an assurance of masculine hegemony.

4. Conclusion

Stefan Cieply discusses how the author was an important figure for *Esquire* in the 1960s (and, I would argue, into the 1980s), especially in relation to the Establishment. Cieply argues that *Esquire* advertises "lifestyle" as the arena in which masculinity can be fashioned. Quoting Mike Featherstone, Cieply argues that,

> under the regime of lifestyle, the self is an aesthetic project that reflects a 'stylisation of life'. Inherent in this sense of lifestyle as a 'life project', is a self-consciousness and an awareness of the 'in-process' nature of the self as a work-in-progress. Thus, the author and ... [*Esquire*'s ideal readership] share a common language of creation, destruction and rejuvenation. The creative agonies the writer suffers, in short, become the folklore of masculine individualism.[91]

This is to say that, "under the regime of lifestyle," the author is an important exemplar of masculinity – a white-collar worker who, through suffering and heroic accomplishment, can make sense of the world around him and a name for himself.

Esquire's summer reading issues of the 1980s were occasions to reiterate this heroic notion of authorship. Introducing the fiction in the 1986 issue, E.L. Doctorow asserts that "What we call fiction is the ancient way of knowing, the total discourse that antedates all the special vocabularies of modern intelligence."[92] Moving from this mythic idea of fiction, Doctorow then conceives of fiction writing as the ultimate act of individuality:

> Fiction ... reasserts the authority of the single mind to make and remake the world. By its independence from all institutions, from the family to

the government, and with no responsibility to defend their hypocrisy or murderousness, it is a valuable resource and instrument of survival.[93]

Independent from "all institutions," the fiction-writer is able to assert authority without compromising his self and his vision to the corrupting influence of the Establishment. The fiction writer, as presented in *Esquire*, provides answers to the same "problem[s] of the legitimacy of patriarchy"[94] as Mailer's "White Negro" figure – he asserts a form of masculinity that evades the stultifying effects of conformity and diminished agency that otherwise accompany institutionalized patriarchy.

This conception of the writer's masculinity is not new – as noted above, Hemingway set the mold for *Esquire* writers, granting the magazine at its inception a type of masculine legitimacy. Though DeLillo's novel troubles the idea of hegemonic masculinity and overtly denies the ability of the author to "master" the highly mediated, postmodern world in which he finds himself, the publication of his work in *Esquire* nevertheless foregrounds his own familiar role as an exemplar of masculinity. DeLillo's performance of authorship – and moreover, *Esquire*'s staging of DeLillo's authorship – contradicts the explicit argument about authorship staged in *Libra*. Instead, the magazine repurposes DeLillo's fiction, if not DeLillo himself, as a way for its ideal male reader to get a grip on his own runaway world.

Conclusion
How to Be a Man

In 2013, Narrative 4, which describes its goal as promoting empathy "through the exchange of stories across the world,"[1] partnered with *Esquire* to produce a website containing over one hundred contributions, each with the title "How to Be a Man." A selection of eighty, including stories by Salmon Rushdie, Khaled Hosseini, and Chimamanda Ngozi Adichie, was later published as *The Book of Men*. The very nature of Narrative 4's endeavour – to ask the question of "How to Be a Man" to authors, men and women from all over the globe, and to have them respond in a number of genres, whether poetry, essay, or fiction – points to the multiplicity of masculinities that crowd the gender order or seek dominance in different gender regimes.

"How to Be a Man" is a question that endures, because the answer not only promises to explain a man's relationship to his gender, and so make intelligible his relative position in a network of social relations, but also seeks to explain his relationship to power in a persistently patriarchal gender order. Being a man – practicing hegemonic masculinity – has seemingly always been about men's relationship to dominance, and *Esquire* has always advertised its hegemonic masculinity project as an answer, or as several answers, to this persisting question. In *Leading with the Chin*, I have argued that *Esquire* was an important venue for enabling American authors such as Norman Mailer, James Baldwin, Raymond Carver, Truman Capote, Tim O'Brien, and Don DeLillo to work through national fantasies of hegemonic masculinity, as those fantasies intersected with the Civil Rights era, the rise of contemporary consumer culture and neoliberalism, and the literary project of postmodernism.

The writing of canonical male authors is no longer central to *Esquire*; in fact, they seem more likely to publish fiction outside of their pages, such as the Narrative 4 collection, or a short-lived ebook series entitled "Fiction for Men." However, the magazine remains invested in examining the shape of American masculinity in the twenty-first century. The October 2014 issue of *Esquire* seems to tackle the issue of men's relationship to dominance – and, in the final instance, to violence – quite directly. The issue focuses almost entirely on the idea of mentoring or "building" men correctly. The centrepiece of the issue is interviews with dozens of men who identify the influential figures in their lives. The feature is entitled "Who Made You The Man You Are Today?" This idea of masculine mentorship is taken up in Mike Sager's "Are There Still Boy Scouts?,"[2] a feature that discusses the current state of the well-known organization. An interview with Robert Gates, its new national president, takes up much of the article. Gates is the former Secretary of Defence of the United States; in Althusser's terms, he is the former head of America's Repressive State Apparatus.[3] Gates's position as the president of the Boy Scouts highlights that organization's role as an Ideological State Apparatus; moreover, the paramilitary nature of the Boy Scouts reinforces Connell's claim that violence (either explicit or implicit) is central to the construction of certain masculinities.

Sager describes the Boy Scouts as existing in a moment of crisis: "the organization is struggling to find its place in a postmodern, politically correct, multicultural society. The scouts were founded in 1910, at a time when the country was becoming increasingly urbanized, when the familiarity of small-town life was giving way to the anonymity (and godlessness and heterogeneity) of the industrialized city."[4] Though Sager's description of the Boy Scouts' origin might be glib, it demonstrates the way the organization was conceived as a hegemonic masculinity project, one which intended to retrench a highly conservative, white, and heterosexual construction of masculinity against heterogeneous and perhaps irreligious, "othered" constructions of masculinity.

Discussing today's Scouts as a heterogeneous group, Sager focuses on the story of Romulda Vasquez Pena III, a Hispanic Scout leader whose troop is made up of youth from South-Central Los Angeles.[5] Indeed, Sager's story seems to indicate that the Scouts act most effectively when interpellating young, racialized men into a hegemonic, masculine subject position. Here are the workings of hegemonic masculinity writ large: through an act of renegotiation, hegemonic masculinity makes way for "othered" (in this case Hispanic) men, as long as they conform to other traditional masculine characters, ones which continue to symbolically reinforce masculine dominance.

Sager's story suggests that the alternative to the Scouts, at least for the Hispanic youth of Los Angeles, is life in violent criminal gangs. One implication is that male physicality can either be regulated and made to work for patriarchy, or be unregulated and destructive. This point is reinforced by the inclusion in the same issue of *Esquire* of Tom Junod's "Everything We Know About Mass Shooters is Wrong."[6] While the article never explicitly announces that mass shootings are a gendered problem – that is, that mass shooters are almost exclusively young men – the placement in *Esquire*, and especially this issue of *Esquire*, nonetheless indicates that mass shootings are a problem connected to masculinity. The "mass shooter" is a failed masculine figure, the poignant alternative to the Boy Scout. The "mass shooter" is the failure of hegemonic masculinity projects, but also – the placement in *Esquire* implies – a product of them. As Antonio Gramsci argues, hegemony is primarily established through leadership (the Boy Scouts model), but also through direct (i.e., violent) subordination.[7] Mass shootings are the nightmare version of masculine hegemony; *Esquire* argues that men must be properly educated into positions of dominance.

Concerns about the role of domination and violence in the construction of masculinity appear, also, in Narrative 4's collection. It is perhaps telling that female authors address these concerns most directly. For example, Liz Moore's contribution – named, like all the rest, "How to Be a Man"[8] – describes in graphic detail the sadistic sexual humiliation and gang rape of an unnamed girl. The short story, which is told from the perspective of Jimmy and seemingly takes place at a high school house party, is reminiscent of recent stories circulated in the media; in particular, some of the details are similar to the Stuebenville High School rape case. While the male characters of Moore's story are named, the victim remains unnamed. Not only does this have the effect of reflecting the male narrator's perspective, by denying the victim's individuality, and therefore personhood, but this also has the potential result of universalizing the female victim. In other words, the female character could be any woman – the humiliation and violence to which she is subjected has nothing to do with her, but only with her gender. The party becomes a predominantly homosocial space in which a violent, patriarchal masculinity is compulsively performed for the approval of other men.

The story ends with Jimmy reflecting on pictures of the girl's sexual assault:

> He thought of prisoners – the frightening hooded prisoners in photographs that Mr. Colgan, his favorite teacher, had projected onto the whiteboard in his political science class last fall. The prisoners were from one place and they had been taken to another. One was naked and wearing a dog collar. One had his hands extended out like Jesus on the cross. What is it that the soldiers were trying to teach them?, Mr. Colgan had asked his students, but nobody could say.[9]

Though Jimmy is unable to make sense of his own associations, he seems on the verge of understanding his actions as violent, colonialist othering. Here, Moore draws a direct parallel between the treatment of women in their own patriarchal society, and the inhuman torture of illegally detained "enemy combatants." The violence always at work in the subordination of women is here made physical and explicit.

But there is, perhaps, some small hint of hope at the end of Moore's story. However brief this hope might be, Moore implies that the right teaching, the right education, can change men's perspectives. Masculine domination can be countered, but it can only be countered through an ideological analysis that reveals the workings of hegemonic masculinity, and through masculinity projects that seek to educate and interpellate men as subjects of a more egalitarian gender order. Prose and fiction, like Moore's work itself, and like the work of Baldwin, Capote, and the others discussed in this study, will play a critical role in just such a project. As the feminist scholar Rita Felski has argued in *Uses of Literature*, for example, literary works "force us – in often unforgiving ways – to confront our failings and blind spots rather than shoring up our self-esteem"[10] and "crystallize ... the essential interwovenness of our being in the world."[11] Literary works are the most sophisticated articulation of social knowledge available to us, and it is in the work of great authors of all social stripes that we will find the most complex engagement with the shapes, problems, and desires of American masculinity.

In the current neoliberal moment, in which the marketplace has come to dominate all aspects of life, many literary critics have turned their focus to financial capital, seeing other social differences – race, sexuality, gender – as essentially an aspect of "identity politics" which distract from the real issue of economic inequality. However, patriarchy and capitalism, as our preeminent systems of social dominance, are intimately intertwined. Over twenty years ago, Raewyn Connell stated that "The reassertion of a dominance-based masculinity" is embodied in

> the 1980s cult of the "entrepreneur" in business. Here, gender imagery, institutional change, and political strategy intersect. The deregulation policies of the new-right governments in the 1980s dismantled Keynesian strategies for social integration via expert macro-economic regulation. The credibility of the new policies rested on the image of a generation of entrepreneurs whose wealth-creating energies were waiting to be unleashed. That this stratum was masculine is culturally unquestionable. Among other things, their management jargon is full of lurid gender terminology: thrusting entrepreneurs, opening up virgin territory, aggressive lending, etc.[12]

One lesson to take away from Connell's analysis is that neoliberal capitalism was, and remains, largely driven by a group of men engaged in a hegemonic masculinity practice, "legitimated by an ideology centering on an economic theory whose most distinctive feature is its blanket exclusion from discourse of women's unpaid work."[13] Hegemonic masculinity seeks to legitimate economic practice, and vice versa.

For the authors discussed in this study, like the authors included in the aforementioned *The Book of Men*, masculinity is multiple, tied to the market, and concerned with power. Practicing hegemonic masculinity, or being subordinated to it, is always understood as an act of dominance – an act through which men are terrorized almost as much as they benefit. *Esquire* magazine proposes that men practice a hegemonic masculinity project that maximizes the benefits of masculinity – but perhaps more importantly, tries to reduce the feeling of terror – by offering men agency in the marketplace.

Its solutions to the historic "problems" of patriarchy succeed, to a certain extent, but the writings analysed in this study always betray a discomfort, a discomfort not only with masculinity and the relationship to power that it entails, but also to the marketplace and consumption. Carver's working-class protagonists, for example, find themselves alienated from masculinity practiced in a consumer-culture paradigm.

Similarly, Mailer's Stephen Rojack enacts a fantasy of masculinity as a reaction to consumption and conformity. For as long as *Esquire* has tried to establish masculinity as a lifestyle strategy, the authors published in its pages have responded with uneasiness.

In the face of commodified masculinity, men often envision masculinity projects based on traditional or heroic conceptions of masculinity found in an imaginary, pre-capitalist past. The works under discussion often respond to a nostalgic or melodramatic view of "true" masculinity. That is to say that these works either challenge or reproduce the idea that life in the modern United States is always "too late" for a true, admirable, and unproblematic performance of masculinity, which is understood as having been possible in the past. One could even trace this pattern back to Hemingway, who in the 1930s already saw masculinity as something best performed in ritualized contexts, such as hunting, boxing, and bullfighting – contexts divorced from the everyday and that often take their male practitioners out of the standard confines of society. For Mailer, society is too conformist to allow for the type of individualism required for heroic masculinity. Cold Warrior culture, as represented in the works of O'Brien and DeLillo, looks to America's distant past for the cowboy figure, or to the more recent past of Kennedy's presidency. At least the ostensibly straight, white male authors of this study (or those who write about ostensibly straight, white characters) always interrogate the relationship between contemporary American masculinity and its supposedly superior but inevitably lost version.

The nostalgia for a supposedly true or legitimate form of masculinity shows just how difficult it is for some to give up on hegemonic masculinity and the structures of masculine domination. Their relationship to hegemonic masculinity becomes one of cruel optimism, "a relation of attachment to compromised conditions of possibility whose realization is discovered either to be impossible, sheer fantasy, or *too* possible, and toxic."[14] However, realizing that hegemonic masculinity is a "significantly problematic object" is not enough, since, as Berlant explains, "the fear is that the loss of the promising object/scene itself will defeat the capacity to have any hope about anything."[15] Hegemonic masculinity makes sense of the world, and so even if masculinity is understood as problematic, it is clung to nonetheless, becoming a fantasy that prevents, rather than promises, happiness.

Perhaps this element of cruel optimism is most obvious in those instances in which authors imagine an escape from hegemonic masculinity. The texts under study often express – either explicitly or implicitly – a desire for alternative gender configurations, for an *outside* to a patriarchal gender order. This is true of queer men like Baldwin and Capote, whose works seek to escape masculine domination, either through an elaborate, explicit critique of hegemonic masculinity, or through the creation, in fiction, of queer spaces which engender alternative, less toxic gender relations. It is true, too, of O'Brien's work, which holds up masculinity as a form of insanity and offers glimpses, however brief, of alternatives, in the form of women's writing and futurity. And it is true of Mailer, Carver, and DeLillo, men who seemingly champion masculinity but nonetheless provide queer or feminine role models to emulate, or implicate consumerism and advanced capitalism in a process that alienates men from themselves.

For a strategy intent on countering neoliberal domination and market subjectivity to be successful, it will have to partake of the utopian thinking about gender that this study's authors have begun. It will take the planning of new masculinity projects to create non-sexist, non-exploitative men, prepared to go about the important work of creating a more equal economic and gender order. A more equal gender order will require cisgender men to support – not lead – women and transgender people in a critique of masculine domination. It is only through such a counter-hegemonic bloc that real change can begin to happen. As I have sought to demonstrate in *Leading with the Chin*, many of the twenty-first century's problems, just like the twentieth's, continue to be entangled with the enduring question of "How to Be a Man."

Notes

Introduction

1 "As for General Content," *Esquire*, Autumn 1933, 4.
2 Breazeale, "In Spite of Women," 1. Breazeale's article is the earliest, and the best, meticulous analysis of the construction of masculinity in *Esquire* magazine. The best subsequent study is Cieply's "The Uncommon Man." My study is thoroughly indebted to the work of these two scholars.
3 Merrill, *Esky*, 32.
4 "As for the Fashion Features," *Esquire*, Autumn 1933, 4.
5 "A Magazine for Men Only," *Esquire*, Autumn 1933, 4.
6 "How to Be a Man" is a recurring feature of the magazine. Most recently, *Esquire* used it as the title of their 2014 handbook: *How to Be a Man: A Handbook of Advice, Inspiration, and Occasional Drinking.*
7 Merrill, *Esky*, 155.
8 *Nothing but People*, 81. For the story of Hemingway's role in the early days of *Esquire*, see Merrill, *Esky*, 32–5. These events are also covered in *Nothing but People*, 84–90.
9 Baron's *Author Index to* Esquire, *1933–1973* has been an indispensable resource for this study.
10 "On Fiction: The Strong, the Slick, the Good, and the Dull," *Esquire*, September 1962, 6.
11 "In Spite of Women," 1.
12 Ibid., 6.
13 By 1958, *Playboy* was outselling *Esquire*; by 1960, it was reaching over a million readers. See Fahy, *Understanding Truman Capote*, 100.
14 Merrill's *Esky: The Early Years at* Esquire provides, as its title would suggest, a good historical overview of the magazine under its first editor, Arnold

Gingrich, from 1933 to the early 1950s. Gingrich himself provides an accounting of his time at *Esquire* in his autobiography *Nothing but People: The Early Days at* Esquire, *a Personal History, 1928–1958.* Polsgrove's *It Wasn't Pretty, Folks, but Didn't We Have Fun?: Surviving the '60s with* Esquire*'s Harold Hayes* more-or-less picks up where Gingrich's story leaves off, covering the editorship of the eponymous Hayes through the 1960s and into the 1970s. The brief history sketched out below is in no way meant to be definitive.

15 *Masculinities*, 77.

16 "On Hegemonic Masculinity and Violence," 94.

17 Featherstone, *Consumer Culture and Postmodernism*, 81.

18 Berlant, *Cruel Optimism*, 24.

19 This study contributes to the field of periodical studies, and as such is deeply indebted to several sources in that field. Most pertinent is David Earle's work: specifically, *Re-Covering Modernism*, in which Earle highlights the importance of the pulp medium through which much modernist work was circulated, and *All Man! Hemingway, 1950s Men's Magazines, and the Masculine Persona*, in which Earle investigates the role of magazines in the construction of Hemingway's famous, preeminent masculinity. Similar work is done by Erin Smith, whose *Hard-Boiled: Working-Class Readers and Pulp Magazines* makes important connections between the content of pulp magazines and the social class of their readership. Moreover, Smith provides a model for reconstructing a magazine's readership. *Leading with the Chin* is similar to Smith's study, in that it is concerned with both the ideological work done by the medium of the magazine and its connection to its readership; however, it differs in the type of magazine (a "slick" rather than a pulp) and the class of its readership (upper-middle-class rather than working-class). Both Janice Winship's *Inside Women's Magazines* and Joke Hermes's *Reading Women's Magazines* provide crucial analyses of the role of lifestyle magazines in constructing and defining gender; this study differs in its focus on masculinity, but also in its primary attention to fiction.

20 *Masculinities*, 78.

21 Ibid., 79.

22 Bourdieu, *Masculine Domination*, 1.

23 Ibid., 34. Emphasis in original.

24 For more on Bourdieu's symbolic violence, see, e.g., his *Masculine Domination*, 33–42, and Bourdieu and Wacquant, *An Invitation to Reflexive Sociology*, 167–74.

25 *Gender and Power*, 120.

26 *Gender*, 2 ed., 72.
27 Bridges, "Gender Capital and Male Bodybuilders," 92.
28 *Gender*, 73.
29 *Gender and Power*, 134.
30 See "Ideology and Ideological State Apparatuses."
31 Hammill et al., "Introducing Magazines," 2.
32 Ibid., 11.
33 *Shaping Our Mothers' World*, xi.
34 Benwell, "Introduction," 6.
35 *Making Sense of Men's Magazines*, 14.
36 Ricciardelli et al., 67.
37 *Masculinities*, 77.
38 "Towards Comparative Masculinity Studies," in Horlacher and Floyd, 4.
39 Breazeale, "In Spite of Women," 9.
40 Specifically, McGann describes radial reading as a variety of reading "in which the activity of reading regularly transcends its own ocular physical bases ... The elementary sign of radial reading is probably illustrated by a person who rises from reading a book in order to look up the meaning of a word in a dictionary or to check some historical or geographical reference." SeeMcGann, *The Textual Condition*, 116.
41 Bornstein, *Material Modernism*, 30–1.
42 "Notes on Deconstructing 'the Popular,'" in *Cultural Theory and Popular Culture: A Reader*, ed. John Storey (Pearson Longman, 2009), 18.
43 Hammill et al., "Introducing Magazines and/as Media," 3.
44 *Shaping Our Mothers' World*, vii.
45 "The Professional-Managerial Class," in Walker, 9, 12. Barbara and John Ehrenreich have recently revisited this influential class marker, and discussed its history, in their article "The Real Story Behind the Crash and Burn of America's Managerial Class."
46 Speaking of the magazine in the 1930s, Kenon Breazeale notes that the magazine "sought to create a comprehensive set of expectations about what constitutes a desirable upper-middle-class identity" (6). Stefan Cieply refers to a marketing survey from 1963 that identifies 90 per cent of the readers as men, 80 per cent as professionals or executives, and the majority as being in their late thirties and early forties. The same survey asked men to describe the *Esquire* reader: 33 per cent selected the descriptor "sophisticated, urbane, up-to-date," and 23 per cent identified the magazine's readers as "intellectuals, eggheads, well-educated" (161–2). Cieply further points to an advertisement for *Esquire* that ran in *Time*, proclaiming that "Like Russian caviar, Dutch gin,

and Swedish movies, *Esquire* isn't for everybody. To be precise, it is edited
for only one man in 59.4" (162). *Esquire* therefore made itself attractive
by advertising its audience as elite, sophisticated, and affluent – all
desirable categories.

Discussing *Esquire* in the 1980s, Denise Kervin argues that the
magazine "has always had a specific male audience in their late 20s to 40s
age group, middle to upper-middle class, educated beyond high school,
and holding a white-collar job" (56). This description of the readership
matches *Esquire*'s current narrative of its readership. Based on polling
data published in 2013 and used for promoting the magazine to
potential advertisers, the magazine claims that "Only *Esquire* readers have
both the influence and wealth to serve as luxury brand promoters,
affecting the purchasing decisions of other consumers – their family,
friends, and colleagues" ("Affluence & Influence"). They claim that
Esquire readers have the highest median net worth when compared to the
readership of other men's magazines (i.e., *Men's Health, Men's Journal,
GQ,* and *Details*) ("Wealthiest Adults"). In addition, the statistics
regarding their male readership find that 78.8 per cent are college
graduates, 37 per cent have studied at the postgraduate level, 63 per cent
are in professional/managerial positions, and 24.7 per cent are defined
as "Top Management" ("Male Profile"). Today's *Esquire* readers, like
the original *Esquire* readers, are members of the professional-managerial
class.

47 "In Spite of Women," 3.
48 *Creating the Modern Man,* 217.
49 *Playboys in Paradise,* 74.
50 "The Uncommon Man," 152–3.
51 Ibid., 162.
52 Ibid., 153.
53 See, for instance, a discussion of these works as they relate to the
    masculine figure of the "square" in Penner (100–4). For a discussion
    of the Organization Man as a problematic male figure, see Cieply,
    "Lineaments" (176–90), or Osgerby, "Two-Fisted" (179–83); Barbara
    Ehrenreich (29–37) includes a discussion of how the issues discussed
    by Riesman led to increased misogyny. See, in particular, Gilbert
    (34–61).
54 Other pertinent books include *The Decline of the American Male* (1960),
    published by the editors of *Look* magazine, and Sloan Wilson's *The Man
    in the Gray Flannel Suit* (1955). For a more modern take on the
    discussion of the role of the organization and individual agency, see
    Andrew Hoberek, who argues that "this discourse of constrained agency

is best understood as a product of the transition from small-property ownership to white-collar employment as the basis of middle-class status. In brief, the postwar period constitutes a tipping point in the history of the middle class, when PMC [professional-managerial class] efforts to rewrite individual and class agency in managerial terms give way to skepticism about organization as such and nostalgia for the putative autonomy of the property-owning old middle class" (8).

55 Cieply, "Lineaments," 180.
56 *Empire of Conspiracy*, 57.
57 *White Collar: The American Middle Classes*, xviii.
58 Ruark, "Mystery Unincorporated," *Esquire*, November 1950, 168.
59 Ruark, "What Hath God Wrought?," *Esquire*, October 1950, 61.
60 J.B. Rice, "Woman: The Overrated Sex," *Esquire*, February 1950, 30.
61 Reddy, "Papa Is a Patsy," *Esquire*, July 1954, 31.
62 "Uncommon," 151. For Cieply, this essay is crucial for defining *Esquire*'s male readership. See "Uncommon" (151) and "Lineaments" (54–5).
63 "The Crisis of American Masculinity," *Esquire*, November 1958, 63.
64 See, e.g., Traister, "Academic Viagra," and Whitehead, *Men and Masculinities* (47–59).
65 Judith Halberstam makes a similar point, arguing that "This notion that the destabilization of masculinity results in crisis and, that crisis demands the immediate re-consolidation of male authority, underpins much of what I am calling imperial masculinity" ("Thugs" 155–6).
66 "Crisis," 63.
67 Ibid., 64.
68 Ibid., 65.
69 *Advertisements for Myself*, 465.
70 *Understanding Truman Capote*, 98.
71 Ibid.
72 Ibid., 108.
73 Pugh, "Capote's Breakfast at Tiffany's," 51.
74 *Understanding Truman Capote*, 107.
75 Government of Mexico Tourist Department, "Advertisement," *Esquire*, November 1958, 40; Aeronaves de Mexico, "Advertisement," *Esquire*, November 1958, 41.
76 Ballantine's advertisement, *Esquire*, November 1958, 18; Cutty Sark advertisement, *Esquire*, November 1958, 23; Cinzano advertisement, *Esquire*, November 1958, 47.
77 Winthrop Shoes, "Advertisement," *Esquire*, November 1958, 12; Jockey Underwear, "Advertisement," *Esquire*, November 1958, 38; California Sportwear Company, "Advertisement," *Esquire*, November 1958, 108.

1 American Dreams, Gendered Nightmares

1 Junod, "The Last Man Standing," *Esquire*, January 2007, 110.
2 Millett, *Sexual Politics*, 314.
3 For an excellent discussion of Mailer's masculine fixation and his macho pose, see, e.g., Schwenger, *Phallic Critiques*, 16–35.
4 Mailer, "The Language of Men," *Esquire*, April 1953.
5 Mailer, "Superman Comes to the Supermart," *Esquire*, November 1968.
6 Mailer, "Norman Mailer versus Nine Writers," *Esquire*, July 1963, 63, 64.
7 See Mailer's letter to the editor in *Esquire*, January 1961.
8 Willingham, "The Way It Isn't Done: Notes on the Distress of Norman Mailer," *Esquire*, December 1963, 307, 308.
9 Mailer, "The Big Bite," *Esquire*, December 1963, 22.
10 Ellmann, *Thinking about Women*.
11 Millett, *Sexual Politics*, 15.
12 Fetterley, *The Resisting Reader*, 155.
13 Meloy, "Tales of the 'Great Bitch,'" 341.
14 Shaw, "Destabilizing Sexistentialism,"46.
15 McKinley, *Masculinity*, 68.
16 Ibid., 67.
17 Parker, "Norman Mailer's Revision," 409.
18 Ibid., 412.
19 Ibid., 411–12.
20 Ibid., 413.
21 Ehrenreich, *The Hearts of Men*, 29, 31.
22 Gingrich, "Public into Private and the New Boom in 'Unreal Estate,'" *Esquire*, January 1964, 4.
23 Ibid.
24 Melley, *Empire*, 7.
25 The *Esquire* essay was a revised version of "Notes on the Establishment in America," published in *American Scholar*.
26 Toropov, *Encyclopedia of Cold War Politics*, 58.
27 Rovere, "The American Establishment," *Esquire*, May 1962, 108.
28 Gentile, "Letter to the Editor," *Esquire*, July 1962, 6.
29 Rovere, "American Establishment," 157.
30 "As for General Content," 4.
31 "A Word to Our Readers," *Dissent*, Winter 1954, 3.
32 Mailer, *Advertisements*, 283.
33 Ibid., 199–200.
34 In comparing the "White Negro" to a "frontiersman," Mailer summons up the classic ideal of American masculinity, the cowboy, an exemplary form of masculinity discussed in subsequent chapters of this study.

35 Mailer, *Advertisements*, 284. Mailer's (frequent) use of the term "existential-ist" is idiosyncratic. As Nigel Leigh explains, "Deracinated, pushed to the margins of culture – radicalized, individual responsibilities become even more acutely felt. Mailer is fond of labelling this condition existential, but it is a mistake to conclude from this that he is greatly influenced by such European thinkers as Sartre, Kierkegaard and Heidegger ... his use of the term consistently emphasizes the individual's problem of knowledge, his epistemological gaps, and the uncertainties of agency" (92).

36 Ibid., 285.

37 For jazz musicians, see, e.g., 337, 341, 345; for orgasms, 341, 347.

38 Mailer, *Advertisements*, 287.

39 Cieply, "Uncommon," 164.

40 Konstantinou, *Cool Characters*, 51, 52.

41 Connell, *Masculinities*, 77.

42 Leigh, *Radical Fictions*, 88.

43 Other critics have similarly contextualized the novel, though not always with the same focus; Michael Glenday, for instance, sees the assassination of President John F. Kennedy as being crucial to understanding the novel (89). This seems slightly problematic, since the first part of the novel had already gone to print in *Esquire* when the assassination occurred. Still, I would agree with Glenday that *An American Dream* should be viewed as a novel that "dramatized the national mood" (88); I would merely suggest that this particular dramatization of the national mood is best under-stood in light of the discourses on constrained masculinity.

44 Mailer, *An American Dream*, 36, hereafter cited in-text. Unless otherwise noted, citations are to the Vintage paperback edition, based on the Dial printing.

45 Whitehead, *Men and Masculinities*, 91.

46 Althusser, "Ideology," 109–11.

47 In this way, Rojack's story appears, at least initially, as yet another iteration of what Richard Slotkin has identified as America's national myth: "regeneration through violence."

48 Several scholars see Rojack's murder of Deborah in symbolic terms. Leigh succinctly explains that "killing Deborah cancels Rojack's social contract with the 'dream' world of capitalist success, status and privilege" (105). Stanley Gutman discusses the murder at length (106–9), in particular stating that "Murder requires an extraordinary commitment to discover the self, since it violates the most basic mandates and taboos of society," and that in doing so Rojack "frees himself from the armature that was stifling his existence" (106, 107). Lost in this discussion is any notion of Deborah's personhood, and that Rojack's act is primarily a misogynistic act of homophobia (as will be discussed in this chapter).

49 Mailer, *Advertisements*, 283.
50 Rojack's narrative is punctuated by highly detailed descriptions of odors, usually associated with other characters. From Ruta, the maid, comes "a smell which spoke of rocks and grease and the sewer-damp of wet stones in poor European alleys" (43); sitting in a room with one officer, Rojack notes that "an odor of violence came off him, a kind of clammy odor of rut, and O'Brien, on my other side, who had shown a pronounced smell already, oversweet and very stale, was throwing a new odor, something like the funk a bully emits when he heads for a face-to-face meeting" (74).
51 These are perhaps most obvious during a rather bizarre section of chapter 4, in which Rojack engages in a sort of mental duel with the denizens of Eddie Ganucci's night club (97–102), during which he develops "a small manufactory of psychic particles" (97) which he wields as "magic bullets" (98).
52 Mailer, *Advertisements*, 294.
53 Miller, "A Small Trumpet of Defiance," 80.
54 Connell, "An Iron Man," 94.
55 Connell, "On Hegemonic," 90.
56 Connell, *Masculinities*, 81.
57 Bufithis, *Norman Mailer*, 70.
58 Leeds, *The Structured Vision of Norman Mailer*, 158.
59 See Messner and Sabo, *Sport, Men, and the Gender Order*.
60 Shago's character is highly racialized: Mailer seems to be parroting several racist notions of black men, and fear of black sexuality, to which James Baldwin responds in the next chapter of this study.
61 Leigh, *Radical Fictions*, 88.
62 As Penner has noted, the hipster differs from the traditional ideal masculine figure (what he calls "hard-boiled" masculinity) in two important ways: first, the "White Negro" is irrational, which is a characteristic traditionally associated with the feminine; second, the hipster is sexually ambiguous (118–20).
63 Mailer, *Advertisements*, 295.
64 Ibid., 289.
65 Ibid., 292.
66 Gutman also notes that, while Rojack "fleshes out the vision in 'The White Negro,'" he seems further divorced from the hipster's world by his "intellectual acuity and his concern with the upper social and economic strata of American society" (96).
67 As Connell states, physically violent men (especially in instances of violence against women) "feel they are entirely justified, that they are

exercising a right. They are authorized by an ideology of supremacy" (*Masculinities* 83).

68 Millett, *Sexual Politics*, 16.

69 Shaw, "Destabilizing Sexistentialism," 59.

70 Connell, *Masculinities*, 77.

71 Mailer, *Advertisements*, 285.

72 While jazz, and the figure of the jazz musician, were embraced by the magazine, anything related to African Americans that seemed politically threatening – dangerous to hegemony – was treated with hostility. The October 1964 issue of *Esquire* features a story by William Worthy entitled "The Red Chinese American Negro"; the blurb reads, "Radical Negro militants are turning to Mao Tse-Tung for support in overturning the U.S. Government" (132). The same issue contains an advertisement for the Mid-Century Book Society, highlighting one of their featured selections: *The Cradle of Erotica* by Allen Edwardes and R.E.L. Masters. The description reads, "A close scrutiny of the unusual and unrestrained sexual practices of Afro-Asian peoples as evidenced in their literature (which is copiously quoted)" (17). *Esquire* had a complicated relationship with African Americans during the Sixties, but there was a strong strain of fetishization, commensurate with a denial of actual political power. See the next chapter of this study for a more in-depth analysis.

73 Newman and Benton, "The New Sentimentality," *Esquire*, July 1964, 25.

74 Ibid.

75 Ibid.

76 *Esquire*'s use of the term "sentimentality" is indeed confusing, as the editorial makes little reference to affect. As Mary Chapman and Glenn Hendler have shown, sentimentality has traditionally been feminized in popular American discourse; however, there remains a tradition of sentimental men pertinent to American literature. See their *Sentimental Men*.

77 Mailer, "The Harbors of the Moon," *Esquire*, January 1964, 77.

78 RelaxAcizor, "Advertisement," *Esquire*, February 1964, 44. Emphasis added.

79 Perfect Voice Institute, "Advertisement," *Esquire*, January 1964, 156. Emphasis added.

80 Executive Research Institute, "Advertisement," *Esquire*, January 1964, 153. Emphasis added.

81 For "hailing" and "interpellation," see Althusser's "Ideology."

82 Many scholars have noted this pattern in Mailer's work; for instance, Howard Silverstein notes that "becoming a man in Mailer's fiction implies competing with and defeating other men" (v), while Herbert

similarly claims that "What counts as heterosexual desire in Rojack is a pattern of impulses governed by the effort to assert his manhood in competition with other men and by his need to overcome the contradictions that threaten to collapse that manhood from within" (151).

83 This contest foreshadows the way JFK will be held up as an exemplar of masculinity in Don DeLillo's *Libra*. See chapter 6.

84 Silverstein, "Norman Mailer and the Quest for Manhood," 37.

85 Mailer, "A Messenger from the Maniac," *Esquire*, March 1964, 144.

86 Ibid., 148.

87 Donaldson, "A Million Jockers, Punks, and Queens," 119.

88 Kimmel, "Masculinity as Homophobia," 186–7.

89 Ibid., 186. For Sedgwick's analysis of male homosociality, and the role of homophobia, see *Between Men* (especially 1–5) and *Epistemology of the Closet* (especially 67–90).

90 Ibid., 189. Here, I want to distinguish between two related terms: "homophobia" and "heterosexism." Homophobia, in its popular usage, is a misnomer: far from referring to a fear or phobia, the term is usually used to describe the discrimination against (or heterosexism towards) homosexuals. The problem with this misnomer is that by misattributing hatred as a phobia, it might legitimate the response of the heterosexist (e.g., "I don't hate homosexuals, I'm only afraid of them.") Kimmel's definition of homophobia has the advantage of identifying a specific fear – the fear of being identified as homosexual and therefore subjected to heterosexism, which includes marginalization.

91 Parker, "Norman Mailer's Revision," 411.

92 Ibid., 417.

93 Mailer, "Green Circles of Exhaustion," *Esquire*, April 1964, 148.

94 Gutman, *Mankind in Barbary*, 103.

95 Halberstam, *Female Masculinity*, 4.

96 Chauncey, *Gay New York*, 290.

97 In *Norman Mailer and the Quest for Manhood*, Silverstein claims that Rojack's excessive emphasis on masculinity cloaks his latent homosexuality (v). Similarly, Andrew Gordon argues that "Rojack's repressed homosexual impulses are willfully converted into honorable and manly aggression" (137). Michael Snyder argues that other characters "read" Rojack as homosexual (268), and sees Rojack's fights as instances of homosexual panic.

98 Mailer, "Green Circles of Exhaustion," 148.

99 Penner, *Pinks, Pansies, and Punks*, 123.

100 This omitted passage adds significance to an earlier, much-discussed episode involving Rojack and a German soldier whom he kills. Rojack describes the soldier as having "that overcurved mouth which only great fat sweet young faggots can have" and claims that the soldier's last words were "'*Mutter*,' one yelp from the first memory of the womb" (4). Rojack's admission of his own attachment to his mother turns this passage into an instance of psychological projection.

101 Gutman, *Mankind in Barbary*, 110–11.

102 Mailer, "The Harbors of the Moon," 77. Emphasis added.

103 For more on Jorgensen, see *Christine Jorgensen: A Personal Autobiography* and Docter, *Becoming a Woman*.

104 Gilbert, *Men in the Middle*, 76.

105 Ibid.

106 Mailer, "A Messenger from the Maniac," 148.

107 Meyerowitz, "Transforming Sex," 18–19.

108 Serlin, "Christine Jorgensen," 159.

109 Chauncey, *Gay New York*, 290.

110 Mailer, "Green Circles of Exhaustion," 98.

2 Cooling It with James Baldwin

1 Baldwin, "Here Be Dragons," 678. Here, Baldwin is distinguishing "masculinity," a category created in opposition to femininity (and which, as he describes, establishes an uneven gender hierarchy), from "manhood," which should be understood in opposition to "childhood."

2 Dievler analyses this essay in the specific context of the sexual culture of Greenwich Village in the 1960s. Of this passage, he writes that "Baldwin characterizes that culture as immature. It may also be worth noting that he is primarily concerned with male identities." See Dievler, "Sexual Exiles," 162.

3 Baldwin's treatment of masculinity has been thoroughly analysed by numerous scholars. For some of the strongest analyses – those which identify the ideological dimension of his argument, as well as discussing the connection Baldwin draws between race and gender – see, e.g., Ferguson, Reid-Pharr, and Spurlin.

4 This claim, about the homosocial enactment of masculinity, is also central to Sedgwick's *Epistemology of the Closet*.

5 Kimmel, "Masculinity as Homophobia," 86.

6 Furthermore, this external judgement – the judgement of other men met in face-to-face social relations – is also internalized by the masculine

subject, who judges himself and others accordingly. Thus David Buchbinder finds Michel Foucault's concept of the "panopticon" useful for
explaining how this homosocial construction of masculinity functions.
He argues that men are simultaneously subjects and objects of a
patriarchal panopticon – they both judge others and are judged against
current gender norms. Those who do not meet the currently accepted
masculine criteria are subjected to "disciplinary action" (81), which in
most instances will be some form of subordination or marginalization
from dominant forms of masculinity, resulting in lessened access to the
patriarchal dividend.

7 Scott, *Extravagant Abjection*, 172.
8 Neal, "The Black Arts Movement," 2043.
9 Ibid., 2044.
10 Leiter, *In the Shadow of the Black Beast*, 2–3. Leiter's study focuses on the
placement of "African American male sexuality at the center of black
and white individual and communal identities" (6) in the works of James
Weldon Johnson, George Schuyler, Erskine Caldwell, Walter White,
Margaret Mitchell, Allen Tate, William Faulkner, and Richard Wright.
11 Schmitt, "Large Propagators," 47.
12 Ibid., 51–2.
13 Ditz, "The New Men's History," 11.
14 Schmitt, "Large Propagators," 13.
15 Pochmara, *The Making of the New Negro*, 10.
16 hooks, *Yearning*, 57–8. hooks's criticism is especially pertinent to writers
associated with the Black Arts Movement, who saw the reclamation and
articulation of masculinity as central to their revolutionary goals of Black
Nationalism. The Black Arts Movement – in particular, Amiri Baraka –
saw white men as emasculated because of disengagement from the physical world (in preference to the intellectual/artistic world). Additionally,
they saw this same failing in their literary forbearers, the writers of the
Harlem Renaissance. As Phillip Brian Harper explains, "Black Aestheti-
cians" drew a parallel between a perceived lack of black consciousness
and an inadequate masculinity, meaning that those deemed insufficiently
black were disavowed as homosexuals (50). This kind of devaluation of
the Harlem Renaissance, based on its perceived failure of manhood,
made Baldwin himself a target, especially given the "open secret" of his
homosexuality. Based on this argument, Baldwin's homosexuality made
him insufficiently black.
17 Spurlin, "Culture, Rhetoric, and Queer Identity," 113. The most obvious
Black Nationalist attack on Baldwin's masculinity came from Eldridge

Cleaver, who would later go on to become a leader in the Black Panther Party. Cleaver's heterosexist attack on Baldwin, in his *Soul on Ice*, has received considerable scholarly attention. While the *difference* between the two authors' approaches to black masculinity are fairly obvious (Cleaver's hypermasculinity, Baldwin's nonnormative masculinity), several scholars have thoughtfully elaborated on the convergence of both authors' thinking. See, in particular, Douglas Taylor, Stockton, Nathaniel Mills, Reid-Pharr, Spurlin (112–15), and Ross's "White Fantasies" (17–18).

18 Ross, "White Fantasies," 25.

19 Reid-Pharr, "Tearing the Goat's Flesh," 388.

20 James Baldwin, *Giovanni's Room* (Penguin Books Limited, 2001), 1.

21 For a discussion of the "Mirror Stage," see Lacan, "The Mirror Stage."

22 Armengol, "In the Dark Room,"675. Matt Bell also comments on the connection between homosexuality and blackness in Baldwin's *Another Country*. See his "Black Ground, Gay Figure: Working through *Another Country*, Black Power, and Gay Liberation," *American Literature* 79, no. 3 (2007): 584–90, doi:10.1215/00029831-2007-021.

23 Andrew Shin and Barbara Judson see *Another Country* as a repudiation of Mailer's concept of black masculinity, articulated in "The White Negro", arguing that "the sexual lionizing of the black musician merely appropriates him for white consumption, and, Baldwin warns, if black musicians embrace this myth, they will be destroyed by it, as demonstrated by the case of Rufus Scott, the tragic character at the center of *Another Country*" (256–7). For further discussions of the confluence of masculinity and race in *Another Country*, see, e.g., Keith Clark (55), Susan Feldman, and Matt Bell.

24 Baldwin, *Blues for Mister Charlie*, 50.

25 Ibid., 120.

26 See, e.g., 92–3, 104, 111–12.

27 Fanon, *Black Skin, White Masks*, 170. Also quoted in Bordo, 25.

28 Mailer, *An American Dream*, 201.

29 Baldwin, "Going to Meet the Man," 247–8.

30 Taylor, "Denigration, Dependence, and Deviation, 46.

31 Ibid., 57.

32 Edelman, "The Part for the (W)hole," 48.

33 Leeming, *James Baldwin*, 168.

34 Baldwin, "Fifth Avenue, Uptown," 209. Citations refer to page numbers in *The Price of the Ticket*, unless otherwise noted.

35 Žižek, *Violence*, 2.

36 Baldwin, "Everybody's," 211.

37 Ibid. At the time of Baldwin's writing (1960), two significant riots had occurred in Harlem, in 1935 and 1943. For further discussion and analysis, see, e.g., Abu-Lughod's *Race, Space, and Riots*.

38 Ibid., 211–12.

39 Ferguson, "The Nightmares of the Heteronormative," 420.

40 Ibid., 423.

41 Baldwin, "Everybody's," 210.

42 Christol, "Whose Power?," 86.

43 Polsgrove, *It Wasn't Pretty*, 117–18.

44 Leeming, *James Baldwin*, 184.

45 Baldwin, "Black Boy," 291, 296, 300.

46 Ibid., 290–1, 289.

47 Taylor, "Three Lean Cats," 79.

48 Baldwin, "Black Boy," 290.

49 Taylor, "Three Lean Cats," 79.

50 While "Fifth Avenue" and "Black Boy" are perhaps the best examples of Baldwin's critique, his other contributions to *Esquire* contained elements of his overall argument. See, e.g., "The Northern Protestant," "Color," and "The New Lost Generation."

51 Plymouth Barracuda, "Advertisement," *Esquire*, January 1967, 28–9.

52 Haig Scotch, "Advertisement," *Esquire*, January 1967, 53.

53 "New Year's Eve with Elegance," *Esquire*, January 1967.

54 Joseph, "A Sportsman's Tip Sheet on the West Indies," *Esquire*, January 1967.

55 Iger, "How to Fly to Europe Without Buying a Ticket," *Esquire*, January 1967.

56 Weinraub, "The Brilliancy of Black," *Esquire*, January 1967, 132.

57 "Esquire's Sixth Annual Dubious Achievement Awards," *Esquire*, January 1967, 85.

58 The National Liberation Front for South Vietnam (the Viet Cong).

59 Worthy, "The American Negro Is Dead," *Esquire*, November 1967, 125.

60 Worthy, "The Black Power Establishment," *Esquire*, November 1967.

61 Worthy, "The American Negro Is Dead," 126.

62 Wills, "The Second Civil War," *Esquire*, March 1968, 71.

63 Polsgrove, *It Wasn't Pretty*, 116. Adelman was the photographer for a similar article on LeRoi Jones. Jack Richardson's "Blues for Mister Jones" features a picture of Jones looking odd, with his eyes rolled back in his head. The article features Richardson's snide, paternal voice; in one instance, he says of Jones's plays that, "judged as relevant social observations they evidenced less imagination than delirium tremens; judged as art they argued a poor

future for black literary standards ... I, as LeRoi had told me, was locked
in a decaying white sensibility and from my decomposing prison it just
seemed to me that LeRoi couldn't write" (106).

64 Ibid.

65 Ibid., 116–17.

66 Baldwin, "Interview," *Esquire*, July 1968, 51.

67 Ibid., 52.

68 Ibid., 50.

69 Ibid., 52.

70 Wallace, *Black Macho*, 36.

71 Baldwin, "Everybody's," 211.

72 Baldwin, "Interview," 116.

73 Ibid., 50.

74 Ibid., 49.

75 Ibid., 116.

76 Baldwin, "Black Boy," 290.

77 Baldwin, "Here Be Dragons," 678. Emphasis added.

78 Each cover of *Esquire* magazine is freely available for viewing at the
Esquire Classic website: http://archive.esquire.com/issues. The content
of each magazine is available for a subscription fee.

79 See, e.g., the *Oxford English Dictionary Online*'s entry for "cool, *adj.*, *adv.*,
and *int.*," especially entry 8b.

80 Majors and Billson, *Cool Pose*, xi.

81 Ibid., 79.

82 Ibid., 1.

83 Ibid., 30–1.

84 Ibid., 28.

85 Oddly enough, this was not the first time that Baldwin had somehow
been associated with beverages by the magazine. The November 1967
issue included, as part of its "Black Power" section, a feature on hot
drinks called "What to Drink before the Fire Next Time."

86 Lipnitzki, "Advice for Summer Drinkers: Cool It," *Esquire*, July 1968, 107,
108.

87 Lasker, "A Whiter Shade of Black," *Esquire*, July 1968, 62.

88 Ibid., 63.

89 Ibid., 64. Emphasis added.

90 Ibid., 65.

91 NAACP Legal Defense & Educational Fund, "Advertisement," *Esquire*,
July 1968.

92 Baldwin, "The New Lost Generation," 309.

3 Low-Rent Tragedies of Beset Manhood

1 Carver's writing about alcoholism came from personal experience. James
   Plath notes that Carver's life and career can be divided into the "bad
   Ray" drinking days and the "gravy days" after he married Tess Gallagher
   and quit drinking (11–13).

2 Towers, "Low-Rent Tragedies."

3 Borstelmann, *The 1970s*, 53.

4 My title is a conflation of Towers's phrase and Nina Baym's influential
   essay on American literary critics' investment in "melodramas of beset
   manhood": "Personally beset in a way that epitomizes the tensions of our
   culture, the male author produces his melodramatic testimony to our
   culture's essence – so the theory goes" (1981, 130).

5 "In the Absence of a Hero for the Seventies," *Esquire*, March 1972, 87.
   Italics in original.

6 Ibid.

7 Men were not banished from the cover for too long: a new subtitle, "Man
   at His Best," debuted on the cover of the March 1980 issue. The new
   subtitle was meant to reflect the magazine's "new" target readership:
   "men who were not necessarily macho anymore, but who had feelings.
   Men were being handled with dignity." Heller, "Esquire and Its Art
   Directors," 60.

8 Ben Harker (2007) provides an excellent discussion of Carver and class
   struggle, and directs readers to pertinent sources on Carver as a
   blue-collar writer. See, e.g., both Bruce Weber and Gordon Burn in
   Gentry and Stull's *Conversations with Raymond Carver* (1990). For a
   discussion of class and gender in Carver, see Vanessa Hall.

9 Michael Kimmel discusses the links between working-class masculinity
   "crisis" and the changing neoliberal economy, especially in the wake of
   Reagan-era economic policy, in *Angry White Men*, 199–203.

10 Skenazy, "Life in Limbo," 77.

11 Bottomore et al., *A Dictionary of Marxist Thought*, 411.

12 Discussion on this editor-writer relationship has taken many forms.
    Sklenicka pays a considerable amount of attention to it in *Raymond Carver:
    A Writer's Life* (see, e.g., 185–7, 354–62). The Carver-Lish relationship,
    and its connections to university creative writing programs, is explored in
    McGurl's *The Program Era* (273–97). For some literary-critical discussions
    of the Lish-Carver relationship, see, e.g., Hemmingson and Monti.

13 Bill Buford coined the term "Dirty realism" in *Granta* 8 (Summer 1983).
    The coinage of "Kmart realism" is more difficult to pin down; the earliest

reference I have found is in Edwin J. Kenney's *New York Times* review of Phyllis Naylor's *Unexpected Pleasures* (1986). For "Kmart realism" and "minimalism," see Barth's "A Few Notes About Minimalism."

14 Simmons, "Minimalist Fiction," 49.

15 The editors clearly relate the term to Mark Fisher's short study *Capitalist Realism: Is There No Alternative?* Fisher's work is mostly focused on periodization, labelling the period after postmodernism as capitalist realism. Shonkwiler and La Berge, and Godden have done the most to refine and apply the term to literary and cultural texts.

16 Shonkwiler and La Berge, "Introduction," 6.

17 Ibid., 14–15.

18 Godden, "Money and Things," 188.

19 Lukács, "Reification and the Consciousness of the Proletariat," 91.

20 Shonkwiler and La Berge, "Introduction," 4–5. For a fuller explanation of this term, see Harvey's *A Brief History of Neoliberalism*.

21 Ibid., 16.

22 Goldman, *Reading Ads Socially*, 2. For Goldman's discussion of the relationship between advertising and the commodity form, see 15–36.

23 See, e.g., Elger, *Gerhard Richter*, 32–69, and Hentschel, "Konrad Lueg and Gerhard Richter," 179–87.

24 Shonkwiler and La Berge, "Introduction," 16.

25 Schudson, *Advertising, the Uneasy Persuasion*," 214–15.

26 Ibid., 220.

27 Shonkwiler and La Berge, "Introduction," 11.

28 I'm sensitive to the inevitable objection that another "realism" isn't needed for a discussion of three stories, especially considering the plethora of categories of aesthetic realism already identified (e.g., Kmart realism). My hope in using this term is to show how Carver's fiction can elaborate on the relationship between capitalist realism and (the traditional understanding of) literary realism.

29 Schudson, *Advertising, the Uneasy Persuasion*, 224.

30 Jhally, *The Codes of Advertising*, 136.

31 Kervin, "Advertising Masculinity," 62.

32 These fashion photographs therefore depict the subordination of women to men in many of the ways noted by Erving Goffman in his *Gender Advertisements* (1976). For more on gender ideology and advertising, see, e.g., Strate, Massé and Rosenblum, and Williamson.

33 For a fuller discussion of commodity aesthetics, see Haug, 103–20.

34 See Baudrillard, *The Mirror of Production*, 127–8.

35 Jhally, *The Codes of Advertising*, 127–8.

36 Stetson Shoes, "Advertisement," *Esquire*, April 1972.

37 Ibid.

38 It is also frequently cited by scholars. See, e.g., Campbell (14–17), Nesset (12–13), Harker, and Boxer and Phillips.

39 Schudson, *Advertising, the Uneasy Persuasion*, 224.

40 Carver, "Neighbors," *Esquire*, June 1971, 137. All other page numbers are to the Library of America's *Collected Stories* edition, unless otherwise noted.

41 Sklenicka, *Raymond Carver*, 201.

42 Goldman, *Reading Ads Socially*, 22.

43 Sklenicka, *Raymond Carver*, 201.

44 Westerman, "The Reification of Consciousness," 120.

45 Carver, "Neighbors," 8.

46 Ibid.

47 Ibid., 10–11.

48 Ewen, *Channels of Desire*, 265.

49 Campbell, *Raymond Carver*, 15–16.

50 Carver, "Neighbors," 11, 9.

51 Goldman, *Reading Ads Socially*, 3.

52 Carver, "Neighbors," 11, 12; Campbell, *Raymond Carver*, 15–16.

53 Campbell, *Raymond Carver*, 15. The story is typically associated with voyeurism. See, e.g., Nesset, Bethea (68–71), Bowers (98–101), and Boxer and Philips. Boxer and Philips point to the window which Bill Miller looks through as a symbol of voyeurism (77).

54 Haug, *Commodity Aesthetics*, 107.

55 Carver, "Neighbors," 10.

56 Bethea, *Technique and Sensibility*, 69.

57 Carver, "Neighbors," 10.

58 Bethea, *Technique and Sensibility*, 70.

59 Carver, "Neighbors," 13.

60 Ibid.

61 Schudson, *Advertising, the Uneasy Persuasion*, 231.

62 Carver, "Neighbors," 9. Arthur Bethea also draws attention to this scene, lamenting, "What a lesser substitute for a child; what a lesser life than the Millers imagine" (2001, 69).

63 Carver, "What Is It?," in *Collected Stories*, 157.

64 Sklenicka, *Raymond Carver*, 215.

65 Carver, "What Is It?," 159.

66 Ibid., 164; Nesset, *The Stories of Raymond Carver*, 22.

67 Carver, "What Is It?," 164.

68 Sklenicka, *Raymond Carver*, 215.

69 Carver, "What Is It?," 162.

70 Ibid., 163; Nesset, *The Stories of Raymond Carver*, 21.

71 Carver, "What Is It?," 160.

72 Nesset, *The Stories of Raymond Carver*, 22.

73 Carver, "What Is It?," 163.

74 Ibid., 163, 160.

75 Ibid., 163.

76 Ibid., 164.

77 Ibid., 163–4.

78 Goldman, *Reading Ads Socially*, 32.

79 Carver, "What Is It?," 164.

80 Godden, "Money and Things," 183.

81 Carver, "Collectors," *Esquire*, August 1975, 95.

82 Carver, "Collectors," in *Collected Stories*, 78.

83 Ibid.

84 *The Queen of America*, 96.

85 The narrator of "Fat" is female, and, as Berlant explains, the story largely focuses on embodiment and her fantasies of pregnancy. While the story is thus seemingly unrelated to the themes of masculinity and the mode of consumer realism on which this chapter focuses, Berlant's reading nevertheless deftly illustrates the ways in which Carver's narrators grapple with selfhood, situatedness, and agency in the face of a dehumanizing modern condition.

86 Carver, "Collectors," 80, 81, 82, 80.

87 Jhally, *The Codes of Advertising*, 12.

88 Carver, "Collectors," 79.

89 Bethea, *Technique and Sensibility*, 9.

90 Carver, "Collectors," 79, 81.

91 Ibid., 81. Emphasis added.

92 Ibid., 82.

93 Ibid., 80.

94 Ibid.

95 Bethea, *Technique and Sensibility*, 10.

96 Carver, "Collectors," 2009, 78.

97 Ibid., 81.

98 Ibid., 83.

99 Berlant, *Queen of America*, 89.

100   Carver, "What Is It?," 157.
101   Joseph, "The Perfect Male Shopping Spree," *Esquire*, August 1975, 97.
102   Carver, "Neighbors," 2009, 11.
103   Butler, *Excitable Speech*, 16.

4 True Men and Queer Spaces in Truman Capote's *Answered Prayers*

1   This chapter is derived in part from an article published in *Critique: Studies in Contemporary Fiction*, 28 April 2017, copyright Taylor & Francis, available at www.tandfonline.com/doi/abs/10.1080/00111619.2017.1317233.

2   "Dazzle," in *Music for Chameleons*, 62.

3   "Capote's Artful Nonfiction," *Esquire*, December 1979, 6.

4   It was not until 2015 that the first peer-review article on *Answered Prayers* was published. See Scott St Pierre's "Bent on Candor." A renewed scholarly interest in Capote is evidenced by the recent publication of two articles on his "La Côte Basque, 1965." In the earliest one, Kelly Marsh analyses the narrative techniques used by Capote to refuse empathy with the story's characters; in the other, Douglas Dowland focuses on the role disgust plays in Capote's critique of high society. See Marsh, "Empathy, and Dowland, "How Disgust Works."

5   St Pierre, "'Bent on Candor,'" 12.

6   The details about Capote's plans for *Answered Prayers*, and its troubled publication history, are taken from Joseph M. Fox's "Editor's Note" to the paperback edition.

7   For an overview of the controversy, see, e.g., Kashner, "Capote's Swan Dive," and Fox, "Editor's Note." For contemporaneous responses, see, e.g., Burstein, "Tiny Yes," and Smith, "Truman Capote in Hot Water."

8   Kashner, "Capote's Swan Dive. "

9   *Masculinities*, 185.

10   Connell, "On Hegemonic," 90.

11   "Queer" is a difficult term in criticism, because it both signifies a theoretical position in which all identity is figured as non-essential and constructed, and an identity (as in "queer person") which is increasingly used in addition to, and sometimes instead of, "gay," "lesbian," or other more specific identifiers – in the latter sense, it may contradict the former sense. When referring to queer spaces or queer gender regimes, for instance, I use the term in the former sense, as detailed by Judith Halberstam, who states that the term *queer* "refers to nonnormative logics and organizations of community, sexual identity,

embodiment, and activity in space and time." See Halberstam, *In a Queer Time and Place*, 6. Queer spaces are therefore spaces in which nonnormative gender regimes can be mobilized (as I discuss). In instances when referring to an identity (e.g., "queer masculinity") or groups of individuals, it should be understood that I am invoking the latter sense of the word, though the former lingers in the margin, threatening to undo any simple essentialism.

12 "Ruptures in Hegemonic Masculinity," 198.

13 *Cruising Utopia*, 49.

14 "As for the Fashion Features," 6.

15 *Nothing but People*, 81.

16 Sedgwick's *Epistemology of the Closet* is, of course, the most well-known discussion of homophobia, masculinity, and literature. The sociologist Michael Kimmel also discusses the centrality of homophobia to the performance of heterosexual masculinity.

17 Jones and Bego, *Macho Man*, 52.

18 "Tom Wolfe's Seventies," *Esquire*, December 1979, 37.

19 Ibid., 36.

20 *Macho Man*, 53.

21 "'These Boots Were Made for Walkin,'" 157.

22 "Ruptures in Hegemonic Masculinity," 197.

23 *Masculinities*, 30, 37.

24 "Baldwin's Sissy Heroics," 648n12.

25 Andy Warhol could also be added to the list. He was frequently discussed, and published two pieces with *Esquire*: one of them, an essay on television, sees the artist seemingly misgender himself as he claims to enjoy watching "everything that makes you cry at ten in the morning while you're ironing or cleaning" ("TV," *Esquire*, December 1975, 136). The other piece by Warhol, "Say hello to the Dirty Half Dozen, Sierra Bandit, The American Playground and all the Superstars of the New Theatre," is discussed in Zuromskis' *Snapshot Photography*, 216.

26 In 1969, the magazine interjected itself into the public tiff between Vidal and William F. Buckley, Jr. The feud between the two public intellectuals began with Vidal calling Buckley a "crypto fascist" on national television during the 1968 Democratic Convention, and Buckley responding by threatening Vidal and labelling him a "queer," bringing to mind Ross's assertion that the sissy is "a suspect vestibule that warrants a charge of faggotry" (634). *Esquire* subsequently published Buckley's "On Experiencing Gore Vidal" and Vidal's response, "A Distasteful Encounter with William F. Buckley Jr." The two promptly sued each

other. The following year, Vidal published in *Esquire* "A Memoir in the
Form of a Novel," which was later republished as part of *Two Sisters*
(1970). The section published in *Esquire* features, among other things, a
scene in which Vidal and an associate visit a gay brothel and engage male
prostitutes. It was as though Vidal were challenging Buckley.

27 *How to Be an Intellectual*, 10.
28 Adams, "Dandyism," 220.
29 *White Girls*, 95.
30 "Young, Effeminate, and Strange," 293.
31 Adams, *Dandies and Desert Saints*, 209.
32 "In Cold Comfort," *Esquire*, June 1966, 124.
33 "Checking in with Truman Capote," *Esquire*, November 1972, 136.
34 "A Pleasant Evening with Yukio Mishima," *Esquire*, May 1972, 130.
35 Ibid., 174, 177.
36 Ibid., 127.
37 Ibid., 131.
38 Burke seems to be describing the emergence of the macho or "clone"
   identity within gay male culture. For a discussion of the fashion, see
   Cole's "Macho Man."
39 "The New Homosexuality," *Esquire*, December 1969, 178.
40 Ibid., 308.
41 Ibid., 315.
42 See Johnson "Physique Pioneers," 884–5.
43 Harry M. Benshoff briefly discuss homosexual content in *Esquire* at this
   time, including the specific examples of Ah Men, *A Time in Eden*,
   and Arthur B. Evans's article on Mishima, in *Monsters in the Closet*,
   179.
44 "*A Time in Eden* Advertisement," *Esquire*, May 1971, 208.
45 See Eril Broomes's glowing review of *A Time in Eden* in *The Advocate*, 20.
46 Muñoz, *Cruising Utopia*, 22–3.
47 Johnson, "Physique Pioneers," 885.
48 Evans and Gamman, "The Gaze Revisited," 48.
49 Segal, *Slow Motion*, 156.
50 Edelman, *Homographesis*, 7.
51 "Young, Effeminate, and Strange," 313.
52 Halberstam, *Queer Time*, 6. For a fuller discussion of counterpublics, see
   Warner, especially 56–63, 117–24, and 198–208.
53 Warner, *Publics and Counterpublics*, 57.
54 Delany, *Times Square Red*, 193–4.
55 Sedgwick, *Epistemology of the Closet*, 7.

56 Muñoz, *Cruising Utopia*, 133.
57 On *Other Voices, Other Rooms* as a queer *bildungsroman*, see Valente, "Other Possibilities." Significantly, a recent article by Jess Waggoner approaches the story from a disabilities-studies perspective; see "Cripping the Bildungsroman."
58 *Understanding Truman Capote*, 51.
59 "Camping the Gothic," 108.
60 *Understanding Truman Capote*, 65.
61 Ibid., 78.
62 "Capote's *Breakfast at Tiffany's*," 51.
63 *Understanding Truman Capote*, 107.
64 Farland, "'Total System, Total Solution, Total Apocalypse,'" 383.
65 St Pierre, "'Bent on Candor,'" 19.
66 "Yachts and Things," *Vanity Fair*, 15 November 2012.
67 "Mojave," 267.
68 *Answered Prayers*, 26. Hereafter referred to in-text.
69 See, e.g., masturbation (16), pedophilia (5), incest (15), rape (128), bestiality (49), urolagnia (105), homosexuality (passim), androgyny (13), transvestism (13), cross-dressing (127), and prostitution (passim). This is only a list of examples and is not definitive: page numbers refer to paperback edition.
70 "'Bent on Candor,'" 10.
71 One exception to this rule is Porfirio Rubirosa, the Dominican Ambassador. Rubirosa's inclusion in the jet set can be explained by his whiteness as well as his wealth.
72 Floyd, *The Reification of Desire*.
73 Marcuse, "The Affirmative Character of Culture," 116. Floyd draws attention to, and discusses, this same section of Marcuse's essay at 123–4.
74 Marcuse, *Eros and Civilization*, 201.
75 Segal, *Slow Motion*, 156.
76 Muñoz, *Cruising Utopia*, 1.
77 Désert, "Queer Space," 21.
78 Delany, *Times Square Red, Times Square Blue*, 111.
79 Ibid., 104.
80 Muñoz, *Cruising Utopia*, 134.
81 Warner, *Publics and Counterpublics*, 57.
82 For a fuller discussion of counterpublics, see especially 56–63, 117–24, and 198–208.
83 Ibid., 1.
84 Muñoz, *Cruising Utopia*, 1.

5 Sexual Fallout in Tim O'Brien's *The Nuclear Age*

1 Berlant, *Cruel Optimism*, 1.
2 Much has been written about gender in O'Brien's *The Things They
   Carried*. In particular, Lorrie Smith focuses on the stories in *Things*
   originally published in *Esquire*, arguing that, "Read sequentially, these
   stories make up an increasingly misogynist narrative of masculine
   homosocial behavior under fire" (20). Smith's justification for discussing
   the stories in the context of *Esquire* is that "It seems more than
   coincidental that the stories that most deeply probe and most
   emphatically reassert masculinity should appear in this glossy, upscale
   men's magazine famous, as [Susan] Faludi puts it, for its 'screeds against
   women'" (23). The most engaging answer to Smith's criticism comes
   from Pamela Smiley, who argues that it is through his female characters
   that O'Brien "de-genders the war, constructs an ideal (female) reader,
   and re-defines American masculinity" (602). Smiley's argument would
   be complicated by contextualizing O'Brien's stories in *Esquire*, where
   the ideal reader is not female, but male. An analysis of *The Things They
   Carried*, contextualized in *Esquire*, could greatly add to our understanding
   of not only the homosocial construction of masculinity, but also of the
   masculine construction of femininity. However, for the purposes of this
   study, I have chosen to focus on O'Brien's *The Nuclear Age*, because of its
   focus on the domestic sphere and consumption, both of which are more
   relevant to *Esquire*'s hegemonic masculinity project.
       For further analyses of gender in *The Things They Carried*, especially
   "Sweetheart of the Song Tra Bong," originally published in *Esquire*, see,
   e.g., Piedmont-Marton, Vanderwees, and Martin and Stiner.
3 Duguid, "The Addiction of Masculinity."
4 See Clark's *Cold Warriors*, discussed below, for an account of "Cold Warrior" masculinity.
5 Connell, *Gender and Power*, 183.
6 Jeffords, *The Remasculinization of America*.
7 Reeves, "Getting Ready for War," *Esquire*, April 24, 1979, 10.
8 Ibid.
9 Ibid., 12.
10 Ibid.
11 Schlesinger, "Crisis," 65.
12 May, *Homeward Bound*, 95.
13 The targeting of homosexuals during the "Red Scare" is often referred to
   as the "Lavender Scare." See Johnson's *The Lavender Scare*.

14 May, *Homeward Bound*, 106–7.
15 Foertsch, "Not Bombshells but Basketcases,"472.
16 As May further explains, "To avoid dire consequences, men as well as women had to contain their sexuality in marriage, where masculine men would be in control with sexually submissive, competent homemakers at their side" (95).
17 Heberle, *A Trauma Artist*, 174.
18 O'Brien, *The Nuclear Age*, 34. Hereafter cited in-text.
19 Herzog, *Tim O'Brien*, 130.
20 In a fascinating dissection of Cold War nuclear discourse, Daniel Grausam discusses this episode as a paradigmatic example of how late 1950s and 1960s nuclear rhetoric frequently transformed nuclear war "into a rule-governed exchange (almost, in the end, a conversation) rather than the catastrophe that Cowling dreads" (509).
21 Cordle, *States of Suspense*, 131.
22 Farrell, *Critical Companion to Tim O'Brien*, 21. Farrell makes this comment when discussing the version of the chapter that was first published in *Esquire* as "Civil Defense." The point, however, is equally applicable to the novel version.
23 Saltzman, *The Novel in the Balance*, 19.
24 Cordle, "In Dreams, In Imagination," 109.
25 Clark, *Cold Warriors*, 2; Starck, "The Early Cold Warrior," 17.
26 Clark, *Cold Warriors*, 2.
27 Holbrook, "There Was a Man: Wild Bill Hickok," *Esquire*, May 1950.
28 Holbrook, "There Was a Man: Daniel Boone," *Esquire*, July 1950, 58.
29 Holbrook, "There Was a Man: Davy Crockett," *Esquire*, August 1950.
30 Holbrook, "There Was a Man: Custer, Fighting General," *Esquire*, September 1950.
31 This is a pattern that Robert Rushing also identifies in peplum films. See Rushing, *Descended from Hercules*, 94–7.
32 Kimmel, *The History of Men*, 94–5.
33 *The Nuclear Age* is therefore one of many Cold War texts that criticizes the hypermasculine figures of the cowboy. Christopher Le Coney and Zoe Trodd discuss the more subversive film examples of John Schlesinger's *Midnight Cowboy* (1969) and Andy Warhol's *Lonesome Cowboys* (1969). See Le Coney and Trodd, "John Wayne and the Queer Frontier."
34 Benwell, *Masculinity*, 151.
35 Cuordileone, *Manhood*, viii; also quoted in Starck, "Early Cold Warrior," 16.
36 Kaplan, "The End of the Soft Line," *Esquire*, April 1980, 46.
37 Ibid., 47.

38 Ibid., 45.

39 Wayne was the paradigmatic cowboy of the era. See, e.g., Slotkin, *Gunfighter Nation*, 512–13.

40 In an interview discussing the cowboy myth as it related to his time in Vietnam and his later work *The Things They Carried* (much of which was also published in *Esquire*), O'Brien discusses how the cowboy figure in general – and John Wayne in particular – was held up as an exemplar of masculinity by some during the Vietnam war. See his interview with Twister Marquiss (especially 12).

41 Slotkin, *Gunfighter Nation*, 519–20.

42 Greene, "American Beat: A Wolf in Wolf's Clothing," *Esquire*, September 1980, 12.

43 Duguid, "The Addiction of Masculinity," 30.

44 Le Coney and Trodd, "Reagan's Rainbow Rodeos,"168.

45 *True Grit* (1969), based on the Charles Portis novel of the same name, featured one of Wayne's most iconic cowboy roles, as the marshal Reuben J. "Rooster" Cogburn.

46 Jeffords, *The Remasculinization of America*, 11.

47 Ibid., 12.

48 See, for example, Cohen's "Cowboys Die Hard." The article, focusing on John McTiernan's *Die Hard* (1988), argues that John McClane (Bruce Willis) is a cowboy figure for the 1980s, establishing himself as an exemplary masculinity (though Cohen does not use that term) in comparison to the businessmen figures found elsewhere in the film. As if describing an exemplary masculinity, Cohen writes, "Men like McClane, *Die Hard* suggests, know Westerns because they embody the authentic man's heritage, ideology, and language of being" (74–5).

49 Baudrillard, *Simulations*, 11.

50 O'Brien's *The Nuclear Age* was not the only 1980s text that complicated the cowboy's relationship to gender. See, for example, Le Coney and Trodd for a discussion of Delmas Howe's series of paintings entitled *Rodeo Pantheon* (1977–91), and the founding of the International Gay Rodeo Association (IGRA) in 1985. The authors argue that such individuals and groups "opened a counter-hegemonic space that challenged social marginalization in the public sphere," which allowed them to resist "the imposition of a rigidly heterosexual cowboy mythology and met Reagan's straight-shooting cowboy dreams on a queer frontier" (165).

51 Althusser, "Ideology," 130.

52 Strychacz, *Dangerous Masculinities*, 69.

53 Butler, "Imitation and Gender Insubordination," 21. Emphasis in original.

54 Strychacz, *Dangerous Masculinities*, 50.

55 Butler, *Bodies That Matter*, 2.

56 Butler, "Imitation and Gender Insubordination," 23.

57 Farrell, *Critical Companion to Tim O'Brien*, 21.

58 Throughout O'Brien's *The Things They Carried*, the author subverts the typical heroic war story by equating fighting and dying in Vietnam with cowardice rather than bravery. Both *The Nuclear Age* and *The Things They Carried* engage in a criticism of the "masculinization" of America in the 1980s.

59 Henriksen, *Dr Strangelove's America*, xix.

60 Foertsch, "Not Bombshells but Basketcases," 474.

61 Winkler, *Life under a Cloud: American Anxiety about the Atom* (Oxford University Press, 1993), 112, 133.

62 See, for example: Phillips and Michaelis, "How I Designed an A-Bomb" (1978); Smith, "Dr. Death" (1982); Zuckerman, "How Would the US Survive" (1982); and Schecter and Schecter, "The War Planners" (1983).

63 Smith, "In Case of Cataclysm," *Esquire*, November 1982, 16.

64 Ibid.

65 Henriksen, *Dr Strangelove's America*, 92.

66 Clarke, "VD Control," 4–5; May, *Homeward Bound*, 90.

67 Clarke, "VD Control," 7.

68 May, *Homeward Bound*, 91.

69 Ibid., 101, 102.

70 For an excellent analysis of the Do-It-Yourself fad and its relationship to masculinity and the gendering of the domestic sphere, see Steven Gelber.

71 Lichtman, "Do-It-Yourself Security," 40.

72 May, *Homeward Bound*, 101.

73 Quoted in Lichtman, "Do-It-Yourself Security," 40.

74 Kotkin and Grabowicz, "Dutch Reagan, All-American," *Esquire*, August 1980, 25.

75 O'Brien, "Civil Defense," *Esquire*, August 1980, 82.

76 Berlant, *Cruel Optimism*, 2.

77 Ibid.

78 Appended to the article is the following message: "The Office of Civil Defense Mobilization will send, direct to you, free, a set of simple plans for a home shelter that you can make yourself" ("Frightening" 61).

79 "A Frightening Message for a Thanksgiving Issue," 61.
80 Gelber, "Do-It-Yourself," 94.
81 "A Man's Castle Is His Home," *Esquire,* June 1951, 8.
82 Lichtman, "Do-It-Yourself Security," 39.
83 Baudrillard, *Simulations,* 60. This passage is also referenced by Messmer (399–400) in a study of the interpretation of nuclear culture.
84 Baudrillard also identifies nuclear deterrence as a cultural discourse dominated by hyperreality: "this is how simulation appears in the phase that concerns us – a strategy of the real, neo-real and hyperreal whose universal double is a strategy of deterrence" (12–13).
85 Derrida, "No Apocalypse, Not Now," 23. Both Foertsch and Cordle ("Cultures") reference Derrida's when discussing *The Nuclear Age.* Derrida's essay is central to the 1984 *Diacritics* issue on "Nuclear Criticism" and is often cited by literature scholars discussing nuclear or postnuclear fiction (see, e.g., Brewer's "Surviving Fictions," as well as most of Cordle's scholarship on nuclear fiction).
86 Cordle, *States of Suspense,* 130, 134. Cordle is the novel's most frequent and most compelling critic. His reading of the novel correctly emphasizes how William counters nuclear anxieties with domestic and consumerist fantasies. See *States of Suspense,* chapter 6, "In Dreams, In Imagination," and "Beyond the Apocalypse of Closure."
87 Much of the scholarly disagreement on *The Nuclear Age* focuses on how to read this ending. In Peter Schwenger's psychological reading (*Letter Bomb*), William's actions at the end are a type of therapy, and destroying the hole is an act of erasing William's psychological connection to the nuclear age itself (114). Lee Schweninger, writing from an ecofeminist perspective, finds the recognition of the need for an epistemological (and post-phallocentric) shift (183). Jacqueline Foertsch rather astutely uses the image of the hole to connect the novel to the "overarching homoerotics of the nuclear age" (478). Foertsch's analysis leads to a rather problematic reading of the ending: "the novel's homoeroticism is ultimately equated with bomb-generated madness and paranoia ... this equation forces us in search of curse and redemption not only for nuclear-generated madness, but for any suggestion of queerness as well" (478–9). For Foertsch, William's detonation of the hole can be read as a destruction of queerness. Foertsch backs up this reading by claiming that, following the detonation, William "releases his family, who begin to forgive and reaccept him" (478). This, however, does not occur in the text, and is merely a possible future that William imagines for himself. Responding most directly to Foertsch, but also to anyone who would too easily find in the ending a neat resolution, Cordle explains that William's

final words can only be understood as "self-deception … As readers, therefore, we are alienated from William's new vision and we cannot achieve the sense of closure that he finds" ("In Dreams" 115). Rather, Cordle argues, quite correctly, that "The novel, therefore, explicitly refuses to resolve the tension between the two alternatives – madness (shelter digging) and denial (conformity) – acted out by William in the course of his narrative" (116). Countering Schweninger, he argues that "This is not a radical 'ecofeminist vision' but a suburban fantasy, acquiescent to the primacy of the political status quo, and as much of a hole in which to shelter as the one he has dug in the garden. It is an admission that nothing can be done in the face of power" (114).

88 Connell, *Gender and Power*, 187.

89 In *The Jet Sex*, Victoria Vantoch argues that stewardesses both reflected Cold War gender roles and challenged them. As an example of emphasized femininity, a stewardess was thought of as "A high-flying expert at applying lipstick, warming baby bottles, and mixing a martini" (2), and seen as "a role model for American girls, and an ambassador of femininity and the American way abroad" (1). Vantoch goes on to challenge these assumptions by claiming that "the profession fostered a budding feminist consciousness among these women long before the American women's movement brought inequality into the mainstream national consciousness" (3). Bobbi's career is hardly accidental, then, since concepts of gender roles and gender power were central to her profession.

90 Like stewardesses, cheerleaders are important gendered figures in the American cultural imagination. In "Cheerleading and the Gendered Politics of Sport," Laura Grindstaff and Emily West specifically identify cheerleaders as examples of emphasized femininity. Discussing the activity during the twentieth century, the authors argue that,

> Female involvement changed the nature of cheerleading, shifting emphasis … to notions of physical attractiveness and sex appeal, which led to a white, middle class bias in the selection of female cheerleaders in the aftermath of desegregation and the trivialization and devaluation of cheerleading overall. Icons of "ideal" femininity notwithstanding, cheerleading is often considered a trivial activity and female cheerleaders have been negatively stereotyped as dumb and/or sexually promiscuous, particularly as traditional gender ideologies underwent significant change in the wake of second wave feminism. (504)

Grindstaff and West go on to argue that, as males became more involved in cheerleading in the last decades of the twentieth century, cheerleading became a gender regime "where the boundaries of gender difference are crossed as well as preserved" (515).

91 Connell, *Gender & Power*, 188.
92 Schwenger, *Letter Bomb*, 107.
93 Ibid.
94 Foertsch, "Not Bombshells but Basketcases," 476.
95 Cordle, "Beyond the Apocalypse of Closure, 72.
96 Ibid., 72–3. For a discussion of the significance of the difference between Bobbi's and William's rhetorical approach to the subject of nuclear warfare, see Grausam.
97 Beynon, *Masculinities and Culture*, 6, 159.
98 Gill, *Gender and the Media*, 206–7.
99 Cieply, "Uncommon," 162.

6 Don DeLillo in the American Kitchen

1 DeCurtis, "'An Outsider in This Society,'" 56.
2 Mitgang, "Reanimating Oswald."
3 DeLillo, *Underworld*, 487–9.
4 DeLillo, *Libra*, 181. Hereafter referenced in-text.
5 Green, "Disaster Footage," 586.
6 Boxall, *Don DeLillo*, 133.
7 Osteen, *American Magic and Dread*, 153.
8 Carmichael, "Lee Harvey Oswald," 207.
9 Jameson, *Postmodernism*, 355.
10 Ibid.
11 Gunzenhäuser, "'All Plots Lead toward Death,'" 79.
12 Warren, "Presidential Wounds," 573.
13 Wicker, "Kennedy Without Tears," *Esquire*, June 1964; Wicker, "Kennedy Without End, Amen," *Esquire*, July 1977.
14 Nelson, *National Manhood*, 218.
15 Wesley, *Violent Adventure*, 140–1.
16 Messerschmidt, "Becoming 'Real Men,'" 298.
17 Schlesinger, "Crisis," 65.
18 See *Empire of Conspiracy*, 12.
19 As discussed in the last chapter, the domestic sphere has the potential to be highly patriarchal; it depends on the type of masculinity being practiced by men in the domestic sphere, and whether or not they are able to dominate within that sphere.

20 DeLillo, *White Noise*, 245. Here, Gladney understands his own masculinity in response to the kind of Do-it-Yourself masculinity discussed in the last chapter. To him, his father-in-law demonstrates just such a type of masculinity, one that turns the domestic sphere into a patriarchal realm.

21 Ibid., 253.

22 Ibid., 21.

23 Timothy Melley notes that violence is used as a common response by DeLillo's male characters who feel that their agency is threatened. His principal example is Oswald's attempt on General Walker, stating that "This familiar form of masculine agency recovery is one of DeLillo's obsessions" (148).

24 DeLillo, "In the Men's Room of the Sixteenth Century," *Esquire*, December 1971, 176.

25 Ibid., 177.

26 The importance of the trope of "men and small rooms" – a phrase used in the novel – has been commented on by several critics of the novel. Most pertinent to a discussion of gender in the novel are Wesley and Belleggia, whose discussions will be analysed below.

27 DeLillo, "Human Moments in World War III," *Esquire*, July 1983, 123, 121.

28 DeLillo, "Players," *Esquire*, April 1977, 103.

29 Ibid., 104.

30 Much of the research on gender and the Central Intelligence Agency focuses on the Kennedy era. Dean's *Imperial Brotherhood* discusses the creation of an "Elite Masculinity" in Kennedy's foreign policy establishment, while Cuordileone writes that Kennedy was attracted to the CIA's style, seeing them as "the institution which best reflected the New Frontier's self-image: fast-acting, adventuresome, impatient with conventions, gutsy, and subversive" (215–16).

31 For a discussion of the importance of secrets in the novel, see Melley.

32 Helyer, "DeLillo and Masculinity," 125.

33 Remy Martin, "Advertisement," *Esquire*, September 1988; Food & Wine magazine, "Advertisement," *Esquire*, September 1988.

34 JCPenney, "Advertisement," *Esquire*, September 1988; Foltene Shampoo, "Advertisement," *Esquire*, September 1988.

35 Service Merchandise, "Advertisement," *Esquire*, September 1988.

36 Melley, *Empire*, 152.

37 Wesley, *Violent Adventure*, 157.

38 Belleggia, "Staging and Performing," 172.

39 DeCurtis, "'An Outsider in This Society,'" 57–8.
40 Nel, "Amazons in the Underworld,"434n11.
41 Wesley, *Violent Adventure*, 158.
42 Ibid., 142.
43 McFadden, "Tom Wicker."
44 Wicker, "Kennedy Without End," 67–8.
45 Ibid., 69.
46 Schlesinger, "The New Mood in Politics," *Esquire*, January 1960, 58, 59.
47 Ibid., 60.
48 Friedenberg, "Who Should Be President in 1960? What Should the Issues Be?," *Esquire*, January 1960, 63. Emphasis added.
49 Katz, *Leading Men*, 2.
50 Mailer, "Superman," 123–4.
51 Marche, "Kennedy, John F.," *Esquire*, October 2015, 134, 136.
52 Cuordileone, *Manhood*, 195.
53 Ibid., 169–70, 199.
54 Ibid., 195.
55 Cieply, "Uncommon," 159.
56 Ibid.
57 Ibid., 165.
58 Starck, "The Early Cold Warrior," 17.
59 Dean, *Imperial Brotherhood*, 170.
60 Ibid., 169. For a rhetorical analysis of how the American president uses masculinity as a political strategy, see Coe et al. For example, the authors discuss how two particular themes "suggestive of masculinity" are mobilized in political discourse: "The first theme we call *strength masculinity* because it taps into the traditional notion that, regardless of circumstances, leaders should be strong and resolute … The second theme we call *dominance masculinity* because it emphasizes aggression and/or violence (Coe et al. 34–5).
61 For a discussion of John Wayne's role as an exemplary masculinity, see chapter 5, "Sexual Fallout."
62 Nel, "Amazons in the Underworld," 428.
63 Ibid., 62.
64 Carmichael, "Lee Harvey Oswald," 209–10.
65 Dean, *Imperial Brotherhood*, 169.
66 Wesley, *Violent Adventure*, 140–1.
67 DeLillo's source may be Schlesinger's *A Thousand Days* (725).
68 For a discussion of the figure of the statesman, and how he reverses the democratic structures of representation, see Pease's *Visionary Compacts*, especially 32–5.

69 Pease, *Visionary Compacts*, 34.

70 Nelson, *National Manhood*, 223.

71 Mailer, "Superman," 123.

72 Wesley, *Violent Adventure*, 141.

73 Kavadlo, "Recycling Authority," 386.

74 Baudrillard, *Simulacra and Simulation*, 6. According to Baudrillard, there are four "successive phases of the image":
> It is the reflection of a profound reality;
> It masks and denatures a profound reality;
> It masks the *absence* of a profound reality;
> It has no relation to any reality whatsoever: it is its own pure simulacrum. (*Simulacra* 6)

75 Arensberg, "Seven Seconds," 45–6.

76 See also the description at 146–8.

77 Parrish, "The Lesson of History," 8.

78 Ibid., 12.

79 DeLillo seems to find this fact quite significant; for example, in one interview he quotes Oswald as writing that "He wanted to write 'short stories on contemporary American life'" (DeCurtis 60); he references the same quotation in Arensberg (44).

80 See, e.g., Earle's *All Man!*.

81 Parrish, "The Lesson of History," 10.

82 Ibid., 5. This particular quotation is widely discussed by critics. See, e.g., Tabbi (175), Carmichael (208), Finigan (190), and Kavadlo (396).

83 Gilbert and Gubar, *The Madwoman in the Attic*, 4.

84 Ibid.

85 Arensberg, "Seven Seconds," 46.

86 Updating Nina Baym's argument that male American authors have opposed their supposedly serious writing to encroaching femininity, Kathleen Fitzpatrick's *Anxiety of Obsolescence* similarly discusses DeLillo's work as a response to the perceived threat posed by television, which is associated (through a certain sexist logic) with women and minority writers.

87 Hills, "Literary Heat," *Esquire*, July 1988, 51.

88 DeLillo, "Oswald in the Lonestar State," *Esquire*, July 1988, 52.

89 Kavadlo, "Recycling Authority," 385.

90 DeLillo, "Oswald in the Lonestar State," 54.

91 Cieply, "Uncommon," 164–5.

92 Doctorow, "Ultimate Discourse," *Esquire*, August 1986.

93 Ibid.

94 *Masculinities*, 2nd ed., 77.

Conclusion

1 "What We Do."
2 Sager, "Are There Still Boy Scouts?," *Esquire*, October 2014.
3 Althusser, "Ideology," 110–13.
4 Sager, "Are There Still Boy Scouts?," 147.
5 Ibid., 148.
6 Junod, "Everything We Know About Mass Shooters Is Wrong," *Esquire*, October 2014.
7 Gramsci, "Hegemony," 75.
8 Moore, "How to Be a Man."
9 Ibid., 183.
10 Felski, *Uses of Literature*, 49.
11 Ibid., 104.
12 Connell, "The Big Picture," 614.
13 Ibid., 615.
14 Berlant, *Cruel Optimism*, 24.
15 Ibid.

Works Cited

Abu-Lughod, Janet L. *Race, Space, and Riots in Chicago, New York, and Los Angeles.* Oxford; New York: Oxford University Press, 2007.

Adams, James Eli. *Dandies and Desert Saints: Styles of Victorian Masculinity.* Ithaca: Cornell University Press, 1995.

— "Dandyism and Late Victorian Masculinity." In *Oscar Wilde in Context,* edited by Kerry Powell and Peter Raby, 220–9. Cambridge; New York: Cambridge University Press, 2013.

Aeronaves de Mexico. "Advertisement." *Esquire,* November 1958.

"Affluence & Influence." *Esquire Media Kit,* 2014.

"A Frightening Message for a Thanksgiving Issue." *Good Housekeeping,* November 1958.

Als, Hilton. *White Girls.* San Francisco: McSweeney's, 2014.

Althusser, Louis. "Ideology and Ideological State Apparatuses." In *Mapping Ideology,* edited by Slavoj Žižek, 100–40. London: Verso, 2012.

"A Magazine for Men Only." *Esquire,* Autumn 1933.

"A Man's Castle Is His Home." *Esquire,* June 1951.

Arensberg, Ann. "Seven Seconds." In *Conversations with Don DeLillo,* edited by Thomas DiPietro, 40–6. Jackson: University Press of Mississippi, 2005.

Armengol, Josep M. "In the Dark Room: Homosexuality and/as Blackness in James Baldwin's *Giovanni's Room.*" *Signs* 37, no. 3 (2012): 671–93. doi:10.1086/662699.

"As for General Content." *Esquire,* Autumn 1933.

"As for the Fashion Features." *Esquire,* Autumn 1933.

"*A Time in Eden* Advertisement." *Esquire,* May 1971.

"A Word to Our Readers." *Dissent,* Winter 1954.

Baldwin, James. "The Black Boy Looks at the White Boy." In *The Price of the Ticket: Collected Nonfiction, 1948–1985,* 289–303. New York: St Martin's, 1985.

- *Blues for Mister Charlie: A Drama in Three Acts.* New York: Samuel French, Inc., 1964.
- "Fifth Avenue, Uptown." In *The Price of the Ticket: Collected Nonfiction, 1948–1985*, 205–13. New York: St Martin's, 1985.
- *Giovanni's Room.* New York: Penguin Books Limited, 2001.
- "Going to Meet the Man." In *Going to Meet the Man*, 229–49. New York: Dial Press, 1965.
- "Here Be Dragons." In *The Price of the Ticket: Collected Nonfiction, 1948–1985*, 677–90. New York: St Martin's, 1985.
- "Interview." *Esquire,* July 1968.
- "The New Lost Generation." In *The Price of the Ticket: Collected Nonfiction, 1948–1985*, 305–13. New York: St Martin's, 1985.
Ballantine's. "Advertisement." *Esquire,* November 1958.
Baron, Herman. *Author Index to* Esquire, *1933–1973.* Metuchen: Scarecrow Press, 1976.
Barth, John. "A Few Words About Minimalism." *New York Times.* December 28, 1986, Late City Final Edition, sec. 7.
Baudrillard, Jean. *The Mirror of Production.* St Louis: Telos Press Publishing, 1975.
- *Simulacra and Simulation.* Translated by Sheila Faria Glaser. Ann Arbor: University of Michigan Press, 1994.
- *Simulations.* Los Angeles: Semiotext(e), Inc., 1983.
Baym, Nina. "Melodramas of Beset Manhood: How Theories of American Fiction Exclude Women Authors." *American Quarterly* 33, no. 2 (Summer 1981): 123–39.
Bell, Matt. "Black Ground, Gay Figure: Working through *Another Country*, Black Power, and Gay Liberation." *American Literature* 79, no. 3 (2007): 584–90. doi:10.1215/00029831-2007-021.
Belleggia, Lino. "Staging and Performing in Small Rooms: Don DeLillo's *Libra.*" *Critical Engagements: A Journal of Criticism and Theory* 2, no. 1 (Summer 2008): 167–94.
Benshoff, Harry M. *Monsters in the Closet: Homosexuality and the Horror Film.* Manchester, England: Manchester University Press, 1997.
Benwell, Bethan. "Introduction: Masculinity and Men's Lifestyle Magazines." In *Masculinity and Men's Lifestyle Magazines*, 6–30. Oxford, UK; Malden, USA: Blackwell, 2003.
- *Masculinity and Men's Lifestyle Magazines.* Oxford, UK; Malden, USA: Blackwell, 2003.
Berlant, Lauren. *Cruel Optimism.* Durham: Duke University Press, 2011.
- *The Queen of America Goes to Washington City: Essays on Sex and Citizenship.* Series Q. Durham: Duke University Press, 1997.

Bethea, Arthur F. *Technique and Sensibility in the Fiction and Poetry of Raymond Carver.* New York: Routledge Press, 2001.

Beynon, John. *Masculinities and Culture.* Buckingham: Open University Press, 2002.

Bornstein, George. *Material Modernism: The Politics of the Page.* Cambridge: Cambridge University Press, 2001.

Borstelmann, Thomas. *The 1970s: A New Global History from Civil Rights to Economic Inequality.* Princeton: Princeton University Press, 2012.

Bottomore, T.B., Laurence Harris, V.G. Kiernan, and Ralph Miliband, eds. *A Dictionary of Marxist Thought.* Cambridge: Harvard University Press, 1983.

Bourdieu, Pierre. *Masculine Domination.* Translated by Richard Nice. Redwood City: Stanford University Press, 2001.

Bourdieu, Pierre, and Loïc J.D. Wacquant. *An Invitation to Reflexive Sociology.* Chicago: University of Chicago Press, 1992.

Bowers, Abigail L. "Seeing Ourselves from the Outside: Voyeuristic Empathy in Raymond Carver's *Will You Please Be Quiet, Please?*" In *New Paths to Raymond Carver: Critical Essays on His Life, Fiction, and Poetry,* edited by Sandra Lee Kleppe, Robert Miltner, and Kirk Nesset, 92–103. Columbia: University of South Carolina Press, 2008.

Boxall, Peter. *Don DeLillo: The Possibility of Fiction.* New York: Routledge, 2006.

Boxer, David, and Cassandra Phillips. "*Will You Please Be Quiet, Please?* Voyeurism, Dissociation, and the Art of Raymond Carver." *Iowa Review* 10, no. 3 (1980): 75–90.

Breazeale, Kenon. "In Spite of Women: 'Esquire' Magazine and the Construction of the Male Consumer." *Signs* 20, no. 1 (1994): 1–22.

Brewer, Mária Minich. "Surviving Fictions: Gender and Difference in Postmodern and Postnuclear Narrative." *Discourse: Journal for Theoretical Studies in Media and Culture* 9 (Spring-Summer 1987): 37–52.

Bridges, Tristan S. "Gender Capital and Male Bodybuilders." *Body & Society* 15, no. 1 (1 March 2009): 83–107. doi:10.1177/1357034X08100148.

Broomes, Eril. "Roy Dean's Artistry Makes Volume of Rare Beauty." *Advocate,* July 1970.

Buchbinder, David. *Studying Men and Masculinities.* New York: Routledge, 2012.

Bufithis, Philip H. *Norman Mailer.* New York: Frederick Ungar Publishing Company, 1978.

Buford, Bill. "Editorial." *Granta,* 1983.

Burke, Tom. "The New Homosexuality." *Esquire,* December 1969.

Burn, Gordon. "Poetry, Poverty and Realism Down in Carver Country." In *Conversations with Raymond Carver,* edited by Marshall Bruce Gentry and William L. Stull, 113–19. Jackson: University Press of Mississippi, 1990.

Burstein, Patricia. "Tiny Yes, but a Terror?" *People*, 10 May 1976.

Butler, Judith. *Bodies That Matter: On the Discursive Limits of "Sex."* New York: Routledge, 1993.

— *Excitable Speech: A Politics of the Performative*. New York: Routledge, 1997.

— "Imitation and Gender Insubordination." In *Inside/Out: Lesbian Theories, Gay Theories*, edited by Diana Fuss, 13–31. New York: Routledge, 1991.

California Sportwear Company. "Advertisement." *Esquire*, November 1958.

Campbell, Ewing. *Raymond Carver: A Study of the Short Fiction*. New York: Twayne, 1992.

Capote, Truman. *Answered Prayers*. Reissue edition. New York: Vintage, 2012.

— "Dazzle." In *Music for Chameleons*, 51–64. Random House, 1980.

— "Mojave." In *The Complete Stories of Truman Capote*, 267–86. New York: Random House, 2004.

— "Yachts and Things." *Vanity Fair*, 15 November 2012. www.vanityfair.com/culture/photos/2012/11/truman-capote-unseen-manuscript-unfinished-novel-answered-prayers.

"Capote's Artful Nonfiction." *Esquire*, December 1979.

Carmichael, Thomas. "Lee Harvey Oswald and the Postmodern Subject: History and Intertextuality in Don DeLillo's *Libra, The Names*, and *Mao II*." *Contemporary Literature* 34, no. 2 (Summer 1993): 204–18.

Carver, Raymond. "Collectors." *Esquire*, August 1975.

— "Collectors." In *Collected Stories*, edited by William Stull and Maureen Carroll, 1st ed., 78–84. New York: Library of America, 2009.

— "Neighbors." *Esquire*, June 1971.

— "Neighbors." In *Collected Stories*, edited by William Stull and Maureen Carroll, 1st ed., 8–13. New York: Library of America, 2009.

— "What Is It?" In *Collected Stories*, edited by William Stull and Maureen Carroll, 1st ed., 157–64. New York: Library of America, 2009.

Chapman, Mary and Glenn Hendler, eds. *Sentimental Men: Masculinity and the Politics of Affect in American Culture*. Berkley: University of California Press, 1999.

Chauncey, George. *Gay New York: Gender, Urban Culture, and the Making of the Gay Male World, 1890–1940*. New York: Basic Books, 1994.

Christol, Hélène. "Whose Power? Baldwin and the 'American Legend of Masculinity.'" In *James Baldwin: His Place in American Literary History and His Reception in Europe*, edited by Jakob Köllhofer, 79–88. Frankfurt: Peter Lang, 1991.

Cieply, Stefan. "The Lineaments of Personality: 'Esquire' and the Problem of the Male Consumer." ProQuest Dissertations Publishing, 2006. http://hdl.handle.net/1903/4149.

– "The Uncommon Man: *Esquire* and the Problem of the North American Male Consumer, 1957–63." *Gender & History* 22, no. 1 (2010): 151–68. doi:10.1111/j.1468-0424.2010.01583.x.

Cinzano. "Advertisement." *Esquire*, November 1958.

Clark, Keith. *Black Manhood in James Baldwin, Ernest J. Gaines, and August Wilson.* Chicago: University of Illinois Press, 2002.

Clark, Suzanne. *Cold Warriors: Manliness on Trial in the Rhetoric of the West.* Carbondale: Southern Illinois University Press, 2000.

Clarke, Charles Walter. "VD Control in Atom-Bombed Areas." *Journal of Social Hygiene* 37, no. 1 (January 1951): 3–7.

Clarke, Gerald. "Checking in with Truman Capote." *Esquire*, November 1972.

Coe, Kevin, David Domke, Meredith M. Bagley, Sheryl Cunningham, and Nancy Van Leuven. "Masculinity as Political Strategy: George W. Bush, the 'War on Terrorism,' and an Echoing Press." *Journal of Women, Politics & Policy* 29, no. 1 (18 December 2007): 31–55. doi:10.1300/J501v29n01_03.

Cohen, Paul. "Cowboys Die Hard: Real Men and Businessmen in the Reagan-Era Blockbuster." *Film & History: An Interdisciplinary Journal of Film and Television* 41, no. 1 (Spring 2011): 71–81.

Cole, Shaun. "'Macho Man': Clones and the Development of a Masculine Stereotype." *Fashion Theory* 4, no. 2 (2000): 125–40.

Connell, Raewyn. "The Big Picture: Masculinities in Recent World History." *Theory and Society* 22, no. 5 (1993): 597–623.

– *Gender.* 2nd ed. Cambridge: Polity, 2009.

– *Gender and Power: Society, the Person, and Sexual Politics.* Redwood City: Stanford University Press, 1987.

– "An Iron Man: The Body and Some Contradictions of Hegemonic Masculinity." In *Sport, Men, and the Gender Order: Critical Feminist Perspectives,* edited by Michael A. Messner and Donald F. Sabo, 83–95. Champaign: Human Kinetics Books, 1990.

– *Masculinities.* 2nd ed. Berkeley: University of California Press, 2005.

– "On Hegemonic Masculinity and Violence: Response to Jefferson and Hall." *Theoretical Criminology* 6, no. 1 (1 February 2002): 89–99. doi:10.1177/136248060200600104.

Cordle, Daniel. "Beyond the Apocalypse of Closure: Nuclear Anxiety in Postmodern Literature of the United States." In *Cold War Literature: Writing the Global Conflict,* edited by Andrew Hammond, 63–77. New York: Routledge, 2006.

– "In Dreams, in Imagination: Suspense, Anxiety and the Cold War in Tim O'Brien's *The Nuclear Age.*" *Critical Survey* 19, no. 2 (2007): 101–20.

— *States of Suspense: The Nuclear Age, Postmodernism and United States Fiction and Prose.* Manchester; New York: Manchester University Press, 2008.

Cuordileone, K.A. *Manhood and American Political Culture in the Cold War.* New York: Routledge, 2005.

Cutty Sark. "Advertisement." *Esquire*, November 1958.

Dean, Robert D. *Imperial Brotherhood: Gender and the Making of Cold War Foreign Policy.* Amherst: University of Massachusetts Press, 2001.

DeCurtis, Anthony. "'An Outsider in This Society': An Interview with Don DeLillo." In *Conversations with Don DeLillo*, edited by Thomas DiPietro, 52–74. Jackson: University Press of Mississippi, 2005.

Delany, Samuel R. *Times Square Red, Times Square Blue.* New York; London: New York University Press, 1999.

DeLillo, Don. "Human Moments in World War III." *Esquire*, July 1983.

— "In the Men's Room of the Sixteenth Century." *Esquire*, December 1971.

— *Libra.* New York: Penguin Books, 2011.

— "The Lone Gunman Theory." *Esquire*, September 1988.

— "Oswald in the Lonestar State." *Esquire*, July 1988.

— "Players." *Esquire*, April 1977.

— *Underworld.* New York: Scribner, 1998.

— *White Noise.* New York: Penguin Books, 1986.

Derrida, Jacques. "No Apocalypse, Not Now (Full Speed Ahead, Seven Missiles, Seven Missives)." Translated by Catherine Porter and Philip Lewis. *Diacritics: A Review of Contemporary Criticism* 14, no. 2 (Summer 1984): 20–31.

Désert, Jean-Ulrick. "Queer Space." In *Queers in Space: Communities, Public Places, Sites of Resistance*, edited by Gordon Brent Ingram, Anne-Marie Bouthillette, and Yolanda Retter, 17–26. Seattle: Bay Press, 1997.

Dievler, James A. "Sexual Exiles: James Baldwin and *Another Country*." In *James Baldwin Now*, edited by Dwight McBride, 161–83. New York: New York University Press, 1999.

Ditz, Toby L. "The New Men's History and the Peculiar Absence of Gendered Power: Some Remedies from Early American Gender History." *Gender & History* 16, no. 1 (2004): 1–35. doi:10.1111/j.0953-5233.2004.324_1.x.

Docter, Richard. *Becoming a Woman: A Biography of Christine Jorgensen.* New York: Routledge, 2008.

Doctorow, E.L. "Ultimate Discourse." *Esquire*, August 1986.

Donaldson, Stephen. "A Million Jockers, Punks, and Queens." In *Prison Masculinities*, edited by Terry Allen Kupers, Willie James London, and Donald F. Sabo, 118–26. Philadelphia: Temple University Press, 2001.

Dowland, Douglas. "How Disgust Works: Truman Capote's 'La Côte Basque.'"
Journal of Modern Literature 39, no. 4 (29 September 2016): 67–84.

Duguid, Scott. "The Addiction of Masculinity: Norman Mailer's *Tough Guys
Don't Dance* and the Cultural Politics of Reaganism." *Journal of Modern
Literature* 30, no. 1 (Fall 2006): 23–30.

Earle, David M. *All Man! Hemingway, 1950s Men's Magazines, and the Masculine
Persona.* Kent: Kent State University Press, 2009.

– *Re-Covering Modernism: Pulps, Paperbacks, and the Prejudice of Form.*
Burlington: Ashgate, 2009.

Edelman, Lee. *Homographesis: Essays in Gay Literary and Cultural Theory.* New
York: Routledge, 1994.

– "The Part for the (W)hole: Baldwin, Homophobia, and the
Fantasmatics of 'Race.'" In *Homographesis: Essays in Gay Literary and
Cultural Theory,* 42–75. New York: Routledge, 1994.

Ehrenreich, Barbara. *The Hearts of Men: American Dreams and the Flight from
Commitment.* Garden City: Anchor Press/Doubleday, 1983.

Ehrenreich, Barbara, and John Ehrenreich. "The Professional-Managerial
Class." In *Between Labor and Capital,* edited by Pat Walker, 5–45. Boston:
South End Press, 1979.

– "The Real Story Behind the Crash and Burn of America's Managerial
Class." *AlterNet,* 19 February 2013. www.alternet.org/print/economy/
barbara-and-john-ehrenreich-real-story-behind-crash-and-burn-americas-
managerial-class.

Elger, Dietmar. *Gerhard Richter: A Life in Painting.* Chicago; London:
University of Chicago Press, 2009.

Ellmann, Mary. *Thinking about Women.* San Diego: Harcourt, Brace & World,
1968.

"Esquire's Sixth Annual Dubious Achievement Awards." *Esquire,* January
1967.

Evans, Caroline, and Lorraine Gamman. "The Gaze Revisited, or
Reviewing Queer Viewing." In *A Queer Romance: Lesbians, Gay Men and
Popular Culture,* edited by Paul Burston and Colin Richardson, 12–61. New
York: Routledge, 2005.

Evans, Oliver. "A Pleasant Evening with Yukio Mishima." *Esquire,* May 1972.

Ewen, Stuart, and Elizabeth Ewen. *Channels of Desire: Mass Images and the
Shaping of American Consciousness.* New York: McGraw-Hill, 1982.

Executive Research Institute. "Advertisement." *Esquire,* January 1964.

Fahy, Thomas Richard. *Understanding Truman Capote.* Columbia: University
of South Carolina Press, 2014.

Fanon, Frantz. *Black Skin, White Masks.* New York: Grove, 1968.

Farland, Maria. "'Total System, Total Solution, Total Apocalypse': Sex
  Oppression, Systems of Property, and 1970s Women's Liberation
  Fiction." *The Yale Journal of Criticism* 18, no. 2 (10 February 2006): 381–407.
  doi:10.1353/yale.2006.0006.

Farrell, Susan Elizabeth. *Critical Companion to Tim O'Brien: A Literary Reference
  to His Life and Work.* New York: Facts on File, 2011.

Featherstone, Mike. *Consumer Culture and Postmodernism.* 2nd ed. Los
  Angeles: SAGE, 2007.

Feldman, Susan. "Another Look at *Another Country*: Reconciling Baldwin's
  Racial and Sexual Politics." In *Re-Viewing James Baldwin: Things Not Seen,*
  edited by D. Quentin Miller, 88–104. Philadelphia: Temple University
  Press, 2000.

Felski, Rita. *Uses of Literature.* Malden, USA; Oxford: Blackwell, 2008.

Ferguson, Roderick. "The Nightmares of the Heteronormative." *Cultural
  Values* 4, no. 4 (2000): 419–44. doi:10.1080/14797580009367210.

Fetterley, Judith. *The Resisting Reader: A Feminist Approach to American Fiction.*
  Bloomington: Indiana University Press, 1978.

Finigan, Theo. "'There's Something Else That's Generating This Event': The
  Violence of the Archive in Don DeLillo's *Libra.*" *Critique: Studies in
  Contemporary Fiction* 55, no. 2 (2014): 187–205.

Fisher, Mark. *Capitalist Realism: Is There No Alternative?* Winchester: Zero
  Books, 2009.

Fitzpatrick, Kathleen. *The Anxiety of Obsolescence: The American Novel in the Age
  of Television.* Nashville: Vanderbilt University Press, 2006.

Floyd, Kevin. *The Reification of Desire: Toward a Queer Marxism.* Minneapolis:
  University of Minnesota Press, 2009.

Foertsch, Jacqueline. "Not Bombshells but Basketcases: Gendered Illness in
  Nuclear Texts." *Studies in the Novel* 31, no. 4 (Winter 1999): 471–88.

Foltene Shampoo. "Advertisement." *Esquire,* September 1988.

Food & Wine magazine. "Advertisement." *Esquire,* September 1988.

Fox, Joseph M. 1987. "Editor's Note." In *Answered Prayers,* xiii–xxii.

François, Anne-Lise. "'These Boots Were Made for Walkin'': Fashion as
  'Compulsive Artifice.'" In *The Seventies: The Age of Glitter in Popular Culture,*
  edited by Shelton Waldrep, 155–75. New York: Routledge, 2000.

Frank, Marcie. *How to Be an Intellectual in the Age of TV: The Lessons of Gore
  Vidal.* Durham: Duke University Press, 2005.

Friedenberg, Walter. "Who Should Be President in 1960? What Should the
  Issues Be?" *Esquire,* January 1960.

Gelber, Steven M. "Do-It-Yourself: Constructing, Repairing and Maintaining Domestic Masculinity." *American Quarterly* 49, no. 1 (1997): 66–112. doi:10.1353/aq.1997.0007.

Gentile, John. "Letter to the Editor." *Esquire*, July 1962.

Gentry, Marshall Bruce, and William L. Stull, eds. *Conversations with Raymond Carver.* Jackson: University Press of Mississippi, 1990.

Gilbert, James. *Men in the Middle: Searching for Masculinity in the 1950s.* Chicago: University of Chicago Press, 2005.

Gilbert, Sandra M., and Susan Gubar. *The Madwoman in the Attic: The Woman Writer and the Nineteenth-Century Literary Imagination.* New Haven: Yale University Press, 1979.

Gill, Rosalind. *Gender and the Media.* Polity, 2007.

Gingrich, Arnold. *Nothing but People: The Early Days at Esquire, a Personal History, 1928–1958.* New York: Crown Publishers, 1971.

– "On Fiction: The Strong, the Slick, the Good, and the Dull." *Esquire*, September 1962.

– "Public into Private and the New Boom in 'Unreal Estate.'" *Esquire*, January 1964.

Glenday, Michael K. *Norman Mailer.* New York: St Martin's Press, 1995.

Goddard, James L. "The Drug Establishment." *Esquire*, March 1969.

Godden, Richard. "Money and Things: Capitalist Realism, Anxiety, and Social Critique in Works by Hemingway, Wharton, and Fitzgerald." In *A Companion to the Modern American Novel, 1900–1950,* edited by John T. Matthews, 181–201. Malden, USA: Wiley-Blackwell, 2009.

Goffman, Erving. *Gender Advertisements.* New York: Harper & Row, 1979.

Goldman, Robert. *Reading Ads Socially.* London; New York: Routledge, 1992.

Gordon, Andrew. *An American Dreamer: A Psychoanalytic Study of the Fiction of Norman Mailer.* Rutherford: Fairleigh Dickinson University Press, 1980.

Government of Mexico Tourist Department. "Advertisement." *Esquire*, November 1958.

Gramsci, Antonio. "Hegemony, Intellectuals and the State." In *Cultural Theory and Popular Culture: A Reader,* edited by John Storey, 4th ed., 75–80. London: Pearson, 2009.

Grausam, Daniel. "Games People Play: Metafiction, Defense Strategy, and the Cultures of Simulation." *ELH* 78, no. 3 (Fall 2011): 507–32.

Green, Jeremy. "Disaster Footage: Spectacles of Violence in DeLillo's Fiction." *MFS: Modern Fiction Studies* 45, no. 3 (Fall 1999): 571–99.

Greene, Bob. "American Beat: A Wolf in Wolf's Clothing." *Esquire*, September 1980.

Grindstaff, Laura, and Emily West. "Cheerleading and the Gendered Politics of Sport." *Social Problems* 53, no. 4 (2006): 500–18. doi:10.1525/sp.2006.53.4.500.

Gunzenhäuser, Randi. "'All Plots Lead toward Death': Memory, History, and the Assassination of John F. Kennedy." *Amerikastudien/American Studies* 43, no. 1 (1998): 75–91.

Gutman, Stanley T. *Mankind in Barbary: The Individual and Society in the Novels of Norman Mailer.* Hanover: University Press of New England, 1975.

Haig Scotch. "Advertisement." *Esquire,* January 1967.

Halberstam, Judith. *Female Masculinity.* Durham: Duke University Press, 1998.

– *In a Queer Time and Place: Transgender Bodies, Subcultural Lives.* New York: New York University Press, 2005.

– "Thugs and Kings: Post-Imperial Masculinities in Recent Movies on Men and Masculinities." In *Un-Sichtbarkeiten Der Differenz: Beiträge Zur Genderdebatte in Den Künsten,* edited by Annette Jael Lehmann, 145–64. Tübingen: Stauffenburg, 2001.

Hall, Stuart. "Notes on Deconstructing 'the Popular.'" In *Cultural Theory and Popular Culture: A Reader,* edited by John Storey, 508–18. Edinburgh: Pearson Longman, 2009.

Hall, Vanessa. "Influences of Feminism and Class on Raymond Carver's Short Stories." *Raymond Carver Review* 2 (Spring 2009): 54–80.

Hammill, Faye, Paul Hjartarson, and Hannah McGregor. "Introducing Magazines and/as Media: The Aesthetics and Politics of Serial Form." *English Studies in Canada* 41, no. 1 (March 2015): 1–18.

Harker, Ben. "'To Be There, Inside, and Not Be There': Raymond Carver and Class." *Textual Practice* 21, no. 4 (December 2007): 715–36.

Harper, Phillip Brian. *Are We Not Men? Masculine Anxiety and the Problem of African American Identity.* New York: Oxford University Press, 1996.

Harvey, David. *A Brief History of Neoliberalism.* Oxford: Oxford University Press, 2005.

Haug, Wolfgang Fritz. *Commodity Aesthetics, Ideology & Culture.* New York: International General, 1987.

Heberle, Mark A. *A Trauma Artist: Tim O'Brien and the Fiction of Vietnam.* Iowa City: University of Iowa Press, 2001.

Heller, Steven. "*Esquire* and Its Art Directors: A Survivor's Tale." In *Graphic Design History,* edited by Steven Heller and Georgette Balance, 51–63. New York: Allworth Press, 2001.

Helyer, Ruth. "DeLillo and Masculinity." In *The Cambridge Companion to Don DeLillo,* edited by John N. Duvall, 125–36. Cambridge, UK: Cambridge University Press, 2008.

Hemmingson, Michael. "Saying More without Trying to Say More: On Gordon Lish Reshaping the Body of Raymond Carver and Saving Barry Hannah." *Critique: Studies in Contemporary Fiction* 52, no. 4 (2011): 479–98.

Henriksen, Margot A. *Dr Strangelove's America: Society and Culture in the Atomic Age.* Oakland: University of California Press, 1997.

Hentschel, Martin. "Konrad Lueg and Gerhard Richter, Living with Pop – A Demonstration on Behalf of Capitalist Realism." In *Shopping: A Century of Art and Consumer Culture*, edited by Christoph Grunenberg and Max Hollein, 179–87. Ostfildern-Ruit, Germany: Hatje Cantz, 2002.

Herbert, Thomas Walter. *Sexual Violence and American Manhood.* Cambridge: Harvard University Press, 2002.

Hermes, Joke. *Reading Women's Magazines: An Analysis of Everyday Media Use.* Oxford: Wiley, 1995.

Herzog, Tobey C. *Tim O'Brien.* New York: Twayne, 1997.

Hills, Rust. "Literary Heat." *Esquire,* July 1988.

– "The Structure of the American Literary Establishment." *Esquire,* July 1963.

Holbrook, Stewart H. "There Was a Man: Custer, Fighting General." *Esquire,* September 1950.

– "There Was a Man: Daniel Boone." *Esquire,* July 1950.

– "There Was a Man: Davy Crockett." *Esquire,* August 1950.

– "There Was a Man: Wild Bill Hickok." *Esquire,* May 1950.

Hooks, Bell. *Yearning: Race, Gender, and Cultural Politics.* New York: South End Press, 1990.

Horlacher, Stefan. "Towards Comparative Masculinity Studies: On the Independence of National Identity and the Construction of Masculinity." In *Post-World War II Masculinities in British and American Literature and Culture: Towards Comparative Masculinity Studies*, edited by Stefan Horlacher and Kevin Floyd, 1–14. Burlington: Ashgate, 2013.

Horlacher, Stefan, and Kevin Floyd, eds. *Post-World War II Masculinities in British and American Literature and Culture: Towards Comparative Masculinity Studies.* Burlington, VT: Ashgate, 2013.

Iger, Eve Marie. "How to Fly to Europe without Buying a Ticket." *Esquire,* January 1967.

"In the Absence of a Hero for the Seventies." *Esquire,* March 1972.

Jackson, Peter, Nick Stevenson, and Kate Brooks. *Making Sense of Men's Magazines.* Oxford: Wiley, 2001.

Jameson, Fredric. *Postmodernism, or, the Cultural Logic of Late Capitalism.* Durham: Duke University Press, 2005.

JCPenney. "Advertisement." *Esquire,* September 1988.

Jeffords, Susan. *The Remasculinization of America: Gender and the Vietnam War.* Bloomington: Indiana University Press, 1989.

Jhally, Sut. *The Codes of Advertising: Fetishism and the Political Economy of Meaning in the Consumer Society.* New York: Routledge, 1990.

Jockey Underwear. "Advertisement." *Esquire*, November 1958.

Johansson, Thomas, and Andreas Ottemo. "Ruptures in Hegemonic Masculinity: The Dialectic Between Ideology and Utopia." *Journal of Gender Studies* 24, no. 2 (March 4, 2015): 192–206. doi:10.1080/09589236.2013.812514.

Johnson, David K. *The Lavender Scare: The Cold War Persecution of Gays and Lesbians in the Federal Government.* Chicago: University of Chicago Press, 2004.

– "Physique Pioneers: The Politics of 1960s Gay Consumer Culture." *Journal of Social History* 43, no. 4 (2010): 867–92.

Jones, Randy, and Mark Bego. *Macho Man: The Disco Era and Gay America's "Coming Out."* Westport: Praeger, 2009.

Jorgensen, Christine, and Susan Stryker. *Christine Jorgensen: A Personal Autobiography.* San Francisco: Cleis Press, 2000.

Joseph, Richard. "The Perfect Male Shopping Spree." *Esquire*, August 1975.

– "A Sportsman's Tip Sheet on the West Indies." *Esquire*, January 1967.

– "Travel Notes: Mexico." *Esquire*, November 1958.

Junod, Tom. "Everything We Know about Mass Shooters Is Wrong." *Esquire*, October 2014.

– "The Last Man Standing." *Esquire*, January 2007.

Kaplan, Peter W. "The End of the Soft Line." *Esquire*, April 1980.

Kashner, Sam. "Capote's Swan Dive." *Vanity Fair.* Accessed 5 July 2016. www.vanityfair.com/culture/2012/12/truman-capote-answered-prayers

Katz, Jackson. *Leading Men: Presidential Campaigns and the Politics of Manhood.* Northampton, USA: Interlink Books, 2013.

Kavadlo, Jesse. "Recycling Authority: Don DeDillo's Waste Management." *Critique: Studies in Contemporary Fiction* 42, no. 4 (Summer 2001): 384–401.

Kenney, Edwin J. "Take April as She Is." *New York Times.* November 2, 1986.

Kervin, Denise. "Advertising Masculinity: The Representation of Males in *Esquire* Advertisements." *Journal of Communication Inquiry* 14, no. 1 (1990): 51–70.

Kimmel, Michael. *Angry White Men: American Masculinity at the End of an Era.* New York: Nation Books, 2013.

– *The History of Men: Essays on the History of American and British Masculinities.* New York: SUNY Press, 2005.

– "Masculinity as Homophobia: Fear, Shame and Silence in the Construction of Gender Identity." In *Men and Power*, edited by Joseph Kuypers, 84–103. Halifax, NS: Fernwood Press, 1999.

Konstantinou, Lee. *Cool Characters: Irony and American Fiction.* Cambridge: Harvard University Press, 2016.

Kotkin, Joel, and Paul Grabowicz. "Dutch Reagan, All-American." *Esquire,* August 1980.

Kraft, Joe. "Washington's Most Powerful Reporter." *Esquire,* November 1958.

Lacan, Jacques. "The Mirror Stage as Formative of the I Function as Revealed in Psychoanalytic Experience." In *Contemporary Critical Theory,* edited by Dan Latimer, translated by Alan Sheridan, 502–9. Orlando: Harcourt Brace, 1989.

Lasker, Lawrence. "A Whiter Shade of Black." *Esquire,* July 1968.

Le Coney, Christopher, and Zoe Trodd. "John Wayne and the Queer Frontier: Deconstructions of the Classic Cowboy Narrative during the Vietnam War." *Americana: The Journal of American Popular Culture (1900-Present)* 5, no. 1 (Spring 2006). www.americanpopularculture.com/journal/articles/spring_2006/le_coney_trodd.htm.

– "Reagan's Rainbow Rodeos: Queer Challenges to the Cowboy Dreams of Eighties America." *Canadian Review of American Studies/Revue Canadienne d'Etudes Américaines* 39, no. 2 (2009): 163–83.

Leeds, Barry H. *The Structured Vision of Norman Mailer.* New York: New York University Press, 1969.

Leeming, David Adams. *James Baldwin: A Biography.* New York: Knopf, 1994.

Leigh, Nigel. *Radical Fictions and the Novels of Norman Mailer.* St Martin's Press, 1990.

Leiter, Andrew B. *In the Shadow of the Black Beast: African American Masculinity in the Harlem and Southern Renaissances.* Baton Rouge: Louisiana State University Press, 2010.

Lichtman, Sarah A. "Do-It-Yourself Security: Safety, Gender, and the Home Fallout Shelter in Cold War America." *Journal of Design History* 19, no. 1 (20 March 2006): 39–55. doi:10.1093/jdh/epk004.

Lipnitzki, Bernard. "Advice for Summer Drinkers: Cool It." *Esquire,* July 1968.

Long, Barbara. "In Cold Comfort." *Esquire,* June 1966.

Look magazine, ed. *The Decline of the American Male.* New York: Random House, 1958.

Lukács, Georg. "Reification and the Consciousness of the Proletariat." In *History and Class Consciousness: Studies in Marxist Dialectics,* translated by Rodney Livingstone, 83–222. Cambridge: MIT Press, 1971.

Mailer, Norman. *Advertisements for Myself.* London: Andre Deutsch, 1961.

– *An American Dream.* New York: Vintage Books, 1999.

– "The Big Bite." *Esquire,* December 1963.

- "Green Circles of Exhaustion." *Esquire*, April 1964.
- "The Harbors of the Moon." *Esquire*, January 1964.
- "The Language of Men." *Esquire*, April 1953.
- "Letter to the Editor." *Esquire*, January 1961.
- "A Messenger from the Maniac." *Esquire*, March 1964.
- "Norman Mailer versus Nine Writers." *Esquire*, July 1963.
- "Superman Comes to the Supermart." *Esquire*, November 1968.

Majors, Richard, and Janet Mancini Billson. *Cool Pose: The Dilemmas of Black Manhood in America*. New York: Lexington Books, 1992.

"Male Profile." *Esquire Media Kit*, 2014.

Marche, Stephen. "Kennedy, John F." *Esquire*, October 2015.

Marcuse, Herbert. "The Affirmative Character of Culture." In *Negations: Essays in Critical Theory*, translated by Jeremy J. Shapiro, 88–133. Boston: Beacon Press, 1968.

- *Eros and Civilization: A Philosophical Inquiry into Freud*. London: Ark Paperbacks, 1987.

Marquiss, Twister. "Westward Ho! (Chi Minh): Tim O'Brien and the Wounding of the American Cowboy Mythos." *Southwestern American Literature* 29, no. 2 (Spring 2004): 9–15.

Marsh, Kelly A. "Empathy, Authority, and the Narrative Ethics of Truman Capote's 'La Côte Basque, 1965.'" *Journal of Narrative Theory* 43, no. 2 (2013): 218–44. doi:10.1353/jnt.2013.0023.

Martin, Terry J., and Margaret Stiner. "'Sweetheart of the Song Tra Bong': Tim O'Brien's (Feminist?) Heart of Darkness." *Short Story* 9, no. 2 (Fall 2001): 94–104.

Massé, Michelle A., and Karen Rosenblum. "Male and Female Created They Them: The Depiction of Gender in the Advertising of Traditional Women's and Men's Magazines." *Women's Studies International Forum* 11, no. 2 (1988): 127–44.

May, Elaine Tyler. *Homeward Bound: American Families in the Cold War Era*. New York: Basic Books, 2008.

McFadden, Robert D. "Tom Wicker, Journalist and Observer, Dies at 85." *The New York Times*, 25 November 2011. www.nytimes.com/2011/11/26/us/tom-wicker-journalist-and-author-dies-at-85.html.

McGann, Jerome J. *The Textual Condition*. Princeton: Princeton University Press, 1991.

McGurl, Mark. *The Program Era: Postwar Fiction and the Rise of Creative Writing*. Cambridge: Harvard University Press, 2009.

McKinley, Maggie. *Masculinity and the Paradox of Violence in American Fiction, 1950–75*. New York: Bloomsbury Academic, 2015.

Melley, Timothy. *Empire of Conspiracy: The Culture of Paranoia in Postwar America*. Ithaca: Cornell University Press, 2000.

Meloy, Mike. "Tales of the 'Great Bitch': Murder and the Release of Virile Desire in *An American Dream*." *The Mailer Review* 3, no. 1 (22 September 2009): 337–56.

Merrill, Hugh. *Esky: The Early Years at Esquire*. New Brunswick: Rutgers University Press, 1995.

Messerschmidt, James W. "Becoming 'Real Men': Adolescent Masculinity Challenges and Sexual Violence." *Men and Masculinities* 2, no. 3 (1 January 2000): 286–307. doi:10.1177/1097184X00002003003.

Messner, Michael A., and Donald F. Sabo, eds. *Sport, Men, and the Gender Order: Critical Feminist Perspectives*. Champaign: Human Kinetics Books, 1990.

Meyer, Karl E. "The Washington Press Establishment." *Esquire*, April 1964.

Meyerowitz, Joanne. "Transforming Sex: Christine Jorgensen in the Postwar U.S." *Magazine of History* 20, no. 2 (2006): 16–20.

Mid-Century Book Society. "Advertisement." *Esquire*, October 1964.

Miller, Gabriel. "A Small Trumpet of Defiance: Politics and the Buried Life in Norman Mailer's Early Fiction." In *Norman Mailer*, edited by Harold Bloom, 67–81. Philadelphia: Chelsea House, 2003.

Millett, Kate. *Sexual Politics*. New York: Columbia University Press, 2016.

Mills, C. Wright. *White Collar: The American Middle Classes*. Oxford: Oxford University Press, 2002.

Mills, Nathaniel. "Cleaver/Baldwin Revisited: Naturalism and the Gendering of Black Revolution." *Studies in American Naturalism* 7, no. 1 (Summer 2012): 50–79.

Mitchell-Peters, Brian. "Camping the Gothic: Que(e)ring Sexuality in Truman Capote's *Other Voices, Other Rooms*." *Journal of Homosexuality* 39, no. 1 (2000): 107–38. doi:10.1300/J082v39n01_07.

Mitgang, Herbert. "Reanimating Oswald, Ruby et al. in a Novel on the Assassination." *New York Times on the Web*, 19 July 1988. www.nytimes.com/books/97/03/16/lifetimes/del-v-oswald.html.

Monti, Enrico. "*Il Miglior Fabbro?* On Gordon Lish's Editing of Raymond Carver's *What We Talk about When We Talk about Love*." *Raymond Carver Review* 1 (2007): 53–74.

Moore, Liz. "How to Be a Man." In *The Book of Men*, edited by Colum McCann, Tyler Cabot, and Lisa Consiglio, 181–3. New York: Picador, 2013.

Muñoz, José Esteban. *Cruising Utopia: The Then and There of Queer Futurity*. New York: NYU Press, 2009.

NAACP Legal Defense & Educational Fund. "Advertisement." *Esquire*, July 1968.

Neal, Larry. "The Black Arts Movement." In *The Norton Anthology of African American Literature,* edited by Henry Louis Gates and Nellie Y. McKay, 2nd ed., 2039–50. New York: W.W. Norton, 2004.

Nel, Philip. "Amazons in the Underworld: Gender, the Body, and Power in the Novels of Don DeLillo." *Critique: Studies in Contemporary Fiction* 42, no. 4 (Summer 2001): 416–36.

Nelson, Dana D. *National Manhood: Capitalist Citizenship and the Imagined Fraternity of White Men.* Durham: Duke University Press, 1998.

Nesset, Kirk. *The Stories of Raymond Carver: A Critical Survey.* Athens: Ohio University Press, 1995.

Newman, David, and Robert Benton. "The New Sentimentality." *Esquire,* July 1964.

"New Year's Eve with Elegance." *Esquire,* January 1967.

O'Brien, Tim. "Civil Defense." *Esquire,* August 1980.

– *The Nuclear Age.* New York: Penguin Books, 1985.

Osgerby, Bill. *Playboys in Paradise: Masculinity, Youth and Leisure-Style in Modern America.* Oxford; New York: Berg, 2001.

– "Two-Fisted Tales of Brutality and Belligerence: Masculinity and Meaning in the American 'True Adventure' Pulps of the 1950s and 1960s." In *Masculinity and the Other: Historical Perspectives,* edited by Heather Ellis and Jessica Meyer, 163–89. Newcastle upon Tyne: Cambridge Scholars, 2009.

Osteen, Mark. *American Magic and Dread: Don DeLillo's Dialogue with Culture.* Philadelphia: University of Pennsylvania Press, 2000.

Parker, Hershel. "Norman Mailer's Revision of the *Esquire* Version of *An American Dream*: The Authority of 'Built-In' Intentionality." *Bulletin of Research in the Humanities* 84, no. 4 (1981): 405–30.

Parrish, Timothy L. "The Lesson of History: Don DeLillo's Texas Schoolbook, *Libra.*" *CLIO: A Journal of Literature, History, and the Philosophy of History* 30, no. 1 (Fall 2000): 1–23.

Pease, Donald E. *Visionary Compacts: American Renaissance Writings in Cultural Context.* Madison: University of Wisconsin Press, 1987.

Pendergast, Tom. *Creating the Modern Man: American Magazines and Consumer Culture, 1900–1950.* Columbia: University of Missouri Press, 2000.

Penner, James. *Pinks, Pansies, and Punks: The Rhetoric of Masculinity in American Literary Culture.* Bloomington: Indiana University Press, 2011.

Perfect Voice Institute. "Advertisement." *Esquire,* January 1964.

Phillips, John Aristotle, and David Michaelis. "How I Designed an A-Bomb My Junior Year at Princeton." *Esquire,* 1 August 1978.

Piedmont-Marton, Elisabeth H. "Doing Gender and Going Native in 'Sweetheart of the Song Tra Bong.'" In *Approaches to Teaching the Works of*

Tim O'Brien, edited by Alex Vernon and Catherine Calloway, 163–70. New York: Modern Language Association of America, 2010.

Plath, James. "On Raymond Carver." In *Raymond Carver*, edited by James Plath, 3–18. Ipswich, MA: Salem, 2013.

– ed. *Raymond Carver*. Ipswich, MA: Salem, 2013.

Plymouth Barracuda. "Advertisement." *Esquire*, January 1967.

Pochmara, Anna. *The Making of the New Negro: Black Authorship, Masculinity, and Sexuality in the Harlem Renaissance*. Amsterdam: Amsterdam University Press, 2011.

Polsgrove, Carol. *It Wasn't Pretty, Folks, but Didn't We Have Fun?: Surviving the '60s with* Esquire*'s Harold Hayes*. Oakland: RDR Books, 2001.

Pugh, Tison. "Capote's *Breakfast at Tiffany's*." *The Explicator* 61, no. 1 (2002): 51–3. doi:10.1080/00144940209597753.

Reddy, Dick. "Papa Is a Patsy." *Esquire*, July 1954.

Reeves, Richard. "Getting Ready for War." *Esquire*, 24 April 1979.

Reid-Pharr, Robert. "Tearing the Goat's Flesh: Homosexuality, Abjection and the Production of a Late-Twentieth-Century Black Masculinity." *Studies in the Novel* 28, no. 3 (1996): 372–94.

RelaxAcizor. "Advertisement." *Esquire*, February 1964.

Remy Martin. "Advertisement." *Esquire*, September 1988.

Ricciardelli, Rosemary, Kimberley A. Clow, and Philip White. "Investigating Hegemonic Masculinity: Portrayals of Masculinity in Men's Lifestyle Magazines." *Sex Roles* 63, nos. 1–2 (31 March 2010): 64–78. doi:10.1007/s11199-010-9764-8.

Rice, J.B. "Woman: The Overrated Sex." *Esquire*, February 1950.

Riesman, David, Reuel Denney, and Nathan Glazer. *The Lonely Crowd: A Study of the Changing American Character*. Edited by Todd Gitlin. Abridged and rev. ed. New Haven; London: Yale Nota Bene, 2001.

Rosenberg, Harold. "The Art Establishment." *Esquire*, January 1965.

Ross, Marlon Bryan. "Baldwin's Sissy Heroics." *African American Review* 46, no. 4 (Winter 2013): 633–51.

– "White Fantasies of Desire: Baldwin and the Racial Identities of Sexuality." In *James Baldwin Now*, edited by Dwight McBride, 13–55. New York: New York University Press, 1999.

Rovere, Richard H. "The American Establishment." *Esquire*, May 1962.

– "Notes on the Establishment in America." *American Scholar*, Autumn 1961.

Ruark, Robert C. "Mystery Unincorporated." *Esquire*, November 1950.

– "What Hath God Wrought?" *Esquire*, October 1950.

Rushing, Robert A. *Descended from Hercules: Biopolitics and the Muscled Male Body on Screen*. Bloomington: Indiana University Press, 2016.

Sager, Mike. "Are There Still Boy Scouts?" *Esquire*, October 2014.

Saltzman, Arthur M. *The Novel in the Balance*. Columbia: University of South Carolina Press, 1993.

Schecter, Jerrold L., and Leona P. Schecter. "The War Planners." *Esquire*, January 1983.

Schlesinger, Arthur. "The Crisis of American Masculinity." *Esquire*, November 1958.

– "The New Mood in Politics." *Esquire*, January 1960.

– *A Thousand Days: John F. Kennedy in the White House*. 1965. Boston: Houghton Mifflin Harcourt, 2002.

Schmitt, Richard. "Large Propagators: Racism and the Domination of Women." In *Revealing Male Bodies*, edited by Nancy Tuana, William Cowling, Maurice Hamington, and Greg Johnson, 38–54. Bloomington: Indiana University Press, 2002.

Schudson, Michael. *Advertising, the Uneasy Persuasion: Its Dubious Impact on American Society*. New York: Basic Books, 1984.

Schwenger, Peter. *Letter Bomb: Nuclear Holocaust and the Exploding World*. Baltimore: Johns Hopkins University Press, 1992.

– *Phallic Critiques: Masculinity and Twentieth-Century Literature*. London; Boston: Routledge & Kegan Paul, 1984.

Schweninger, Lee. "Ecofeminism, Nuclearism, and O'Brien's *The Nuclear Age*." In *The Nightmare Considered: Critical Essays on Nuclear War Literature*, edited by Nancy Anisfield, 151–85. Bowling Green: Popular, 1991.

Scott, Darieck. *Extravagant Abjection: Blackness, Power, and Sexuality in the African American Literary Imagination*. New York: NYU Press, 2010.

Sedgwick, Eve Kosofsky. *Between Men: English Literature and Male Homosocial Desire*. New York: Columbia University Press, 1985.

– *Epistemology of the Closet*. Berkeley: University of California Press, 1990.

Segal, Lynne. *Slow Motion: Changing Masculinities, Changing Men*. New Brunswick: Rutgers University Press, 1990.

Serlin, D.H. "Christine Jorgensen and the Cold War Closet." *Radical History Review* 1995, no. 62 (1 April 1995): 137–65. doi:10.1215/01636545-1995-62-137.

Service Merchandise. "Advertisement." *Esquire*, September 1988.

Shaw, Justin. "Destabilizing Sexistentialism and Hegemonic Masculinity in Norman Mailer's *An American Dream*." *Canadian Review of American Studies* 44, no. 1 (1 January 2014): 44–64. doi:10.3138/cras.2013.030.

Shin, Andrew, and Barbara Judson. "Beneath the Black Aesthetic: James Baldwin's Primer of Black American Masculinity." *African American Review* 32, no. 2 (Summer 1998): 247–61.

Shonkwiler, Alison, and Leigh Claire La Berge. "Introduction: A Theory of Capitalist Realism." In *Reading Capitalist Realism*, edited by Alison Shonkwiler and Leigh Claire La Berge, 1–25. Iowa City: University of Iowa Press, 2014.

Silverstein, Howard. "Norman Mailer and the Quest for Manhood." Eastern Illinois University, 1973.

Simmons, Philip E. "Minimalist Fiction as 'Low' Postmodernism: Mass Culture and the Search for History." *Genre: Forms of Discourse and Culture* 24, no. 1 (Spring 1991): 45–62.

Skenazy, Paul. "Life in Limbo: Ray Carver's Fiction." *Enclitic* 11 (1988): 77–83.

Sklenicka, Carol. *Raymond Carver: A Writer's Life.* New York: Scribner, 2009.

Slotkin, Richard. *Gunfighter Nation: The Myth of the Frontier in Twentieth-Century America.* Norman: University of Oklahoma Press, 1992.

Smiley, Pamela. "The Role of the Ideal (Female) Reader in Tim O'Brien's *The Things They Carried*: Why Should Real Women Play?" *Massachusetts Review: A Quarterly of Literature, the Arts and Public Affairs* 43, no. 4 (January 2003): 602–13.

Smith, Adam. "Dr. Death Will See You Now." *Esquire*, February 1982.

– "In Case of Cataclysm." *Esquire*, November 1982.

Smith, Erin. *Hard-Boiled.* Philadelphia: Temple University Press, 2000.

Smith, Liz. "Truman Capote in Hot Water." *New York*, 9 February 1976.

Smith, Lorrie N. "'The Things Men Do': The Gendered Subtext in Tim O'Brien's *Esquire* Stories." *Critique: Studies in Contemporary Fiction* 36, no. 1 (Fall 1994): 16–40.

Snyder, Michael. "Crises of Masculinity: Homosocial Desire and Homosexual Panic in the Critical Cold War Narratives of Mailer and Coover." *Critique: Studies in Contemporary Fiction* 48, no. 3 (Spring 2007): 250–77.

Solomon, Jeff. "Young, Effeminate, and Strange: Early Photographic Portraiture of Truman Capote." *Studies in Gender and Sexuality* 6, no. 3 (15 July 2005): 293–326. doi:10.1080/15240650609349279.

Spurlin, William J. "Culture, Rhetoric, and Queer Identity: James Baldwin and the Identity Politics of Race and Sexuality." In *James Baldwin Now*, edited by Dwight McBride, 103–21. New York: New York University Press, 1999.

Starck, Kathleen. "The Early Cold Warrior on Screen: An All-Purpose Signifier?" In *Post-World War II Masculinities in British and American Literature and Culture: Towards Comparative Masculinity Studies*, edited by Stefan Horlacher and Kevin Floyd, 15–33. Farnham, UK: Ashgate, 2013.

Stetson Shoes. "Advertisement." *Esquire*, April 1972.

Stockton, Kathryn Bond. *Beautiful Bottom, Beautiful Shame: Where "Black" Meets "Queer."* Durham: Duke University Press, 2006.

Storey, John, ed. *Cultural Theory and Popular Culture: A Reader.* Edinburgh: Pearson Longman, 2009

St Pierre, Scott. "'Bent on Candor': Gossip, Shame, and Capote's *Answered Prayers.*" *Textual Practice*, 25 July 2015, 1–24. doi:10.1080/0950236X.2015.1057217.

Strate, Lance. "Beer Commercials: A Manual on Masculinity." In *Men, Masculinity, and the Media*, edited by Steve Craig, 78–92. London: SAGE, 1992.

Strychacz, Thomas F. *Dangerous Masculinities: Conrad, Hemingway, and Lawrence.* Gainesville: University Press of Florida, 2008.

Tabbi, Joseph. *Postmodern Sublime: Technology and American Writing from Mailer to Cyberpunk.* Ithaca: Cornell University Press, 1995.

Taylor, Douglas. "Three Lean Cats in a Hall of Mirrors: James Baldwin, Norman Mailer, and Eldridge Cleaver on Race and Masculinity." *Texas Studies in Literature and Language* 52, no. 1 (2010): 70–101.

Taylor, Sara. "Denigration, Dependence, and Deviation: Black and White Masculinities in James Baldwin's Going to Meet the Man." *Obsidian* 9, no. 2 (Fall 2008): 43–61.

Toropov, Brandon. *Encyclopedia of Cold War Politics.* New York: Infobase Publishing, 2000.

Towers, Robert. "Low-Rent Tragedies." *The New York Review of Books*, 14 May 1981. www.nybooks.com/articles/1981/05/14/low-rent-tragedies/.

Traister, Bryce. "Academic Viagra: The Rise of American Masculinity Studies." *American Quarterly* 52, no. 2 (2000): 274–304.

Valente, Joseph. "Other Possibilities, Other Drives: Queer, Counterfactual 'Life' in Truman Capote's *Other Voices, Other Rooms.*" *MFS Modern Fiction Studies* 59, no. 3 (27 September 2013): 526–46. doi:10.1353/mfs.2013.0044.

Vanderwees, Chris. "Resisting Remasculinization: Tim O'Brien's 'Sweetheart of the Song Tra Bong.'" *Feminist Studies in English Literature* 17, no. 2 (Winter 2009): 191–210.

Vantoch, Victoria. *The Jet Sex: Airline Stewardesses and the Making of an American Icon.* Philadelphia: University of Pennsylvania Press, 2013.

Veeck, Bill. "The Baseball Establishment." *Esquire*, August 1964.

Waggoner, Jess. "Cripping the Bildungsroman: Reading Disabled Intercorporealities in Truman Capote's *Other Voices, Other Rooms.*" *Journal of Modern Literature* 38, no. 1 (10 January 2015): 56–72.

Walker, Nancy A. *Shaping Our Mothers' World: American Women's Magazines.* Jackson: University Press of Mississippi, 2000.

Walker, Pat, ed. *Between Labor and Capital.* Boston: South End Press, 1979.

Wallace, Michele. *Black Macho and the Myth of the Superwoman.* New York: Dial Press, 1979.

Warhol, Andy. "Say Hello to the Dirty Half Dozen, Sierra Bandit, The American Playground and All the Superstars of the New Theatre." *Esquire*, May 1969.

– "TV." *Esquire*, December 1975.

Warner, Michael. *Publics and Counterpublics.* New York: Zone Books, 2005.

Warren, Craig A. "Presidential Wounds: The JFK Assassination and the White Male Body." *Men and Masculinities* 10, no. 5 (August 1, 2008): 557–82. doi:10.1177/1097184X06291917.

"Wealthiest Adults." *Esquire Media Kit*, 2014.

Weber, Bruce. "Raymond Carver: Chronicler of Blue-Collar Despair." In *Conversations with Raymond Carver*, edited by Marshall Bruce Gentry and William L. Stull, 84–97. Literary Conversations Series, xxviii, 259. Jackson: University Press of Mississippi, 1990.

Weinraub, Bernard. "The Brilliancy of Black." *Esquire*, January 1967.

Wesley, Marilyn C. *Violent Adventure: Contemporary Fiction by American Men.* Charlottesville: University of Virginia Press, 2003.

Westerman, Richard. "The Reification of Consciousness: Husserl's Phenomenology in Lukács's Identical Subject-Object." *New German Critique: An Interdisciplinary Journal of German Studies* 111 (Fall 2010): 97–130.

"What We Do." *Narrative4.* Accessed 15 July 2016. http://narrative4.com/mission-vision/.

Whitehead, Stephen. *Men and Masculinities: Key Themes and New Directions.* Cambridge; Malden, USA: Polity, 2002.

Whyte, William H. *The Organization Man.* Philadelphia: University of Pennsylvania Press, 2013.

Wicker, Tom. "Kennedy without End, Amen." *Esquire*, July 1977.

– "Kennedy without Tears." *Esquire*, June 1964.

Williamson, Judith. *Decoding Advertisements: Ideology and Meaning in Advertising.* London: Boyars, 1978.

Willingham, Calder. "The Way It Isn't Done: Notes on the Distress of Norman Mailer." *Esquire*, December 1963.

Wills, Gary. "The Second Civil War." *Esquire*, March 1968.

Wilson, Sloan. *The Man in the Gray Flannel Suit.* New York: Thunder's Mouth, 2002.

Winkler, Allan M. *Life under a Cloud: American Anxiety about the Atom.* Oxford: Oxford University Press, 1993.

Winship, Janice. *Inside Women's Magazines.* New York; London: Pandora, 1987.

Winthrop Shoes. "Advertisement." *Esquire*, November 1958.

Wolfe, Tom. "Tom Wolfe's Seventies." *Esquire*, December 1979.

Worthy, William. "The American Negro Is Dead." *Esquire*, November 1967.

– "The Black Power Establishment." *Esquire*, November 1967.

– "The Red Chinese American Negro." *Esquire*, October 1964.

Žižek, Slavoj. *Violence: Six Sideways Reflections*. New York: Picador, 2008.

Zuckerman, Ed. "How Would the U.S. Survive a Nuclear War?" *Esquire*, March 1982.

Zuromskis, Catherine. *Snapshot Photography: The Lives of Images*. Cambridge: MIT Press, 2013.

Index